THE ENTERPRISING AMERICANS

Books by John Chamberlain

THE ENTERPRISING AMERICANS

THE ROOTS OF CAPITALISM

THE AMERICAN STAKES

FAREWELL TO REFORM

The Enterprising Americans:

A Business History of

the United States

NEW AND UPDATED EDITION

BY JOHN CHAMBERLAIN

HARPER & ROW, PUBLISHERS

NEW YORK, EVANSTON, SAN FRANCISCO, LONDON

*For Ernestine, who understands the likeness
of all creative people*

Contents

Introduction   IX

1. Free Enterprisers Before the Revolution   1

2. Businessmen Join in an Unbusinesslike War   24

3. The Quest for Capital and the Sprouting of Invention   43

4. Early America Goes Places   63

5. Frontier and Factory   81

6. The Pre–Civil War Speedup   100

7. The Civil War and Its Aftermath   119

8. The Gilded Age   140

9. The Rise of the Money Power   163

10. The Age of Edison   185

11. F.O.B. Detroit   202

12. The New Frontier of the Depressed Thirties   223

13. The Modern World of Enterprise   243

Bibliography   265

Index   273

Introduction

This book, which in a somewhat condensed form ran through thirteen successive issues of *Fortune* magazine, had a double origin. First of all, John Davenport, one of *Fortune's* assistant managing editors, had been dismayed by a daughter's request for something to counteract the "robber baron" approach to American business history for a class paper she had to write. Looking for a history which would treat business as a prime creative force, Mr. Davenport found nothing made to his hand. His suggestion to Duncan Norton-Taylor, *Fortune's* managing editor, that the deficiency be repaired fell on ready ears.

How I came into the picture as a chosen instrument derived from conversations with Mr. Davenport. He had listened to my complaints, voiced in certain reviews of "new" American histories, that the books all seemed to be written by authors who looked to politics for their guiding thread. The ancient tradition of Bancroft had never been overthrown. True enough, the Beards, Charles and Mary, had suggested the importance of a Carnegie, an Armour, a Cornelius Vanderbilt, to the "rise of American civilization." But, having suggested the "Elizabethan" contributions of such figures, the Beards had returned to the mode of their times, which was to let economic matters provide the ground tone for the usual political history. Later on, Garet Garrett, in *The American Story,* really did accept the great U.S. business innovators as the equivalent of Drake and Hawkins, the adventurous mariners who, in the age of Elizabeth, laid the basis for Britain's world mercantile empire. But the emphasis of Mr. Garrett's history was still on the political story.

Mr. Davenport's search for an author and my own inclinations to correct what seemed to me an ancient bias coincided, with what justification the reader of this book must decide for himself. It is not that either Mr. Davenport or myself takes an anarchic view of things: man is, after all, a political animal, as Aristotle was prob-

ably not the first to observe. But politics, since it is a result of collid-
ing energies, is a secondary manifestation: even the most powerful
statesmen work with forces and sentiments already in play. Chanti-
cleer may crow on the political hustings, but the sun rises by itself.
At its best, government provides the institutional framework for
the release of energies. Where government tries to substitute itself
for the economic motor, there is the inevitable confusion between
the starter, the accelerator, and the brake. Resources can be allo-
cated by political fiat, sometimes based on "broadly felt social
needs," sometimes on the political compromises of log-rolling
minorities, but nobody actually knows whether such allocation has
any relationship to true individual desires. Without the free play
of prices, profits, and wages, the calculation of human choice breaks
down.

The Sixties opened with talk about a "new" frontier. But the pioneer on any frontier, new or old, is the unharnessed man free to
walk at will over the horizon. In the United States, it is business
that has kept the pioneer's adaptability and ingenuity alive. The
constant innovation of inventors, technicians, and enterprisers (see
Schumpeter's economics) has been the main factor in the rise of
real wages. Investment has kept the national income and gross
product on a broadly rising curve despite cyclical dips and depressions. And it is to enterprise that the government, sometimes biting
its tongue, is compelled to turn when seeking new patterns of
growth at home or providing the tools for use in "underdeveloped"
countries abroad.

The contribution of American business and the market economy
goes far beyond the mere feats of production. To a significant degree the business system, which gives free play to the decisions of
individuals and voluntary groups, has allowed for a kind of un-
coerced social collaboration that is wholly impossible under centralized government planning. Without the creative infusions of
business, the ideal of liberty under law that has animated the American experiment would lack concrete realization.

In complaining about the lack of a comprehensive history of
American business, it will not do to suggest that there is any dearth
of works that touch on business development, or that scholars,
notably at Harvard, haven't done first-rate work in the field. Books

by John Moody and Burton Hendrick, now sixty years old, are still useful. But, as Allan Nevins has pointed out in a notable paper on "Business and the Historian," the historians have generally regarded "trade and manufacturing with disdain." The writers of historical syntheses have left the subject of business history to those whose taste runs to test-borings undertaken for depth in deliberately narrow compass.

There are, of course, the purely economic histories, grounded in a predominantly statistical treatment of events, of which Harold Underwood Faulkner's work stands as an excellent example. There are pertinent and provoking analyses of economic *forces* as they have shaped our history: Louis M. Hacker's *The Triumph of American Capitalism* and *The Age of Enterprise,* by Thomas C. Cochran and William Miller, come immediately to mind. There are studies of institutional changes in American business, some of them done quite admirably by Professor Cochran. There is a vast literature of attack, ranging from Theodore Dreiser's novelistic portrayal of a corrupt traction monopolist (patterned on the character of Charles T. Yerkes) to the type of study that is exemplified by Matthew Josephson's colorful and animated *The Robber Barons* which, in its turn, was a more sophisticated ordering of the material (often gleaned from the prejudiced records of Congressional hearings) that Gustavus Myers used so vitriolically in his *History of the Great American Fortunes.* As for business biographies, they have been as plentiful as Falstaff's blackberries, but they usually bear the telltale marks of their times and origins. Biographies written in the twenties (or subsidized at a later period in the spirit of that decade) ordinarily err on the puff side; those that came in the thirties and forties are more often than not savagely or urbanely iconoclastic, dealing with alleged "merchants of death," or depicting J. P. Morgan as a creature of tainted magnificence.

In recent years, the biographical mode has taken on a new balance. Allan Nevins' individual or co-authored studies of key figures (Abram Hewitt, the ironmaster; Eli Whitney, the inventor; John D. Rockefeller; the creators of the Ford Motor Company) are keen blends of narrative and judicial appraisal; the Hidys, Ralph W. and Muriel E., have explored the genesis of the Standard Oil Company without recourse to the indignation of a Henry Dem-

arest Lloyd or an Ida Tarbell; and a younger generation of writers
(Edwin P. Hoyt, author of *The Vanderbilts and Their Fortunes,*
and the John Tebbel of *The Inheritors* are cases in point) have
added a bit of good clean fun to the art of biographical exhuma-
tion. And Edward C. Kirkland, professor emeritus at Bowdoin,
has, in his *Industry Comes of Age: Business, Labor, and Public
Policy, 1860–1897,* happily recreated the scene of the so-called
Gilded Age without animus. But the literature, whether of attack
or judicial appraisal, offers no running story of the whole stream
of entrepreneurial decision from colonial times to the present.
Though there are excellent histories of production (beginning with
J. Leander Bishop's *A History of American Manufactures from
1608 to 1860,* and continuing with Victor S. Clark's *History of
Manufactures in the United States*), and stirring accounts which
treat of business under such headings as "The Telephone," "The
Horseless Carriage," and "The Glamor Business" (James Blaine
Walker's *The Epic of American Industry*), there is a dearth of
books that try to set the key creative business acts in chronological
perspective.

One reason for the lack is that the businessman has usually been
somewhat contemptuously contrasted to the creative artist. (The
artists, who have written the books, have seen to that—and the businessman has not ordinarily heeded St. Clair MacKelway's old ad-
monition, "Business man, get yourself a writer.") Yet the innovator,
in both business and the arts, is always to be contrasted in the same
way with the routineer: innovation deals with unknowns and refrac-
tory materials which must be fused and made effective by the creative act. Between an Edison, trying to make a going industry out of
the invention of a practical light bulb, and a sculptor trying to
fashion an image of human love or despair by taking mallet and
chisel to stone, there is not so much difference after all. In each
case the human will seeks to impose itself on chaos, to the end of
creating significant form. Choreography is something for the stage;
it is also something for the factory floor, as Walter Flanders demonstrated when he rearranged the machine sequences in the primitive
days of the Ford Motor Company.

A second reason for the lack of a story of creative "busy-ness"
is the modern compartmentalization of the social disciplines and

even of our thought processes. As has been suggested, political historians concentrate on the Age of Jackson or the Age of Roosevelt, as the case may be. Economists trace the evolution of the market economy from the first incipient revolt against feudalism. Sociologists and sociological novelists indulge in a peculiar jargon that concentrates on the group and the social class. And theoreticians like the late Thorstein Veblen have attempted to drive distinctions between engineers and businessmen, with the idea that production and money-making have little in common, and that a price system lives and flourishes only through planned sabotage of fecundity.

Thus everything tends to be pushed into abstract categories. Categorizing as he did, Veblen never could explain why a supposed monopoly like the Aluminum Corporation of America progressively lowered its prices while the older brick-and-mortar building trades, in which there were thousands of competitors, were afflicted with chronic price stiffness. The categorizing of today makes it popular to oppose Business to Labor, and to set both of these off in opposition to Agriculture. But this tripartite class division does not reckon with the fact that the farmer is or should be a businessman whether he incorporates his establishment or continues to work in the immemorial tradition of the family-owned farm. Nor does it stress the creative relationship of the worker to the business firm. Long ago Amos Lawrence, one of the famous Boston Associates of pre-Civil War days, set a seal on the basic likeness of Americans in business. "We are literally all workingmen," said Lawrence, "and the attempt to get up a 'workingmen's party' is a libel upon the whole population, as it implies that there are among us large numbers who are not workingmen." As a man who rose from storekeeping to give his name to a new textile city on the Merrimack, Lawrence was speaking from experience. The Lawrence text would be equally applicable from a psychological standpoint if it had begun, "We are literally all *businessmen* . . ."

Business, in short, is both a *process* that cuts across class lines, and a system wherein production and individual effort are geared to consumer and public need by the operation of the price-profit mechanism. It is *creative busy-ness* within the rules of the marketplace, which harnesses the hunger of man and his work together. While the business process thus includes just about everybody, the role of the profit-seeking entrepreneur is obviously of critical importance. For far from being some kind of surplus value extorted from the worker, profit is the evanescent margin of return for the risk an enterpriser takes when he brings factors of production together. In a static economy, where consumer taste and technology are by definition frozen, there might be no mathematical room for profit—or loss. But the American story has never been a static one; from the days of Eli Whitney to those of Alfred P. Sloan there has been a constant upending of equilibrium. In the process whole industries have gone to the wall—the canals, the early toll roads, the carriage business, the traffic in whale oil. But always new ventures have arisen to fulfill and to create new demands.

The manner in which creative busy-ness has worked its wonders in America will be detailed as our business story progresses. When the early colonists arrived in the New World, and indeed at the time when they formed the Republic, there was no Point Four Program to help them. Yet the very shortages of men, money, and capital inspired a tremendous inventiveness. In 1810 we were still stealing industrial secrets from England, which had an anti-Point Four policy; but by 1850 the British were inviting gunmaker Samuel Colt of Hartford to appear before a parliamentary committee in London to explain the secrets of American production. By 1906 America was already the world's greatest producer.

It had all been a matter of a couple of generations wherein small-business ventures proliferated into larger ones, and big business in turn found itself faced with new competition. The Washburn & Moen Co., wire makers of Worcester, Massachusetts, got a boost when the crinoline dress trade began demanding wire stays. Forty years later, as part of the American Steel & Wire Company, the old Worcester concern was merged into the U.S. Steel Corp., the frightening new behemoth conjured up by J. P. Morgan to do 66 per cent of the steel business in America. In another forty years U.S. Steel itself, challenged by the growth of Bethlehem, Republic, Jones & Laughlin, and other new giants, had to solace itself with a mere 33 per cent of total steel output. And in 1962 it could no longer make a price rise stick by mere say-so.

Monopolies—oil was the most notorious of them—waxed fat only to recede into the pack, sometimes pursued by antitrust laws, as later arrivals came on the scene. Meanwhile new products and processes continually rose to compete with the old. Aluminum, even when there was only one company in the field, had to fight it out with wood at one extreme and steel at the other. Du Pont artificial fibers freed the textile business from dependence on cotton, silk, and wool. The railroads were controlled more effectively by competition from automobile and truck and airplane than they were by the ICC. From telephones to television, the electrical revolution leaped from dependence on wires to dependence on wave lengths in God's free ether. Came, too, the supermarkets and consumer credit, washing machines, home freezers, and the split-level ranchhouse which never looked upon a longhorn steer.

So it went—a success story if there ever was one. How to account for it? It is true that Americans inherited a rich and almost empty continent that had hitherto been peopled by a few nomadic red men. It is also true that the ever expanding western "frontier" profoundly shaped American institutions, as William Graham Sumner and Frederick Jackson Turner among others have emphasized. Even so, the inviting presence of an unspoiled continent meant little when taken by itself. Siberia, though admittedly a more difficult country, was equally unspoiled, but the early Russian settlers never managed to cut the apron strings that bound them to St. Petersburg. And Spaniards to the south of the British colonists inherited equally empty spaces yet never developed those spaces in the manner that came naturally to the descendants of the Cavaliers and Puritans.

The point is that before there can be a real frontier there must be creative frontiersmen. And here the American story owes much to its *selective* inheritance from the Old World. In crossing the Atlantic the "new men" of America left behind them much that was to impede European development in the seventeenth and eighteenth centuries—vestiges of feudal master-servant relationships, traditions of absolute monarchical allegiance, a society of "status" and classes as opposed to a society of free men. Yet the American development is also entirely incomprehensible without reference to what its frontiersmen brought with them across 3,000 miles of ocean. They enjoyed, after all, a common language; they were heir to three hundred years of the development of English common law. More profoundly, they were animated by the religious and moral traditions stemming from the freer aspects of medieval Christendom and the search for an "ideal law" that stands above the law of parliaments. Both Americans and Englishmen built on Magna Carta and the "rights of Englishmen" as defined by Lord Coke in the seventeenth century. And when the chips were down at the time of the Revolution it seemed entirely natural to Americans to draw on the philosopher John Locke and his theory of "natural rights."

It is the impact of this whole tradition and mind-set of freedom on a continent full of challenge and promise that best explains the emergence of America. In economics, to be sure, the story has a peculiar twist. For the Colonies grew up under the system of mercantilism—a philosophy in which the state attempted to direct foreign trade with a view to building up a gold balance at home and under which the colonists were expected to stick to raw-material production for the benefit of the manufacturers of the mother country. Yet even mercantilism was profoundly modified in early America by a noble race of smugglers who saw little reason to obey a continuous flow of royal ukases and restrictions: and when England applied the screws too hard, the "new men" of America naturally revolted. In this revolt the colonists had the sympathy of many Englishmen: it was no accident that Adam Smith's *Wealth of Nations* and the American Declaration of Independence were published to the world in the same year. In a profound sense America, for the next few generations, gave the principles of the *Wealth of Nations* their first great trial run.

There never would have been a trial run, however, had there not been a political frame for the business process. Luckily the Founding Fathers were highly conscious students of political philosophy as tested by history. In the eighteenth-century fashion the Founders had recourse not to a shallow contemporary pragmatism, but to first principles as defined by the centuries. They began, not with economics, but with values and with law—the "law of Nature's God." The Constitution was consciously designed to protect *all* the rights of the individual, whether political, religious, ethical, or economic. And in offering protection for the individual in *all* his rights, the Founders recognized that economic and political liberties stand or fall together. As Hamilton put it, power over a man's subsistence is power over his will.

As it turned out, the political frame set up by the Founders and preserved by Chief Justice Marshall's great Supreme Court decisions has served America a thousand times better than would have been the case had they attempted to draw up a master economic blueprint. For what emerged was a unique system wherein power was constantly dispersed not only between the federal government and the states but likewise across the whole range of human endeavor. In countries where the state substitutes central planning for the market it must pretend to omniscience and enforce its decrees by arbitrary authority. In America, save in periods of great war or in moments of social aberration such as those exemplified by the NRA or the threat to dictate steel prices, we have had a different dispensation. Historically, our government has laid down the rules of the road, maintained the common defense and internal order, and generally left the rest to the initiative of the individual and free association.

Out of this unsystematic system have come our cities, our skyscrapers, our industries, and the trade and the foreign investment that can help transform a world. In this transforming endeavor the American businessman stands in the front rank not because the pursuit of business is a sanctified end in itself but because it palpably makes the achievements of higher ends possible. The history of American business becomes in the broadest sense the history of a people—a people who, looking to government for the performance of certain indispensable functions, nevertheless has put its ultimate faith in its own creative energies. For such a people a new frontier, the real frontier, will always be open.

In offering this story of American business I have had to be highly selective. Certain service and insurance aspects of business have been skimped; there is little here about such things as the refinement of actuarial science, or the development of business forecasting, or the many ramifications of banking and credit. To many sins of omission, the author pleads guilty. But a book, after all, must have limits. When one is writing about decisive campaigns, one has, necessarily, to forgo minute forays into the history of tactical maneuver.

As for acknowledgments, some are implicit in this introduction; and many more must be made to the books mentioned on pages xi and xii and thereafter in the bibliography. Some of the material in the latter chapters derived from the author's fifteen-year experience doing corporation stories for *Fortune* and writing industry articles for *Barron's Business and Financial Weekly* and *The Wall Street Journal*. The author wishes to thank many people for help in both general approach and specific detail: John Dos Passos for his suggestions about the men of the colonial and post-colonial generations; Bernard Knollenberg and Edward M. Riley, Director of Research for Colonial Williamsburg, for insight into the workings of British mercantilism and into the ideas of George Washington as a businessman; Robert Cantwell, for pointing out the value of the work of J. Leander Bishop on early manufacturing; Professor David McCord Wright of McGill University for items about the business system of the South; Professor Louis Hacker of Columbia University for shrewd general counsel; Christy Borth, formerly of the Automobile Manufacturers Association, for the use of material from his files on the automobile age; many willing representatives of corporations that are too numerous for special mention; the helpful staffs of various libraries, including the New York Society Library, the New York Historical Society Library, the Nicholas Murray Butler Library of Columbia University, the New York Public Library, the Library of Yale University, the Rhode Island Historical Society Library, and the library of the Time Inc. Editorial Reference department; and *Fortune* publisher Ralph D. Paine, Jr., for making books from his historian-father's library available for consultation. Among living authors who have offered themselves willy-nilly for paraphrase at certain critical points, the author wishes to single out Roger Burlingame for his many insights into the impact of technology on business development, and the Messrs. John Jewkes, David Sawers, and Richard Stillerman for their detailed case histories of modern inventions. E. James Ferguson of the University of Maryland also deserves special mention for bringing clarity to the tangled financial history of the Revolutionary epoch and for putting Robert Morris into proper perspective as the man who prepared the way for Alexander Hamilton. In the special field of gun manufacture, the Messrs. Melvin Maynard Johnson, inventor of the Johnson machine gun, and Howard Greene made their informed services available.

Finally, the author owes a profound debt to Mrs. Mireille Gerould, a research assistant who offered many constructive ideas, checked the manuscript with a passion for exactitude that carried her far back of many a slipshod secondary source, and whose indefatigable probing of sources multiplied the reach of the writer's eyes, ears, and legs many times over. The same sort of debt is owed to *Fortune* editor John Davenport, both for his eye for backtracking in a manuscript (as keen as Bill Knudsen's for back-looping in an assembly line) and for the general sagacity of his editorial suggestions; and to *Fortune* managing editor Duncan Norton-Taylor and assistant to the publisher Brooke Alexander for making the whole project possible.

Needless to say, none of the people mentioned above should feel the slightest compunction should he or she choose to disown responsibility for any of the author's opinions or general interpretations.

1 Free Enterprisers Before the Revolution

Pepperrell at Kittery creates a business barony.

Whale-spermaceti candles and privateering enrich the coastal towns.

A complex of forges and ironworks rises in Pennsylvania.

Indigo, rice, and tobacco bring wealth, and trouble, to the South.

An energetic George Washington becomes the Colonies' most imaginative businessman.

WHEN the first Americans faced the rocky woodlands and inter-vales of New England and the humid valleys of the Delaware and James rivers, they were already on the way toward becoming the "new men" later celebrated by those visiting Frenchmen, Michel de Crèvecoeur and Alexis de Tocqueville. The "new man" was inher-ently a self-starter. Religion was the main propelling urge behind his trek across the seas and, as Tocqueville emphasized, cast a lasting and indispensable influence over the development of free American institutions. But the man of the seventeenth century saw no opposition between faith and practical works. The high-pooped ships that bore the colonists westward were launched, after all, by joint stock companies, and carried the dreams of merchant adven-turers no less than those of men seeking religious freedom.

Once here as colonizers, the first English invaders engaged the extremes of summer heat and winter freezing with what shiftiness they could muster. Inhospitable until the first tricks of adaptation

1

had been learned (a dead fish to each cornhill, the early central heating of chimneys offering fireplaces on more than one side), the land tended to resist politically dominated enterprise. In Virginia, Acting Governor Sir Thomas Dale discovered that "martial law did not grow corn," and turned the cultivatable plots over to individual families. And in Plymouth, Governor Bradford followed suit, having learned that communal planting of crops not only entailed "tiranie and oppression" but also led to starvation.

It is not to be argued that "private enterprise" sprang full-panoplied from the soil of the New World without a hundred checks and much sidewise motion. The colonists were, after all, Europeans, with a feudal heritage of a "relational" society and a tradition of church control, even to the setting of price ranges. But with man-power at a premium, the stress almost from the start was on the individual—and the individual tended to make his own decisions if only because he could walk off into the forests if unsatisfied. If not a full-fledged entrepreneurial society in the seventeenth and eighteenth centuries, coastal North America was at least the embryo of one.

The achievement of the Puritan and Quaker enterprisers was apparent to early observers. One of the shrewdest was a Dr. Alexander Hamilton of Annapolis, Maryland (no kin to his more famous namesake), who in 1744 made a 1,624-mile trip through the colonies by horseback with his Negro servant. Though Dr. Hamilton's prime concern was with the entrepreneurship of the innkeepers, he had an eye and an ear for other things. Philadelphia looked to him like an English country market town, "the buildings low and mean, streets unpaved. . . ." But the doctor sensed more than that in the city that had been settled by the solid burghers, mechanics, and craftsmen imported by the Quaker William Penn. "A few years hence," so Dr. Hamilton predicted, Philadelphia would be "a great and flourishing place and the chief city of North America." The Philadelphians, so the doctor noted, "apply themselves strenuously to business, having little or no turn to gayety." They had "that accomplishment peculiar to all our American colonies: subtlety and craft in their dealings."

New York, by contrast, suffered because the grip of the Dutch on the Hudson Valley still persisted. The third generation of Ranslaer (Dr. Hamilton's spelling) still held on to a manor forty-eight miles long, twenty-four miles wide. Moving into Connecticut, Dr. Hamilton noted the "large towns and navigable rivers . . . people are chiefly husbandmen and farmers . . . the staples same as Massachusetts' . . . horses are shipped to the West Indies, one town is famous for its onions, a sloop is loaded with them." But Connecticut oppressed him a bit with "its ragged money, rough roads, and enthusiastick people."

Boston was better, the Bostonians "more decent and polite in their dress, tho more fanatical in their doctrine. . . ." They gave "indirect and dubious answers to the plainest questions . . . but there is more hospitality shown to strangers than in New York and Philadelphia . . ." and an "abundance of learning and parts. . . ."

The local talk was "on commerce and trade," the staples were "shipping, lumber, and fish." Salem, a "pretty town" with a long street, had pleasing architecture; at Marblehead, just next door, there was little but fish to talk about: fish flakes—or racks—spread out to dry on 200 rocky acres around the town; ninety fishing sloops employed out of the port; the yearly value of the fishing industry £34,000 sterling for some 30,000 quintals (or three million pounds) of dried and salted fish. At Portsmouth, New Hampshire, where geese were kept in the fort to give alarm in case of a night attack by the French from the north, the trade was in fish and in masting for ships.

As Dr. Hamilton noted, the New Englanders had really to scrape for their sustenance. They were the New World's first real business leaders because, with them, it was a case of root hog, or die. They bulk larger than the Pennsylvania Quakers in the first commercial annals of North America, partly because they made more noise about their affairs and partly because, in the words of the Englishman Edward Randolph, their lack of a rich hinterland compelled them "to trye all ports to force a trade." As early as 1713 the New Englanders began building schooners for the nascent Grand Banks fishing fleet; and it was in the first part of the eighteenth century that their distilleries made rum into a ubiquitous medium of exchange that flowed to the Guinea coast of Africa (to pay for gold dust and slaves), to the fishing stations off Newfoundland and Nova Scotia (where, as grog, it kept the hardy suppliers of the fish mar-

Sir William Pepperrell

kets from freezing to death), and to the inland frontier only a few miles from tidewater (where it bought beaver skins from the Indians and paid the bribe money that kept Deerfield massacres from becoming everyday occurrences).

The curious thing about the invigorating uses of adversity is that the hardiest and least likely clime, that of Massachusetts-owned Maine, produced the greatest of the early colonial tycoons, William Pepperrell. This merchant of the North Country (who lived at Kittery Point in Maine, just across the river from Portsmouth, New Hampshire) inherited from his pioneer father a thriving fishing business that multiplied out in all directions. Kittery Point was just "downriver" on the Piscataqua from the White Mountains and the Maine woods, which made it the logical place for assembling the "king's masts" (cut from the straight pines marked with the "king's arrow"), and for building ships for the fisheries and the West Indies trade. The Pepperrells' shop in Kittery dealt in lumber, in naval stores, in fish, and in provisions (meaning rum); Pepperrell coasters brought corn and tobacco from the southern colonies; and the larger Pepperrell vessels voyaged to England, Spain, and Portugal for sails, cordage, dry-goods, wines, and fruit and to the West Indies for sugar. The Pepperrells frequently sold their ships and cargoes as a unit, which led to more shipbuilding; their bankers in London and Plymouth acted as clearing agents in their exchange of New and Old World products and drew bills of exchange on Boston merchants for goods the Pepperrells could not get in direct trade for their own cargoes.

Whenever the Pepperrells did come by some hard money, they plowed it into real estate, as was the fashion in those days. William Jr. bought the land on which the cotton-mill town of Saco was to grow (he was still a minor when he acquired it, and his father had to sign for him). Later he managed the lottery that put a bridge over the Saco River. He became the great public personage of his frontier world—a justice of the peace, a member of the Massachusetts province board of councilors, and, at the age of thirty, commander of the Maine militia. As a tribute to his practical abilities and experience with frontier weapons and levies, Pepperrell was placed in charge of the 4,300 colonials who sailed in 1745 from Boston to besiege the vaunted French fort of Louisburg on Cape

Breton Island, which guarded the approach to the Grand Banks fishing grounds. After forty-nine days of siege the supposedly impregnable fortress fell. To the colonists' distress, Louisburg was returned to the French after the war. Nevertheless, the colonists got something out of the Louisburg expedition, for the British Parliament refunded the expenses of it to the New Englanders in gold specie, to help put the local currencies on a sound basis for the first time in half a century.

Pepperrell himself did extremely well out of the whole show: he was the first native-born New Englander to become a baronet. The baronetcy tied him to the British Crown and made him a magnifico beyond local compare. In 1747 he built four ships of war for England. At the age of fifty-one, at the height of his resplendence, he is not only a chief justice and a commander of militia; he is also a president of the governor's council, a colonel in the regular British Army, a superintendent and accountant of the recruiting service, a commissioner of Indian affairs (he has had a long experience in patrol duty as a boy during the Indian wars), he is an owner of sawmills, and he is still extensively engaged in the fisheries. He is fond of gay plumage, appearing at his log landings along the Saco River in bright scarlet. During this period he lives in a style befitting his baronetcy; his house, as Hunt's *Lives of American Merchants* tells us, has "walls hung with costly mirrors and paintings, his sideboards loaded with silver, his cellar filled with choice wines, his park stocked with deer, a retinue of servants, costly equipage, and a splendid barge with a black crew dressed in uniform." His portrait is painted by John Smibert, who preceded Copley as the fashionable portraitist of the colonial merchant aristocracy. The town of Saco becomes Pepperrellboro—and between the Piscataqua and Saco rivers, a distance of some thirty miles, Sir William can travel through Maine entirely on his own soil.

While Sir William was expanding his Maine dynasty (which petered out with the Revolution when Sir William's Loyalist grandson fled to England) other and better known New Englanders were extracting wealth from the sea. An effigy of the "sacred cod" hangs suspended in the Massachusetts House of Representatives to this day for a very good reason: as early as the 1740's, a Salem or Boston ship carrying a load of cod from the Newfoundland banks to the West Indies or southern Europe could make a 200 per cent profit—or £2,000—in a single trip and this despite an insurance rate that ran as high as 11 per cent on ship and cargo to Madeira, 14 per cent to Jamaica, and 23 per cent to Santo Domingo. Besides ordinary shipwreck, a ship had to risk capture by privateers or pirates, and since under the British rules of trade the voyages were often fundamentally lawless in the first place, there was much excuse for British men-of-war to pick off a Salem sloop and detain it. The nature of a voyage to the West Indies to pick up French molasses or salt in exchange for fish is indicated by a letter of instruction given to Captain Richard Derby of Salem, who was about to take the schooner *Volante* to the southern islands in 1741: ". . . and if you should fall so low as [the Dutch island of] Statia, and any Frenchman should make you a good Offer with good security, or by making your vessel a Dutch bottom, or by any other means practicable in order to your getting among ye Frenchmen, embrace it . . . Also secure a permit so as for you to trade there next voyage, which you may undoubtedly do through your factor or by a little greasing some others." In other words, sail under Dutch colors to avoid the British Navigation Acts, and be prepared to bribe the customs officials.

By 1765, so prosperous had the trade built on dried cod, mackerel, and haddock become that more than 31,000 men were engaged on fishing boats putting out from Salem, Marblehead, and other Massachusetts ports; and more than 350 ships were busy carrying the fish to the markets of the West Indies and Catholic Europe and bringing back molasses, Malaga grapes, salt, and "pipes" of Madeira wine. Whaling, too, became a prosperous business, especially after the conquest of Quebec in the French and Indian War had opened the St. Lawrence and the Strait of Belle Isle to the Yankees. Eighty or more Yankee whalers put into the St. Lawrence in 1763—and in 1764 some 1,500 hundredweight of whalebone were sent by the colonists to England duty free. And 4,000 tons of whale oil were being exported annually just before the Revolution.

How did a man without capital (and there was practically no liquid capital in the Colonies other than specie obtained from pirates) become a well-to-do merchant in the days before the

Thomas Hancock

Revolution? If he was the younger son of a minister, as was Thomas Hancock of Lexington, he might be apprenticed to a bookbinder. After seven years of indenture in Boston, Thomas Hancock scraped together £100, probably with the help of his father, the famous "Bishop of Lexington," and set up in business for himself. By 1728 we find Thomas Hancock contracting to dispose of 3,000 volumes for another book dealer. A few years later he begins pushing books to his back shelves and offering tea, cloth, and cutlery to his patrons.

It is all very hit-or-miss. To barter for tea and cutlery, he exports codfish, whale oil, whalebone, and lumber; possibly he deals in bowls and buckets and ax handles made by the farmers in winter evenings by the fire. But how did he get the wherewithal to buy the codfish in the first place? Perhaps he would take hogs from farmers in exchange for Bibles, sending the pork on to Newfoundland and picking up fish from there to go to England for knives. Getting richer out of such huckstering, he might buy a "piece of a ship" bound for Surinam (Dutch Guiana) to bring contraband home to Boston. Taking precautions, Hancock writes to his shipmaster before one such trip to Surinam: "Closely observe, when you come on our coasts, not to speak with any vessels nor let any of your men write up to their wives when you arrive at our lighthouse." In other words, slip in without any Empire customs officer seeing you.

By such devious and resourceful trafficking the House of Hancock grows with the century. Building a big two-story house of Braintree granite on Boston's Beacon Hill, Thomas Hancock asks his merchant friend John Rowe, who is traveling in Europe, to pick up an English wallpaper for him with a pattern of flowers, peacocks, macaws, and squirrels. He sends for a chiming clock of black walnut, he rifles Europe for yews and hollies for his lawn, and for mulberry, nectron, peach, and apricot trees for his garden. He is pleased with the "chariot" he has imported to drive out on the cobbled Boston streets amid the clamors of the fishmongers and peddlers. When he goes forth he dresses in coats of lavender or peachbloom, in satin waistcoats, with velvet smallclothes and silver knee and shoe buckles.

In time, Thomas Hancock adopts his suddenly fatherless nephew Johnny, sending him to Harvard and taking him into the business to become his partner, his heir, and one of the merchant subsidizers of the American Revolutionary cause. Johnny was never the equal of his Uncle Thomas in jumping from one ice cake to another as wars—usually profitable while they were being waged—begat depressions. His sloop, the *Liberty,* was seized for smuggling when the British finally applied the screws to those who flouted the Navigation Acts. He missed out on an attempt to corner the whale-oil market. In the days of the Stamp Act, the Boston Massacre, and the Tea Party, Hancock was to blow hot on the subject of independence from England, then cold, then hot again. (Eventually he affixed his signature to the Declaration of Independence with such a flourish that George III would need no glasses to see it.) After the war, he becomes Governor of Massachusetts, and stuffily insists that President Washington should come to see *him,* not vice versa, when the Father of Our Country is making a tour of New England. Known to the end as the "Prince of Smugglers," he died in 1793, leaving £20,000 less than he had inherited from his Uncle Thomas some twenty years before. His excuse for dipping into capital— always a prime sin in Boston—might have been that the times had not been good, and besides there were other things to do.

The exploits of the Hancocks by sea and land were endlessly repeated by other pushing Boston families. Less self-made than Thomas Hancock, Peter Faneuil inherited a merchant estate from a Huguenot uncle. He grows richer by acting as a commission merchant at the standard rate of 5 per cent; he too takes "pieces of ships"; he gives credit to Boston merchants at a heavy discount, even charging 350 per cent in 1732 to cover depreciation. His legacy to the future is Faneuil Hall, the Hall of Markets, which gives Boston merchants a place to congregate out of the rain. (Much later the first economic historian of New England, William B. Weeden, lectures the shade of Peter Faneuil for having built his hall out of the blood of Negroes bought on the coast of Africa.) Meanwhile, in nearby Salem, another tough breed of seafarers, the Derbys, are making their mark. Richard Derby, a representative of the third generation of a family of notable seafarers, sailed with his own small ships up to 1757, carrying the usual fish and lumber to the West Indies and bringing home sugar, molasses, cotton, and claret wine. When, after 1763, the British tried to stop his trade under the stiffened imperial attitude, he and his fellow shipowners of Salem haughtily replied that "they were His Majesty's Vice Admirals . . . and would do that which seemed good to them." And when the British marched on Salem in February of 1775 to seize some stored cannon some two months before Paul Revere's ride and the Battle of Lexington, it was Captain Richard Derby who refused the British the use of a drawbridge into town. After all, he owned most of the cannon personally. "Find the cannon if you can," he roared across a stream. "Take them if you can. They will never be surrendered."

Down the coast, in Rhode Island, the Browns of Providence, a family dynasty like the Hancocks of Boston and the Derbys of Salem, had been doing business as merchants for a half-century before the Revolution. Captain James Brown ran a general merchandise shop, operated rum distilleries, owned a slaughterhouse and ships, acted as a banker, and traded with South Carolina, where he bartered for rice with Rhode Island cattle. His younger brother, Obadiah, who took over the business when James died in 1739, built a mill to grind "chocklit." Obadiah owned an early business textbook, *A Guide to Book Keepers According to the Italian Manner*, and presumably inaugurated the art of double-entry bookkeeping in America. It was Obadiah who undertook to rear James Brown's sons—and the quartet of "Nicky, Josey, John, and Mosey" Brown was to dominate Rhode Island trade and commerce for a long generation.

In the 1760's, Nicholas Brown & Co. (the business partnership of the four brothers) is the leading candle-maker of the Colonies, selling its product in New York and Philadelphia and as far away as the Caribbean under the Brown copperplate label. At one point the Browns try with other candle-makers to establish price control through the "United Company of Spermaceti Chandlers," one of the earliest American "trusts." The United Company set prices on "head matter" from sperm whales and maintained the selling price of completed candles. Within two years the "trust" collapsed, which was only poetic justice. The Browns themselves hated the British monopolies; it was brother John who led the seizure and burning of the British schooner *Gaspee* when it pursued smugglers into shoal water once too often.

By 1765 the Browns are in the iron business, in which they flounder until they hire a foundry master from Baron von Stiegel's Lancaster Furnace in Pennsylvania to put their own Hope Furnace in Rhode Island on a paying basis. This iron business is part of a growing complex of blast furnaces and forges in the Colonies—by 1775 there will be more furnaces and forges in America than in England and Wales, and statisticians will shortly be estimating that America is producing almost a seventh of the world's output of iron pigs and bars. The Browns' ledger books begin in 1723; the records kept by later son-in-law partners and their descendants have continued in uninterrupted sequence until today, covering a span of over two centuries. The estate still owns property in Ohio— and keeps books pertaining thereto. And the name of Brown, of course, is enshrined in a great Rhode Island university.

Newport, which flourished earlier than Providence as the first commercial capital of Rhode Island, was a cosmopolitan center with an atmosphere of great tolerance. Jews were free to worship there in what is said to be the first synagogue in America, and both Bishop Berkeley, the philosopher, and Ezra Stiles, an early Yale president, found the place much to their liking. But in spite of its tolerant charm Newport represents one of the darker strands of our early business history. It was not alone in the development of the slave trade with West Africa: ships from Massachusetts frequently visited the Guinea coast, where they crammed black men into their 'tween-deck spaces for export to the sugar lands of the West Indies and the tobacco plantations of the South. Newport ships, however, made a more or less regular thing of the traffic in human flesh. In 1770, Samuel Hopkins wrote in his reminiscences that "Rhode Island has been more deeply interested in the slave trade, and has enslaved more Africans than any other colony in New England." Later, Mr. Hopkins amplified his words to point specifically to Newport, whose "trade in human species has been the first wheel of commerce . . . on which every other movement in business has depended."

Why should it have been Newport that led in the development of a grisly business? It will not do to accuse the early Newporters of being less sensitive than other people of their time; they were not. Newport moved into the slave-running vacuum for reasons that can be largely deduced from its position. Lacking a hinterland to supply them with lumber and other trade goods, farther than the Boston and Salem men from the cod fisheries, Newporters might have felt more dependent than their competitors on a strictly triangular form of trade. Once out to Africa, they would load slaves for the West Indies. The next step would be to pick up a cargo of molasses in Statia or St. Domingo for the many Rhode Island distilleries. Finally it would be rum for shipment to Africa, and the cycle would start up anew. In justice to Newport, its eighteenth-century captains—such as the redoubtable David Lindsay, who prided himself on landing his slave cargoes "in helth and fatt"—abstained from the barbarities that were to become the normal disgrace of middle-passage voyages at a later date. Moreover, the American slave traders of the early days did not customarily engage in violent seizures: they bought their "human species" from black chiefs who had already enslaved their brothers in the course of pursuing tribal wars. In some cases the sale of a black man to a Newporter at Anamaboe or Old Calabar was an improvement over the original tribal way of celebrating a victory, which might have culminated in the grand climax of a cannibal feast. The willingness of the whites to buy slaves, however, caused the more enterprising chiefs to conduct raids on their fellow blacks for purely mercenary reasons.

While Boston and Newport flourished, the port of New York, which had the best natural harbor on the coast, lagged for reasons that were wholly political and social. Before it was seized by the English from the Dutch, in 1664, New York (or New Amsterdam) had been run as a port of entry to a land of feudal domains granted to its members by the Dutch West India Co. Great land grants lined the Hudson all the way to Albany—and the self-sufficient manors of the Van Rensselaers, the Philipses, and the Van Cortlandts continued as the fundamental units of the New York economy long after the Duke of York, later King James II of England, had taken possession of his proprietary. The Dutch had done some trading with the Indians at Albany for beaver skins (an article that sold well in faraway Muscovy) and with the "unrighteous, stubborn, impudent and pertinacious . . . English at Hartford" (it is Governor Stuyvesant speaking). But the "good grain country" that had never contained more than 5,000 or 6,000 Dutchmen remained relatively unpopulated under the English. Indeed, the slippery Colonel Fletcher, who governed the province at the end of the seventeenth century, continued the Dutch policy of feudal grants; following the custom of the time in mixing public and private affairs, he lined his pockets by selling great tracts along the Hudson up to 804 square miles each. In 1691 a report to the King described New York City as "a barren island" which "hath nothing to support it but trade, which chiefly flows from flower and bread they make of the corne the west end of Long Island and Zopus produceth. . . ."

If Manhattan Island lacked an upriver hinterland that was productive of other things than beaver skins and land rents, it had neighbors to the east and the west that found its facilities useful. New Jersey, under two proprietary lords, Carteret and Berkeley, had welcomed freehold settlers who took land in small chunks and on easy quit-rent terms. East Jerseyites naturally turned to New York for trade, as did a Major Selleck of Stamford, Connecticut, who kept a warehouse close to the Sound and took illicit goods from deep-water vessels for transshipment into New York on small boats. (Some of the goods from the proscribed sloop of the famous Captain Kidd are supposed to have passed through Selleck's hands.) Pirate specie, "gold of Araby" coming into New York from distant Madagascar, found a welcome—but for investment opportunities New Yorkers would eventually turn to Dover and other places in the "iron mountains of New Jersey," where mines and foundries became "thick as tombstones in Trinity Church graveyard."

In time New York became quietly rich. It was a "nest of privateers" in the middle of the eighteenth century. Stephen De Lancey had made his fortune partly by staking vessels in the "Madagascar trade," asking no questions about piratical doings in a part of the world supposedly monopolized by the British East India Co. His son James, a young politician, married into the Heathcote family, whose founder, Caleb, had combined New York merchandising with being lord of the manor of Scarsdale. The Livingston family got its start through progenitor Robert, who parlayed government jobs into the possession of a manor and entered into a privateering partnership with Captain Kidd, who may have been unjustly hanged as a pirate.

If New York still lagged behind Boston in the years before the Revolution, Philadelphia was already emerging as the leading metropolis of what was shortly to become the American Republic. The town had been planned by William Penn with sober Quaker foresight; a practicing sociologist, Penn had recruited able artisans and mechanics for his city as well as solid middle-class Quakers whose Inner Light seemed to direct them to the main chance as often as to heaven. When Penn himself had cleared his name with King William of Orange some time after the deposition of the Stuarts, he betook himself in person to his colony, where he found things thriving. There was good grain land in back of Philadelphia; there were grist mills along the creeks; the Germans of Germantown had turned industriously to the manufacture of linen and paper; there were ropewalks, breweries, and bakery shops.

Some twenty-five years after Penn's sojourn in his proprietary domain, the canny Benjamin Franklin chose Philadelphia in preference to New York or Newport when, after running away from an apprenticeship in Boston, he went looking for a job. In ten years Franklin had become master of his own Philadelphia printing establishment. As a printer of almanacs—his *Poor Richard's Almanac* collection of exhortations to order, frugality, and industry was a colonial best-seller second only to the Bible—he made money out of the sort of aphorisms that appealed to Yankees. He naturally issued a newspaper, the *Pennsylvania Gazette,* from his printing shop; and, as everybody knows, he indulged an experimental and inventive faculty that led him to make a famous iron stove and to trap electricity from a storm cloud with a kite. Long before the middle of the eighteenth century Franklin had amassed enough money out of business to indulge his scholarly and diplomatic bents; he represented the colonial merchants in London, sending back sage advice about the limits to which American importers could go in flouting the mercantilist acts and get away with it.

The Quaker businessmen of Philadelphia made no such clamor in the world as the Hancocks of Massachusetts; but their "peculiar practices"—the truthful labeling of merchandise, the habit of offering goods at a single open price—did much to make them both trusted and rich. Combining forces with the Germans ("Palatines"), the Welsh, and the Scots who were attracted to Penn's colony,

Quaker merchants provided capital for the earliest corporations. By the time of the Revolution, Pennsylvania was taking the lead as the iron manufacturer of the Colonies; a bloomery forge known as the "Pool" was operating at Pottstown—and brewers and storekeepers were putting their excess capital into sixteenth or fourteenth shares of forges and ironworks. The Paschal furnace in Philadelphia, visited by General Washington, became "the largest and best in America." Meanwhile, the "Palatines" of Lancaster and the back country produced more and more wheat to feed the suddenly vaulting colonial populations, floating some of their produce down the Susquehanna to be shipped from Philadelphia's rival port of Baltimore. Newspaper advertisements in other colonies just prior to the Revolution particularized Pennsylvania flour and iron, Philadelphia beer, potash kettles cast in Salisbury, Connecticut, Rhode Island cheese, Virginia tobacco, and Carolina pitch—which indicates Pennsylvania's place in the scheme of things. In addition, Philadelphia—the home of the Shippens, the Cadwaladers, and the rich Quaker merchant Samuel Powel—evolved as a banking center, producing such famous names as Thomas Willing, Robert Morris, and Stephen Girard, the mean-tempered French shipper whose complex of enterprises centering in a bank was to make him the nation's first multimillionaire. In Philadelphia industry and finance developed in harness, with the result that when Washington needed funds in the Revolution, the city was ready. When the war was over, it was through Philadelphia's leadership that the North, not the South, became the nation's money center.

In the South things were different from the start. Here the soil lent itself to large plantations as contrasted to the small and straggling New England farms where corn, peas, beans, and skimpy grain provided a meager fare. Moreover, the products of the southern soil were needed by Britain and fitted in nicely with prevailing British economic theory. What irked the descendants of the first planters was that in the process of trading with Britain they found themselves accumulating enormous debts to London countinghouses. Still, they might well have remained loyal British subjects had not the British Crown finally cut off their access to free land in the West. For the land was to the Southerners what the sea was to New England—the fundamental generator of their wealth, their way of life, and their culture.

In South Carolina the profitable growing of indigo after 1742 brought profits of 33 to 50 per cent and led to the colonization of the upland interior. Rice, the other staple of the region, became another source of profit when a relaxation of trade restrictions after 1730 permitted the merchants of Charles Town to export some of it directly to southern Europe—or "south of Cape Finisterre," as the charitable exemption read. And in all the southern colonies the English Navy provided a ready market for naval stores (produced by "tar burners") at times when the Baltic had been closed as a prime source.

With the British trade restrictions resting lightly upon them, the merchants of Charles Town had less scrabbling to do than their brothers of the North. There was, to be sure, a stigma attached to "trade" in a country where good livings were to be had from slave-manned plantations—and the Draytons and the Middletons and their descendants lived well on their Cooper and Ashley River showplaces without demeaning themselves by entering the counting-house. But plantations were—or should have been—business enterprises in and by themselves. Though plantation owners frequently lived beyond their means, the injunction to industry was taken seriously even by colonial plantation women: it was the daughter of a British Army officer, Miss Eliza Lucas (later Mrs. Charles Pinckney), who first experimented with indigo when her family left her alone in charge of the ancestral acres a few miles west of Charles Town. In years to come, as Mrs. Pinckney, Eliza was interrupted in her very knowledgeable pleasure-gardening by messages from her overseer complaining about the indigo (it would not get dry), the rice (it needed water), the barn (the Negro carpenter was busy making barrels), the indigo ladles (they were too short), the chickens (they were being eaten by wildcats and foxes), and the boat (it had not come upriver for the tar). These were details of an exacting business that needed profits if slaves were to be imported from Africa and if the lean seasons were to be endured.

To service the growing Carolina economy, at a time when planters expected to double their capital every three years, a generation of canny French Huguenots, sons and grandsons of refugees, led in making Charles Town the first port of consequence in the southern colonies. Here the Manigaults and de Saussures outpaced the English and Scotch-Irish Gadsdens and Rutledges as money-makers. The boldest trader in the Huguenot community was Henry Laurens, the son of a saddlery merchant. As a go-between who was prepared to perform any service for a pyramiding economy, Laurens found he could double his capital much faster than by raising crops on land he himself owned. As a wholesale commission merchant, factor, and independent trader, Laurens dealt in rum, sugar, Madeira wine, coffee from Guadeloupe, indigo, slaves, indentured servants, and such odd items as marble mantels. Sometimes he sailed his own ships; sometimes he took pieces of cargo in ships owned by others. As a banker for an economy that depended on notes of hand and bills of exchange, Laurens frequently took his pay from planters by accepting liens on next year's crops of rice and indigo, sometimes risking as much as £10,000 on future plantings.

At the age of forty, Laurens bought a Santee River plantation and settled down to raise rice and indigo; he acquired more rice lands on the Georgia coast; he created a 3,000-acre estate at Mepkin, on the Cooper River about thirty miles from Charles Town—and, when King George III's Townshend Act duties eventually bore down heavily on Charles Town importers, he tongue-lashed the colonial merchants from his retirement into a more zealous endorsement of nonimportation of English goods. When the Revolution came, he acted as president of the Continental Congress. He was captured by the British in 1780 (he was then fifty-six years old), and returned as an exchange prisoner at the end of the hostilities.

In contrast to Carolina rice, indigo, and naval stores, the tobacco of Virginia, Maryland, and the Albemarle country of North Carolina never received special consideration from the home country. King James I wrote an angry screed against it; and under later kings it was saddled with high import duties, which necessarily limited its market even though duty was remitted on the proportion of the crop that was re-exported from Britain to the European continent.

In addition to these man-made political drawbacks, tobacco quickly exhausted the soil on which it was grown; the plots had to be abandoned after four or five years, finding new use mainly as "school lands." When the price of slaves went up (owing to competition for them in the rice and indigo country), the Virginians were in real trouble, though they eventually found it profitable to breed slaves for sale to the owners of new cotton lands on the Gulf. Freight costs, insurance, commissions, merchants' profits, and the interest on borrowed funds, all of which were dominated by English companies, remained high for the tobacco growers—and with Britain monopolizing the trade there was no way of seeking new markets to meet shifts in the price.

Listen to Thomas Jefferson on the woes of the tobacco planter: "It is a culture productive of infinite wretchedness." (Jefferson was not referring to what smoking or snuff-taking did to users of the "sot weed.") Continuing his damnation, Jefferson said: "Those employed in it are in a continual state of exertion beyond the powers of nature to support. Little food of any kind is raised by them; so that the men and animals on these farms are illy fed, and the earth is rapidly impoverished." As for the dependence of Virginia tobacco farmers on English merchants and Scottish factors, which kept Virginia in hock to the suppliers of overseas credit, Jefferson was equally contemptuous. "These debts," he remarked, "had become hereditary from father to son, for many generations, so that the planters were a species of property, annexed to certain mercantile houses in London."

Yet if tobacco culture earned such opprobrium, it produced fine houses as well as shanties with clay-lined chimneys, able men as well as spendthrifts. The earlier eighteenth-century planters lived well, if precariously, on the proceeds of their wasteful staple crop; and throughout Virginia "tobacco notes"—or warehouse receipts validated by inspectors—passed as money. This money, of course, fluctuated in value with the state of the crops and markets, but it nevertheless was an accepted medium of exchange. Local Anglican clergymen, for instance, were regularly paid in tobacco notes; and when the Virginia state legislature temporarily substituted depreciated paper currency they raised a loud protest.

Tobacco also bred leaders for the Revolutionary period, because it took qualities of command to run a plantation. Supervisors and overseers had to be watched; slave and indentured-servant labor had to be stimulated to action. Cooperage for the hogsheads had to be done at the plantation mills; the hogsheads themselves might have to be rolled a mile or more to shipside. Since there were few towns or ports in the Virginia and Maryland tidewater country, plantation owners had to make their own diversions; hence the drinking and the card playing, the minuets and the horse racing and the endless entertainment of visitors, which were welcomed as a relief from country monotony. The planters might be always in debt, but money, to them, was a bookkeeping matter, and they lived high on the credit that was carelessly renewed from season to season. With the habits of Cavaliers, even such planters as came from lower-middle-class English stock took on a mien of lordliness. The more enterprising among them were stewards of large enterprises (some of them had many farms), and the plantation house, surrounded as it was by kitchens, smokehouses, tobacco houses, kitchen gardens, and Negro cabins, was necessarily the center of a domain.

The palmy days of the tidewater produced the Fitzhughs, the Byrds, and the Carters, whose names evoke a vision of "quality" in Virginia to this day. William Fitzhugh's Bedford estate, consisting of 1,000 acres of which 700 were left in thicket for future use, had 2,500 apple trees, a water gristmill, a dairy, a dovecote, a henhouse, and kept twenty-nine Negroes employed. The plantation house had thirteen rooms, with a big library; a French Huguenot refugee minister resided on the premises to teach Fitzhugh's son, young William. A man of affairs, the elder Fitzhugh was a lawyer as well as a planter; he acted as judge of the county court, as commander of the militia, and he was a member of the House of Burgesses.

Along with Fitzhugh, the first William Byrd was born in England. William Byrd II, born in Virginia, was sent to England by his wealthy planter father to be educated in business matters in London. Unlike some of the later planters whom Jefferson complained about, the Byrds, father and son, believed in diversified interests. The first Byrd had been a shopkeeper and fur trader before he became a tobacco planter; he bought slaves in lots of 500 for resale as well as for his own use; he purchased 1,000 gallons of rum at a time. When he became the lord of Westover, William Byrd II grew all types of vegetables and fruits, ran a tannery and a "one-man coal mine," and manufactured his own coarser textiles. He continued his father's fur trading in the Catawba Indian country, which gave him a cash income denied to other planters.

In planting time, William Byrd II's day was that of any planter who was concerned for his crop. After a chilling May rain the field hands would have to be rushed out to set 4,000 tobacco plants before dark. Since there was an annual poll tax and an initial importation tax on each Negro, the plantation owner had to make the most of his men when he needed them. Both as a reward and as a forestaller of bad colds, Byrd saw to it that each of his field hands got a good serving of rum after the day's labor. Byrd regularly inspected his plantations at the falls of the James and on the Appomattox River, watched over the health of his slaves, and saw that his tannery and coal mine were operating efficiently.

When he died in 1744 at the ripe age of seventy, the younger Byrd left 180,000 acres. The city of Richmond, set up with "streets sixty-five feet wide" on the site of his father's trading house, was Byrd's own development. Life had not been a mere colonial version of the rat race for William Byrd II. A cultivated man, he was in the habit of starting his day by reading passages in Greek from Homer or Thucydides, or something in Hebrew. His library at Westover contained 3,600 volumes. He kept a "secret diary" (published posthumously), wrote a "Discourse Concerning the Plague" commending tobacco as a therapeutic, and was always ready for billiards or cards with his swarming visitors.

Tobacco provided the credit for London cutlery, chinaware, four-poster beds, and serge suits; but it was the land itself, taken up in ever larger quantities both as a hedge against soil exhaustion and with a speculative eye to future sale, that provided the growth of the big planters' fortunes in a perennially inflationary age. At his death Robert Carter, the famous "King Carter," left an estate of 300,000 acres. A "miscellaneous agent" as well as a tobacco grower, Carter bought and sold and shipped tobacco raised on plantations other than his own, sending his sloop up and down the James and Rappahannock rivers to make the collections. He had more than 700 slaves—a huge number for the early part of the eighteenth century. The inducement to buy a Negro was increased by the property "headright" that went with him—an extra grant of fifty acres of land per person, which could be measured against the $10 poll tax levied on both whites and blacks alike and against the small quit-rents that had to be paid on land in any proprietary or royal colony.

As John Rolfe's tobacco plant voraciously ate the nutriment out of unmanured topsoil, the frontier lands to the west became more and more of an obsession with the Virginia planters. With Peter Jefferson, the father of Thomas, they pushed toward the Blue Ridge; and throughout the middle years of the eighteenth century caravans of slaves, overseers, horses, oxcarts, pigs, and kerchiefed women moving to inland sites were a familiar sight in Virginia. George Washington himself was part of the migration, as his father Augustine and his half-brother Lawrence moved upriver to new lands on the Potomac and the Rappahannock. As a young man still in his teens, Washington earned up to $42 a day (1962 value) by toting a surveyor's chain through the Shenandoah country to the headwaters of the Potomac to help lay out the still unbounded acres granted to his employer, Lord Thomas Fairfax. With the proceeds from surveying, Washington patented lands of his own in Frederick County—"My Bullskin Plantation," as he called them. He already had a sizable domain when he inherited Mount Vernon from his half-brother, along with his executor's share in the Principio Iron Works. To this he added shares in the Ohio Company, which had extensive land rights "on the western waters of Virginia."

Washington came to value his western possessions as his own troubles with tobacco multiplied. Although his tobacco brought the highest price in the Alexandria market, he was depressed by the way it ate up the fertility of his lands in spite of everything he could do. He tried alternating tobacco with grain to keep from having to let his ground lie fallow; he made replenishing experiments with mud from the Potomac, with black mold from his gullies, with horse, sheep, and cow dung, and with the new "green manure" crops of lucerne (alfalfa) and clover. Eventually he decided to get out of the tobacco business altogether, stipulating in contracts with his tenants that only enough tobacco should be raised to provide for "chewing and smoking in his own family." He was the first man in America to cultivate alfalfa; and his wheat became famous as the source of a "superfine" flour produced by his own mills and shipped in barrels made at his own cooperage plant. He became the biggest flour producer in the Colonies, gaining most of his cash income from three mills, which enabled him to produce for markets as far away as the West Indies. But it was good real estate, increasing in value against the constantly depreciating colonial currencies, that made Washington one of the richest men in eighteenth-century America. Washington's shrewdness in conducting continual hedging operations against inflation is clearly reflected in a letter to his stepson, John Parke Custis, that is dated October 10, 1778. "A Moment's reflection," so the embattled colonial commander-in-chief wrote, "must convince you of two things: first that Lands are of permanent value, that there is scarce a possibility of their falling in price, but almost a Moral certainty of their rising exceedingly in value; and secondly, that our Paper Currency is fluctuating; that it has depreciated considerably, and that, no human foresight can, with precision, tell how low it may get as the rise or fall of it depends on contingencies which the utmost stretch of human sagacity can neither foresee, nor prevent."

Though he always retained the predilections of landed gentry in his mode of living, Washington had the instincts of a modern business developer. With twenty other Southerners he organized a company in 1763 to drain the Great Dismal Swamp south of the Virginia port of Norfolk. He ran the company himself as managing director from 1763 to 1768, and eventually his executors collected dividends of $18,800 from 1810 to 1825 on the Great Dismal Swamp project; they finally sold the Washington share in it for $12,000.

Working on the Dismal Swamp drainage canals had set Washington to thinking about an all-water route into the Ohio country. But such ideas were rudely shoved aside by the onrush of political events. With the end of the French and Indian War in 1763, and the removal of old threats, Britain came to the conclusion that there was no further reason for allowing the colonists to expand westward. A buffer zone was no longer needed. This was not only a blow to the dreams of a young Washington; it was one more signal that before Americans could further expand their own enterprises they must provide themselves with a new political framework in which business could operate. And as Washington himself was to discover one day in 1775, the frame had to wait the issue of war.

2 Businessmen Join in an Unbusinesslike War

The bitter leaf leads to a bitter excursion.

Cannon and gunpowder are smuggled in via "the rock" of St. Eustatia.

Robert Morris banks the penurious Continental Congress.

Grass grows in the streets of Nantucket.

Alexander Hamilton completes the Constitution's grand design.

W<small>HO</small> boarded the first of the tea brigs at Griffin Wharf to touch off the Boston Tea Party that dark December night in 1773? Lendall Pitts, the scion of a rich merchant family, led the expedition quite openly, and Paul Revere, the silversmith, made no particular attempt to conceal his identity. Revere's contemporary, the redoubtably named George Robert Twelvetrees Hewes, who became an unofficial (though not entirely trustworthy) historian of the exploit, swore that he recognized merchant John Hancock among the "Indians" by his voice as he grunted the password, "Me know you." And Sam Adams was supposedly present. But no matter who did make "salt-water tea" in the "teapot" of Boston Harbor that night, the merchants of Boston stood behind the action and financed and led the subsequent opposition which sparked the American Revolution.

The active participation of merchants and businessmen in the War of Independence was, as matters turned out, crucial to its

24

outcome. This does not mean, of course, that the Revolution can be explained in purely economic terms, as some latter-day historians have made out. The angry merchants of Boston, like other men of their times, believed that liberty was all of a piece; though many of them feared that war might unchain "leveling" passions, life to the thoughtful colonials was not worth the having without liberty, and liberty without a share in private property was all but inconceivable. In taking up the cudgels against the British Crown in such mundane matters as trade and taxation, the colonists felt they were defending their very existence as free men.

This whole tradition of liberty was, moreover, based on the "rights of Englishmen" and inherited from the mother country. At its inception the Revolution was much more of an internal quarrel as to how a great commonwealth should be run than it was a war for "self-determination" in the current usage of that phrase. The Americans of the eighteenth century were above all politically *mature* men—mature in their view of liberty and knowledgeability of the law, and mature in their capacity to conduct their businesses in the far places of the earth. If their English rights had been respected, they would not have rebelled. But such a people could not lightly be pushed around by a head-strong King and Parliament removed by three thousand miles of water. As Edmund Burke reminded Parliament in his great plea for conciliation: "The ocean remains. You cannot pump it dry."

To make the relevance of Burke's warning clear, some under-standing of British eighteenth-century economic history, both in its commissions and omissions, is necessary. The shorthand word for Britain's pre-Adam Smith economic philosophy, which gov-erned the course of the history, was Mercantilism. It was a doctrine that favored the creation of monopolies and the preserva-tion of colonies as sources of raw materials which were to be exchanged for home country finished goods or processed com-modities on terms dictated by the mother nation. Not all raw materials were treated alike by the mother country, and this naturally led to a distinction between colonies.

Tea, originating in the British East and carried in British ships, had one priority. But back of tea there lurked sugar, which had the first priority of all. In Stuart times sugar had been a luxury;

but by the time of the Hanoverian Georges it had become a prime British necessity (in 1767 an English writer complained that "as much superfluous money is expended on tea and sugar as would maintain four millions more subjects on bread"). The new necessity was grown in the "sugar islands" of the British West Indies, which bulked considerably larger than all the North American Colonies together in the British Mercantile Plan. In all, the British investment in Caribbean island plantations—some 60 million in pounds sterling in 1775—was six times the debt owed to London or Bristol agents by southern planters and the merchants of Boston, Newport, and Philadelphia.

The sons of pioneer sugar planters had over the years been returning from the islands to buy rotten borough seats in the British Parliament, leaving their "attorneys" to handle plantations through overseers. In the early 1770's some seventy absentee plantation lords were sitting for county boroughs in the House of Commons. As a spectacular part of English life, with money to spend on brilliant equipages drawn by horses whose hoofs were shod in silver, these lords had identified themselves with the Mercantilist System as no Virginia tobacco grower, in debt to his Bristol factoring house, could possibly consider doing.

The protection of British Caribbean sugar, then, was a political "must" almost from the very start. For a time, the colonists were satisfied to trade for British "sugar island" molasses without making much of an issue of it. But over the years the Dutch and the French sugar plantations in the West Indies became more efficient producers than the British plantations in Barbados and Jamaica— and the New Englanders found they could get greater quantities of molasses from the "foreign" islands in exchange for their own exports of dried cod, barrel staves, horses, hay, and the slaves which they picked up for rum in the famous "triangular" extention of trade to West Africa.

In the England dominated by Robert Walpole, the bluff countryman who was the Whig prime minister during much of the first part of the eighteenth century, the mercantilist philosophy was tempered by a widespread willingness to wink at smuggling. Walpole's spirit of indulgence extended to sugar and molasses. In general, the importance of the various acts of trade and navigation was not that they made any pretense of keeping American colonial merchants, the ancestors of the first hardy race of laissez-faire businessmen, from doing what they felt they must do to live and prosper. The laws were complied with only when the advantage lay with compliance. Since London was the established market for tobacco in Europe, it involved no particular hardship when the Virginia planters were compelled to deliver their product to the "sot weed" factors sent out by London and Bristol mercantile houses to extend them credit. And when bounties were offered for South Carolina indigo (needed for woolen dyes) after 1740, or for naval stores (pitch, tar, turpentine) and hemp, the colonists gladly took the benefits.

When the advantage lay with ignoring the mercantilist restrictions, however, the colonial merchants blandly by-passed such things as Customs Boards and the office of the Surveyor General of the King's Woods, who tried to pre-empt the tallest pines for masts for the King's Navy. The sugar legislation and the white pine acts were often there as a mere felt presence, a daily reminder that there was sometimes a vital difference between positive, or "legal," law and the Natural Law—the Law of "Nature's God"—which the James Otises and the Thomas Jeffersons, echoing John Locke, were soon to be talking about.

In avoiding the Molasses Act, in particular, the colonists did not feel they were behaving in criminal fashion. Their attitude was that of a thirsty American in the 1920's who wanted a drink. Juries would not convict in molasses smuggling cases because they felt that custom in the matter was superior to the regulations demanding high customs. Moreover, the King's collectors acquiesced in the colonial view of things throughout the first half of the eighteenth century. They regularly granted "indulgences" to the molasses traders, letting them off for a small portion of the import duties, some of which presumably stuck to their own fingers as a bribe. Though the tax on molasses was set at sixpence a gallon in 1733, the custom in Boston was, according to James Otis, to settle for "about one-tenth" of the official statutory rate. At New York, the customs men exacted a fourth to a half penny a gallon; at Salem the rate was a half penny. And fresh fruit and wine came direct from southern Europe in distinct violation of an act prohibiting the importation of most European products from any place other than Britain.

The colonists broke with the mother country only when they feared that mercantilism would be enforced to the letter. Though the Southerners had a complementary trade relationship with England—tobacco, rice and indigo for English cloth and furniture— the Virginians needed new lands as their old lands wore out. Mercantilism was there to stop them, for under the terms of the Proclamation Line of 1763 and the subsequent Quebec Act they were sealed off from legitimate expansion into Kentucky beyond the Blue Ridge wall. The British obviously wished to turn the Ohio country into a reserve for Indians and Canadian fur traders. As for the Northerners, they had only salt fish and lumber and wheat to sell in the first instance—and the home island of Britain couldn't absorb these commodities in sufficiently large amounts to balance a trade for British manufactures. The salt fish and lumber had to go outside the Empire if Boston and Newport were to hope for enough specie to buy from London. Hence it was fight or be choked when the government of King George III decided really to crack down, or, in Edmund Burke's language, to apply the "tight rein." The colonists, as befitted men with an English heritage of their own, naturally chose to fight.

The first real crunch came with the Stamp Act and the so-called Townshend duties, which were part of King George III's campaign to compel the colonists to shoulder their share of the costs of the mid-century French and Indian war. The taxes and economic penalties were also accompanied by an effort to stifle ancient colonial charter-guaranteed rights of self-government. In common with other segments of the population the colonial businessmen rose to the challenge, acting virtually as one body to force a repeal of taxes on lead, glass, paint, and paper. As Professor Arthur M. Schlesinger has demonstrated in his trail-blazing *The Colonial Merchants and the American Revolution,* the sustained united front of the importers almost succeeded in making King George III back down.

The London mercantilists, however, couldn't leave well enough alone. They might have gotten away with it if they had limited themselves to imposing a small token tax on tea, which they did in 1767. For the colonists, after all, were prudential men: even the doughty John Adams managed to reconcile himself to drinking the lightly taxed beverage at John Hancock's home; he merely "hoped" that his particular cup might be a smuggled variety from Holland. But in early 1773, the mercantilist advisers to King George III were particularly concerned over the possible failure of the East India Company, a "favored instrument" of the Crown which had a seven-year supply of tea stored in its warehouses along the Thames. The company had to get this tea to market to keep from going bankrupt. Since, unlike the colonists, the East India Company *was* represented in Parliament, the 1767 Tea Act was quickly supplemented to give the company a monopoly of the American market. It was specified that the bitter leaf should be shipped only in the East India Company's own bottoms, and that it should be delivered not to indigenous Boston and Newport retailers, but to favored royal consignees. This cut out both the colonial shipowner and the colonial storekeeper (who were often united in the same person).

The result, quickly felt, was the dark excursion at Griffin Wharf, with the wild "Indians" whooping their defiance in the night. Benjamin Franklin, along with other prominent citizens of the middle colonies, was shocked by the violence of the Tea Party. But as Britain proceeded to punish the town of Boston by cutting off its commerce and literally trying to starve it into submission, the other colonies reacted swiftly to the severity of the retribution. To help keep Boston alive, Charleston, South Carolina, sent rice, which was bootlegged into the port over the neck connecting it with the Massachusetts mainland. Marblehead patriots provided codfish; Baltimore dispatched rye and bread. And Colonel Israel Putnam—"Old Put"—arrived one day from Connecticut driving a flock of sheep. As Esther Forbes has described it, Old Put was so much "caressed" by the grateful Bostonians that he had a hard time getting away. And when the merchant-financed opposition to the British finally erupted in gun smoke near the rude bridge that arched the flood in Concord, enough of the business leaders in New York, Philadelphia, Virginia, and South Carolina stood by Boston to make a united front.

The war itself was not a businesslike war in the modern sense;

indeed, the colonists won largely by combining frontier guerrilla tactics with watchful waiting until the French fleet cut off Cornwallis at Yorktown at a crucial moment. Nevertheless, Washington's straggling army had to be supplied through seven hard years of constant maneuver, and here businessmen continued to play their part. When the colonists couldn't get by on British cannon seized at Ticonderoga, they smuggled their armaments through the West Indies. This, in the language of Helen Augur, was the "secret war"—and the colonial shippers, old hands at dodging the King's customs collectors, took hold here with alacrity. The free Dutch port of St. Eustatia in the Caribbean became Washington's favorite arsenal—and so well did it serve the Colonies as a point of transshipment for gunpowder forwarded from Europe that the British Admiral Rodney, sent out to command in the Leeward Islands in 1780, said of "Statia" that "this rock of only six miles in length and three in breadth has done England more harm than all the arms of her most potent enemies, and alone supported the infamous American rebellion."

In Statia, the profit on gunpowder rose during the war to 700 per cent. The gunpowder came into the Dutch island in tea chests and in rice barrels tucked into the holds of ships that had supposedly cleared in Europe for Africa or the Mediterranean. The agent for the state of Maryland on Statia was Abraham van Bibber; together with Richard Harrison, an American factor on the French island of Martinique, he forwarded to the Continental Congress some of the first war supplies to reach the Colonies. Along with the gunpowder would go a constant dribble of civilian goods—linen and English thread stockings, French gloves, and French sugars. Through certain secret arrangements that are credited to Benjamin Franklin, the English island of Bermuda kept sending salt—and cedar sloops—to the mainland of America throughout the war.

Meanwhile, as envoys in Europe, able men like Silas Deane of Wethersfield, Connecticut, teamed up with Ben Franklin to form a sort of private State Department-*cum*-Board of Trade. By intrigue and negotiation these secret committeemen combed the capitals of the Old World for aid. Closer to Washington's constantly shifting field headquarters, a breed of native quartermasters foraged as best they could, helped by such public-spirited business-men as Jeremiah Wadsworth of Hartford, Connecticut. As an associate of Quartermaster General Nathanael Greene (who was himself a silent partner with Wadsworth in private operations), the "sachem" Wadsworth helped pick Washington's army up after some of its early sufferings. Wadsworth also helped build the frigate *Trumbull* on a 5 per cent commission, and with his partner, Barnabas Deane, held a contract from the Continental Congress to supply masts and spars for ships to all the states.

The food, clothing, and hay that were forwarded to the Continental soldiers as they hacked about New England, the Hudson Valley, and New Jersey had to be paid for somehow. At first Congress tried to foot the bill by an emission of paper money (the continentals). It also issued "loan certificates," and still later asked for "grants" from the separate state governments. Finally the whole business of paying for the war was turned over to the states save in the instances that American representatives abroad managed to cajole loans from the French and the Dutch. The final cost of the war has been estimated at $104 million in terms of gold, but most of it was paid in currency that a few years later was all but worthless. The irrepressible Franklin remarked in 1779: "This Currency, as we manage it, is a wonderful Machine. It performs its Office when we issue it; it pays and clothes Troops, and provides Victuals and Ammunition: and when we are obliged to issue a Quantity excessive, it pays itself off by Depreciation."

Actually, financing the war was not quite so simple as that, and printing-press money alone would never have done the job. Powder and shot from abroad had to be paid for in hard money and Congress relied heavily on merchants to lay their hands on it through manifold trading operations. The best known of these merchants was Robert Morris of Philadelphia, who in the early years of the war co-ordinated foreign procurement. Son of a British trader, Morris served his apprenticeship in the Philadelphia mercantile house of the Willings, and married Mary White, a Philadelphia belle who was the sister of the first Episcopalian bishop of Pennsylvania. By the time of the war he was a full partner of Thomas Willing, and was also a personal friend of Washington. Morris did extremely well by the struggling young confedera-

Courtesy Independence National Historical Park Collection

Robert Morris

tion, masterminding many of the deals with the West Indies. He also continued to grow rich by carrying on his own private transactions in tobacco and other commodities. Though Thomas Paine attacked Morris for this kind of "conflict of interest," Washington as well as most other people was willing to overlook his habit of mingling private and public business.

Toward the end of the war Morris was made Superintendent of Finances. As such he gave America its first lessons in practical banking when he founded the Bank of North America—described as the "first commercial bank in the U.S."—and made his old partner, Thomas Willing, head of it. When "gentlemen of monied interest" refused to invest in the bank, Morris arranged that the government should subscribe $254,000 of hard money that it had received from France. The remainder of the $400,000 needed for incorporation followed from private sources. With this capital in hand, the bank, under Morris' direction, proceeded to make large loans to the government—$1,200,000 in all. It also discounted commercial paper and issued its own bank notes, which were readily accepted as a medium of exchange because of the bank's reputation for redemption and Morris' own financial standing. Indeed, Morris' personal notes were readily accepted at par around Philadelphia and in the middle states. When he severed his official connection with the government in 1784 he had not restored its credit, but he had more than earned his sobriquet as "financier of finances."

Morris' later years proved unhappy ones. Always flamboyant in his operations, he finally overreached himself in real-estate speculation and actually was sent to debtors' prison in Philadelphia in 1798. Despite this disgrace, Washington remained loyal to his wartime financier to the end, and indeed invited Mrs. Morris to spend time at Mount Vernon while her husband was in jail. For Washington correctly sensed that America owed an extraordinary debt to this man. Not only did Morris help the Colonies finance the war, but he also grasped the need for strong and centrally directed finance, which was to prove essential for the revival of business. In and out of office he kept urging the Continental Congress to revise its own powers, to levy more taxes, and to maintain a sound currency system. He also undoubtedly forestalled repudiation of the country's wartime obligations. Thus he set the stage for the great funding operations of Alexander Hamilton, the first U.S. Secretary of the Treasury. Indeed, it was at Morris' behest that Washington chose Hamilton for that office.

Before Hamilton got his opportunity to put Morris' ideas into effect, however, the American people had to discover by sad experience that they needed a stronger form of government than the one supplied by the Continental Congress and the Articles of Confederation. For the war, while successful in a military sense, had taken an enormous economic toll. Despite much privateering, external trade had been completely disrupted, and in Nantucket grass had grown in the streets as the whaling vessels rotted at the piers. Privateering profits, save with the Derbys of Salem, Girard of Philadelphia, and a few others, disappeared as the British Royal Navy swept the small, inadequately armed American vessels from the seas. The New England fisheries needed new ships before the "sacred cod" could move again in commerce—and then there would be the troublesome matter of finding new markets for fish and lumber to replace British Caribbean island ports that had been placed out of bounds by King George's Parliament. As for the southern states, which might have paid for imports with shipments of tobacco, rice, and indigo, their plantations had either deteriorated during the war or been overrun and devastated by the British. The fields could not be revived overnight.

Meanwhile internal domestic commerce was falling to pieces for want of a strong central authority. Every state tried to get the drop on its neighbors—for example, New Jersey, "a cask tapped at both ends," found itself squeezed between the trade discriminations practiced at its expense by Pennsylvania and New York. Connecticut levied duties on imports from Massachusetts and, in turn, discovered that New York had no intention of letting firewood from Stamford and New Haven move through Hell Gate into the East River free. New Yorkers and New Hampshiremen started quarreling over the rights to Vermont maple-sugar-bush country. Even state boundaries were matters of dispute. Connecticut, for instance, claimed that certain land between the Susquehanna and Delaware rivers had been granted to it by the British Crown and tried to enforce this claim against an outraged Pennsylvania.

The whole chaos was compounded by a spotty paper-money inflation in every state save Connecticut ("the land of steady habits") and Delaware. The inflation was kept within reasonable limits in the middle states, but Rhode Island, an old offender in the matter of paper money, went hog-wild. When the merchants of Newport and Providence closed their stores in 1786 rather than sell goods to Rhode Island farmers for worthless paper, the farmers retaliated by burning their corn, pouring their milk on the ground, and letting their apples rot in the orchards. The year 1786 might, with pardonable exaggeration, be called the year in which no business was done.

This is not to say that the American people starved in the post-Revolutionary period; after all, 90 per cent of the population still lived close to the soil. The farmer had his beans, his peas, and his Indian corn; he let his lean pigs forage in the woods for acorns; and when he added to his farm buildings he generally used wooden dowels instead of costly nails to fasten his beams together. The spinning wheel provided him with clothes, which he stained with sumac or butternut dyes—and if his sheep were too poor to supply much wool, such woolen yarn as was available could be mixed with linen fibers from flax to provide the rough cloth known to our ancestors as "linsey-woolsey." People ate out of wooden trenchers shaped by the fireside during long winter evenings; homemade moccasins were used for shoes—and when cash was needed for such things as sewing needles or for salt, or to pay the land tax, the farmer burned some wood and leached the ashes to make pot ashes or potash, an article that usually commanded a good price.

But while life went on, the means of economic expansion were, to say the least, limited. In the 1780's the roads were still so abominable that most travel was by water, though horses and stages clopped and jolted at four or five miles an hour in good weather over the sketchy highways from Portsmouth, New Hampshire, to Baltimore. In the South, land travel was even more difficult. Though Kentucky and Tennessee were attracting settlers, a general movement to the West must wait upon something better than canoes, pack horses, and even broad-horn flatboats. There was, too, the matter of the Indians, who were being egged on against American settlers by British commanders who had not yet departed from U.S. soil at Detroit and Niagara. As for would-be manufacturers, if they had capital they couldn't transport their goods. And a people used to farming in the crudest conventional ways hardly helped improve things by regarding the inventor in quest of a mechanical short cut as an "indolent" and "God-less" man.

The rundown condition of the country after the Revolution— and the inadequacy of the Confederation to deal with it—was well known to the men who became the federal republic's "Founding Fathers." As a member of a Continental Congress that was unceremoniously shuffled about between Princeton, New Jersey, and Annapolis, Maryland, Jefferson experienced at firsthand the make-shift character of a government that could not levy taxes to pay for a permanent capital. To pay his way during his term in a Congress that would not pay him, Madison had to borrow money from a Philadelphia banker, Haym Solomon, who refused to charge interest when he learned of the young Congressman's predicament.

Washington himself had plenty of opportunity to see conditions at firsthand. In 1784, after fighting to get paper notes for his veterans, which were cashed at anywhere from 20 to 50 per cent discount, he returned to Mount Vernon. But he was soon off to the West, where he found squatters on his lands—and he offered the *de facto* claimants a settlement at 25 shillings per acre or leases for ninety-nine years. Over the years he investigated all possible routes to the West. At the end of the war he made a horseback trip up the Mohawk Valley, the future route of the Erie Canal, and even bought over 5,000 acres of New York State land. He also explored the middle and southern approaches and, as the young nation's "first expansionist," pushed for the formation of the Potomac Co. to dig a westward canal from the Potomac's upper reaches to the Monongahela.

The idea never came to much because the terrain proved too difficult. But Washington's activities on behalf of the Potomac Co. gave the young states their first lessons in co-operation. In 1786, Maryland formally agreed to let Delaware construct a canal connecting the Delaware River and Chesapeake Bay. More important, it met with New Jersey and New York in conference at Annapolis to consider "such additions to the powers of Congress as might conduce to a better regulation of trade."

The Annapolis Convention was the first effort to stir the states out of their postwar lethargy. In itself it accomplished little, but it did succeed in setting the stage for the Constitutional Convention at Philadelphia in 1787. The fifty-five delegates from the thirteen sovereign states met at Philadelphia ostensibly to "amend" the Articles of Confederation. Boldly, however, they chose to exceed their powers and sought to form a "more perfect union." Quite aside from the necessity of squaring this action with the folks back home, the delegates had to solve a unique problem in social physics: how to create a stronger central government—a "power of the whole"—without infringing on the individual's rights to life, liberty, and property, and without weakening the ability of the states to conduct their own affairs.

The historic solution was to create a federal structure of delegated authority, with all non-delegated powers reserved under the Tenth Amendment "to the States respectively, or to the people." In good part the Founders trusted to the states to preserve the liberties of their own citizens. But in two critical economic areas pertaining to business they drew the line. As practical men of affairs, the delegates had seen the evils of multiple state currencies, and in 1786 they had witnessed Shays's Rebellion, in which Captain Daniel Shays had attempted to rouse inflationary-minded Massachusetts farmers against the hard-money interests of maritime Boston. Congress, in reaction to this, was given exclusive power to coin money and the states were forbidden to do so. Similarly, the states were expressly forbidden to levy tariffs or embargoes against one another.

This was about all the economic planning there was, but the results were profound. For when the last necessary ratifying vote on the Constitution came through in 1788, merchants and businessmen from the Kennebec to the Savannah River could look forward to moving out into a world of internal free trade that was to become the greatest "common market" in history. And with the "power of the border" secure, Americans could look out on the outside world with confidence that they would no longer be pawns of contending European empires. The great business boon of the Constitution was that it created a legal instrument that permitted individual forward planning without fear of *ex post facto* interruptions by government or undue molestation from mercantilists of any sort, whether home-grown or foreign.

Even so, the Constitution was at best a prospectus, and the job of putting its economic insights into effect still remained to be done. The man who rose to this challenge was Alexander Hamilton. Born in the West Indies, an artillery officer during the war, an able lawyer and negotiator, Hamilton would have preferred a far more centralized government than emerged from the Constitutional Convention. Failing that, however, he set to work as Secretary of the Treasury on three enormous tasks: the funding of the national and state debts; the creation of a viable credit system; and the stimulation of domestic manufacturing.

In the matter of debt Hamilton took on an extraordinarily complex and politically delicate job. During the war and postwar years the old Continental Congress not only borrowed abroad but had also piled up a domestic debt with a face value of some $40 million (not counting the issue of paper currency, which was clearly beyond redemption). In addition, the states had incurred or assumed debts amounting to $25 million. A more timid man might have counseled the scaling down of these obligations, letting the states in particular meet their creditors any way they chose. But to Hamilton such a course seemed neither honorable nor expedient. The new Republic had to restore its credit, and the state debts had, after all, been incurred in fighting a common enemy. It seemed unjust that the states which had been trampled by war should pay more than those which had, so to speak, come home free.

In his great "Report on Public Credit," therefore, Hamilton proposed that the old Continental debt and most of the state debts be bundled together and paid off at par. The proposal met with a storm of opposition in and out of Congress. Madison, for one, was suspicious of the whole scheme, arguing among other things that many of the original holders of state and Continental obligations had sold them off at cut-rate prices to speculators who would be the ultimate gainers. Many other Southerners invoked the doctrine of "states' rights" and opposed the plan. Unable to joust with his opponents on the floor of Congress, Hamilton had to rely on his lucidity as a writer to carry his point. Eventually he won over the votes of Virginia and Maryland by the political deal under which the administration agreed to remove the national capital from New York and locate it on the Potomac River at a site to be chosen by President Washington.

In the final outcome Congress agreed to fund a total of $42 million of debt with the biggest portion of the new obligations drawing 6 per cent interest and a smaller portion at 3 per cent.

In the process, speculators certainly made money, and some latter-day historians have even accused the Founding Fathers of conspiring to feather their own nests by anticipating all along a rise in the value of Continental paper. But in writing the Constitution the Founders made no recommendation about the debt, leaving the matter to the discretion of Congress; and Congress in its turn finally decided that something had to be risked if the public credit were to be re-established. Actually, as Hamilton correctly foresaw, much more than the public credit was at issue. For the assumption of the state debts in particular proved a powerful instrument for drawing the states together and giving their citizens a vital stake in the whole federal experiment.

The funding of the debt was also essential to and interlocked with Hamilton's design for giving the country an efficient monetary and credit system. At his urging Congress defined the U.S. dollar in terms of gold and silver and set up the mint for coining both. Specie of all kinds, however, remained desperately short for a good many years, and the more immediate problem was how to regulate the issue of paper money, in which most business transactions had to be done. Here Hamilton improvised boldly. In 1791 Congress set up the first Bank of the United States with an initial capital of $10 million. Most of this capital came from private investors who purchased bank stock with bonds they had recently acquired under Hamilton's funding plan. With these bonds and a smaller amount of specie as assets, the bank in turn issued its own bank notes, which became a reliable and much-needed medium of exchange.

To head the bank Hamilton recommended Robert Morris' old partner Thomas Willing, commonly called "Square Toes" from the conservative cut of his shoes. A reticent and prudent man with a horror of speculation, Willing helped set the tone of anonymity that bankers have generally cultivated to this day. Scarcely had Square Toes assumed office than the bank, along with Hamilton's whole design for the future, was put to the test by the short-lived panic of 1792. A drop in the money market coincided with the collapse of various land-company schemes of the New York speculator, William Duer. An ex-Assistant Secretary of the Treasury, Duer had sought to enlist European capital for the settlement of lands in the Ohio Valley. When the bubble burst, he was sent to prison for debt, and it looked as if the young nation were in for a long depression. Indeed, Jefferson computed that New York investors and speculators lost some $5 million (equal to the value of all the buildings in the city), and that Philadelphia and Boston losses ran to $1 million each. The *National Gazette* pointed to New York's "languishing condition—vessels lying at the wharves without anyone to receive their cargoes—the speculators either in jail ruminating over bushels of loose papers, locked up in garretts, or fled into remote and desolate parts of New Jersey." Characteristically, Hamilton met the situation by directing the government to support the market for U.S. 6 per cents at par, and within two months the country's banks were discounting as usual. By June, 1792, confidence in the economy was so far restored that 5,000 persons met at the state house in Philadelphia "with $30 in every man's hand" for subscribing to the Lancaster Road, the first big enterprise of its kind.

Despite this initial success, Hamilton's general philosophy never proved popular. When the charter of the first Bank of the United States lapsed in 1811, it was not renewed. A second Bank of the United States was set up after the War of 1812, but was in turn killed off by Andrew Jackson. Thereafter for many years the country rode along with a highly decentralized banking system, suffered many a bank failure and some disastrous panics, and learned to its cost that it is one thing to specify that a central government shall "regulate" the value of money, and another thing to do so. Indeed, even the modern Federal Reserve System—established a hundred and nine years after Hamilton was killed by Burr in their famous duel under the cliff at Weehawken—has scarcely found a magic formula. Nevertheless, Hamilton set a standard to emulate. He was not, as some latter-day agrarians have charged, a skinflint hard-money man. He was that rare phenomenon—an expansionist who knew that growth and good money go together.

Hamilton also sought to encourage manufacturing, though here his ideas leaped far ahead of his time and the country's resources. In his "Report on Manufactures," written in 1791 with the able assistance of a young Philadelphian called Tench Coxe, Hamilton drew heavily on Adam Smith's *Wealth of Nations* and, indeed, as historian Louis Hacker has noted, paraphrased it in a number of places. In one respect, to be sure, he deviated from the principles of free trade and the market economy. With his eyes on the predatory powers of Europe, Hamilton noted that a young and struggling nation needed a certain amount of self-sufficiency lest it be vulnerable in case of embargo and war. The report, therefore, favored a protective tariff to encourage new industries. Yet Hamilton also hedged this proposal. In his view an open bounty, or subsidy, was better than a tariff, and even a bounty should not be continued too long.

The second part of Hamilton's report consisted largely of a census of U.S. manufactures as they existed in the summer of 1791. Aside from household fabrication such as weaving and spinning, Hamilton listed seventeen separate industries that were already flourishing to some extent. These included ironworking, the tanning of hides, the softening of flax fibers for linen, the making of hemp, sugar refining, the many developments of the lumber industry (ships, cabinet wares, etc.), tinware, copper and brass work, and hat-making. Oddly, Hamilton did not count milling of wheat as a "considerable" manufacture, though since colonial times it had contributed substantially to exports.

Here was a beginning, but as Hamilton and Tench Coxe looked around them, they also found much room for improvement. There was, first, the sad state of the "mechanick arts": workers were lazy and untutored; the machinery in use was a ramshackle collection of minor aids to handicraft; and as for capital, it was not to be had without paying exorbitant interest rates. The biggest shortage of all was manpower, since there were at the time fewer than a million white adult males to "shoulder the burden of a continent." Hamilton's answer here was more machinery, which would reduce the need for many hands; and women and children could take over some of the repetitive tasks of factory production.

In an attempt to give point to his report, Hamilton formed what was probably the first true corporation in the United States, the "Society for Establishing Useful Manufactures," chartered by the New Jersey legislature on November 22, 1791. According to the proposed plans for the society, the proprietors hoped to manufacture paper and paper products, heavy linen for sails, women's shoes, brass and iron ware, carpets and print cottons. A "new city" was projected and in time the textile town of Paterson, New Jersey, was to grow up on the site. The society raised $625,000 and actually built a cotton-print mill. But alas for Hamilton's hopes, it could find neither skillful managers nor competent machine designers and artisans; nor could it lure young men away from the farms at costs commensurate with the operation. In 1796 the plant closed down. Hamilton, foreseeing the difficulties of the society, had resigned from it in 1793.

The uncomfortable truth was that the U.S. had few resources on which to erect a "holding company" for "useful manufactures" in the early 1790's. What Hamilton only fitfully grasped was that the manufacturing nation of his dreams had to be born out of long travail and pain. Although the young nation had a going money system, it was short in both investment capital and technical know-how. To be sure, some inspired tinkerers, such as Oliver Evans, Samuel Slater, and Eli Whitney, were already at work on inventions that presently would revolutionize business enterprise. But the fruits of their tinkering lay ahead, and neither Hamilton nor the other Founding Fathers could hurry things. Their glory was that they provided some ideas which freed man as a producer— and the ideas would find their way.

3 The Quest for Capital and the Sprouting of Invention

The Empress of China *links New York harbor with Canton and Macao.*

Salem becomes a pepper emporium.

Gimcracking Oliver Evans automates flour milling.

Samuel Slater brings the Arkwright spinning secrets to Rhode Island.

The Browns and the Lowells found the textile industry.

Paul Revere pioneers metal rolling, and Eli Whitney foreshadows mass production.

IF ANY nation seemingly needed a Marshall Plan or Point Four Program at its launching, it was the young American Republic. For in the late eighteenth century, and indeed well into the nineteenth, the shortage of capital was everywhere, and there was no beneficent power beyond the seas to supply it. Rather the newborn nation had to store up its own reserve of money and energy for new and risky ventures and to rely on its own inventiveness to expand and develop its "infant industries."

As matters turned out, it was shipping that supplied the velvet for getting the investment process going. Trading up had always been congenial business to the colonists, especially the Yankees, and the visible sign of such trading was the acquisition of gold and silver specie from abroad through all kinds of complicated foreign transactions. Tracing the course of any hard bit of currency over the decades must, of course, defeat the ingenuity of even the closest student of the Keynesian "multiplier": gold notoriously leaves no scent. But the success of American trade in the early years of the Republic can be roughly measured from the fact that U.S. reserves of specie, at first desperately short, increased by 1820 to a point that permitted the federal government to pay off most of its foreign creditors in hard coin.

The great American sea story, which culminates in the clipper ships of the 1850's, had its beginnings, of course, in the earliest ventures of New England and Delaware Valley merchants to exploit the wealth of the West Indies and Africa. During the Revolution trade took on a new dimension as the colonists, daring the British blockade, sought new sources of supply. The Cabots of Beverly sent ships to Göteborg, Sweden, and even all the way into Russia to pick up duck (a textile, not a fowl). The war also opened the eyes of other bold men—Girard and Morris of Philadelphia, the Browns of Providence, the patriotic Jeremiah Wadsworth of Hartford—to the possibilities of assembling and delivering goods over long distances and in big bulk. And almost inevitably trade in the post-revolutionary period broke out of the Atlantic and sought the distant Far East.

The first big breakthrough voyage in the grand manner came in 1784, when the *Empress of China,* a promotion of Philadelphia's Robert Morris, New York's William Duer, and Daniel Parker of Watertown, Massachusetts, set sail out of New York Bay bound for Macao and Canton in China. This first venture into the "China trade" set a pattern for what the early economic historian Weeden called "the new order of merchants." The *Empress of China,* 360 tons burden, was loaded with ginseng root, which she carried into the Whampoa roads some six months after leaving New York. Lacking charts, the *Empress* negotiated the perils of Sunda Strait in East Indian waters in company with a French man-of-war. Since there were no cabled analyses of the market in those days, the bartering of the cargo was in the hands of an attractive young man, Major Samuel Shaw, who had served through the Revolution as aide-de-camp to General Knox.

Acting under the title of supercargo, Shaw was the representative aboard ship of the owners and the consigners. Though in some voyages the captain himself doubled as supercargo, Shaw was exclusively a man of business, as befitted a young Army officer who had grown up in the countinghouse of his Boston merchant father. Reverting to family type, he made an instantaneous success. The Chinese merchants of the Hong, as the foreigners' trade center at Canton was known, welcomed the Americans as the "new people," and Shaw got permission to trade in spite of some trouble the English were having because of the accidental killing of a Chinese by a British gunner. The profits of Shaw's trading for teas and silks amounted to $30,000, or 25 per cent on the capital— and when Shaw's report to the U.S. government was published, it started other merchants on the road to the East. Shaw himself made other voyages before his early death from a liver disease contracted in Bombay; he established the first American commercial house in China, and he became the first American consul at Canton.

The *Empress of China* was followed by other famous New York ships, culminating in the 1850's in Donald McKay's *Flying Cloud* and the *Sovereign of the Seas*. For a time, however, the hardy skippers of the Massachusetts North Shore were the great American admirals of the open sea. The fruits of Down East sea-borne enterprise are evident to this day, as the Federalist homes in old Newburyport and the Boston of Charles Bulfinch quite visibly demonstrate. To be sure, the trade of Newburyport, unlike that of Salem and Boston, was always with such relatively close-to-home places as the Baltic and the West Indies, but the town was conveniently situated at the mouth of the Merrimack to build ships for all the ports, and so benefited indirectly from the swelling global ventures.

During the last days of the Revolution, Salem's Elias Hasket Derby had learned the value of faster ships, and had begun to break with ancient conventions of marine design, thus giving an important impetus to the shipbuilding art. His 309-ton *Grand Turk*, built to new specifications, outsailed the vessels of the Royal Navy in 1782 and 1783, and thereafter took off for the "Salem Indies" and Canton by way of the Isle of France in the mid-Indian Ocean.

Soon other Derby ships—the *Peggy,* the *Three Sisters,* the *Light Horse,* and the speedy *Astrea*—were returning full-laden to Salem with manifests that featured Bombay cotton, Mocha coffee from the Red Sea, pepper from Sumatra, and teas, colored muslins, fine porcelains, and silks from India and China. Derby took ingenious calculated risks when insuring his cargoes, and tried to have none of his vessels approach the stormy North Shore coasts between November and March.

Courtesy Peabody Museum of Salem

Crowninshield's Wharf in Salem

A decent man who refused to let his supercargoes pick up slaves on the African coast, Derby also had an eye for the welfare of his crews. The pay on the early ships was good, especially when contrasted with the rewards of the proletarian whaler crews of New Bedford at a later date; an able seaman in the first great days could earn more than a shore laborer in actual cash, and he had his board and lodging, a considerable item, to boot. The Derby officers, like the captains and mates of nearby Boston, were permitted to trade in foreign ports on their own account, as were the seamen to the extent that space in their chests allowed. Many a plowboy who came aboard ship "through the hawsehole" (as distinct from the cabin window) rose to be an officer (and a comparatively rich man) in the Salem fleet; as for other farm sons who made a voyage or two, they often saved enough to return to the soil with farm title, a grubstake, and a wife.

When Elias Hasket Derby died a millionaire in 1799 at the age of sixty, his sons Elias H. and John carried on after him, along with other famous seafaring merchants, the Crowninshields, the prodigious Joseph Peabody, and the famous Billy Gray (who owned 113 vessels before 1815). At the beginning, this canny group directed their imaginative voyages from the gambrel or hip-roofed houses standing back of Derby Street up from Derby Wharf. Lacking both a good harbor and a hinterland, the group nonetheless combined with the Cabots and Israel Thorndike of nearby Beverly to make a couple of unlikely villages on the bleak North Atlantic littoral a self-help legend. After becoming the pepper emporium of the Western world (and everyone needed pepper in those days because of the lack of refrigeration for meat), Salem was eventually killed as a port by Mr. Jefferson's embargo and Mr. Madison's War of 1812—quite senseless ventures in spite-your-face politics from the New England merchant's standpoint. But the money made from the early Salem shipping supported the Bay State economy during a perilous period. And Salem's Nathaniel Bowditch, a supercargo of mathematical genius who discovered 8,000 errors in the tables of the standard English work on navigation, produced his own *New American Practical Navigator*—a guide that was to stand all American sailors in good stead through the high days of the clipper ships, and is still in favored use today.

Where Salem's preferred route to the pepper marts of Asia was by way of Vasco da Gama's Cape of Good Hope, the merchants and seafarers of Boston tended to prefer Magellan's way of Cape Horn. John Ledyard's account of fur trading in the Pacific Northwest, plus a hint or two in Captain Cook's chronicles, gave these men the idea that the skin of the sea otter would prove a key to the Canton market, and so it proved. The great pioneering Boston voyage was that of the *Columbia,* which was outfitted by seven shareholders (including John Derby and Charles Bulfinch, the architect of the Capitol in Washington and Boston's State House).

On her second voyage the *Columbia* under Captain Robert Gray poked her way, in 1792, into the mouth of a great river, the "Oregon" of William Cullen Bryant's "Thanatopsis." Having opened a valid U.S. claim to the Oregon country, the *Columbia* took furs from the Columbia River Indians for copper and cheap bolts of cloth, and was off again to China. Many another Boston ship followed her in the years to come, varying the sea-otter peltry cargoes by picking up sandalwood in the islands of "Owyhee." Through trading with the Cantonese by way of the American Northwest, a Cape Cod boy like Captain Bill Sturgis could become a Boston merchant of high consequence and, later, a manager of investment capital.

When the sea-otter pelts and the Hawaiian sandalwood ran out, Sturgis and others turned to trafficking in California hides. To quote George R. Russell, a merchant scholar of the era, the typical Yankee merchant was soon sending his "merchandise all over the earth; [he] stocks every market; makes wants that he may supply them; covers the New Zealander with Southern cotton woven in Northern looms; builds blocks of stores in the Sandwich Islands; swaps with the Feejee cannibal; sends the whaleship among the icebergs of the poles . . . piles up Fresh Pond [a reference to exported ice] on the banks of the Hoogly . . . and makes life tolerable in the bungalow of an Indian jungle." American merchant shipping had its many "downs" before the English eventually took the business away from both Boston and New York with the advent of the tramp steamer. But, despite the interruptions caused by the Jeffersonian Embargo of 1807, the Non-Intercourse Act, the War of 1812, and the long depression of 1837–43, shipping continued for a full half-century to be a mainstay of the young Republic's economy.

During the early Napoleonic troubles, when the British and the French were locked in a deleterious trade war that accompanied the military campaigns, the Yankees took over a major part of the carrying trade of the world. And for a period after the Napoleonic wars Americans fought the British successfully for their share of world commerce. It was not until the discovery of gold in California in 1848 that American businessmen began to forget the outer world in the excitements of developing the new continental market. Meanwhile Stephen Girard of Philadelphia had joined the merchants of Salem, Boston, and New York in assembling great cargoes for the Far East (including Turkish opium), and bringing home a fabulous wealth in return. New Bedford, Nantucket, Sag Harbor, and New London specialized in whaling, a hard-bitten business which became notorious after 1830 for its cruel skippers and its tight-fisted owners who often cheated their crews of their "lays" (titles to a proportion of a voyage's profits). The cheating was done by various stratagems such as reckoning a crew's shares in prices below the actual market. Until "rock oil," or petroleum, began to service the lamps of China (along with those of the United States), whaling and the manufacture of whaling products followed after cotton textiles and shoes as Massachusetts' leading industry.

It was commerce that provided the vital capital needed to stimulate and expand domestic U.S. manufacturing and businesses of all kinds. With money made out of the China trade, Stephen Girard of Philadelphia moved into banking, offering in 1812 a "complete service under one-man management." Money made by the Browns of Providence out of foreign trading and by the Lowells and Jacksons of Boston and Newburyport out of shipping spilled over into textile manufacturing. So, too, did the whaling money of New Bedford, Sag Harbor, and New London. In the 1830's and 1840's came the really dramatic shifts. For example, John Murray Forbes, brother of the charming Robert Bennet Forbes who had originally gone to sea at the age of thirteen "with a capital consisting of a Testament, a Bowditch, a quadrant, a chest of sea clothes, and a mother's blessing," took his own capital won in the China trade and, with a number of merchant friends, bought into the unfinished Michigan Central Railroad. John P. Cushing, Thomas Handasyd Perkins' Canton agent, put his money into banks, insurance companies, and railroads, most of them in New England. Perkins himself, working anonymously behind the scenes, became one of the early investment capitalists. Thus the original merchant capital became the first investment capital of the New World. It had all come out of the sea.

This capital never could have gone to work, however, had not a bold breed of inventors developed new machines and technologies. Some inventions sprang from the ingenuity of boys seeking to escape the endless chores of hardscrabble subsistence farms; others came from England, in the heads of immigrants or the first generation of Yankee travelers. The men who built our first industries, which were usually set up in crude wooden structures at the fall lines of the rivers where gristmills, sawmills, and paper mills had long been operating, scarcely knew they were pioneering what was to become a complete system of industrial production and eventually mass merchandising. Generally speaking, these men were primarily interested in adding a bit of speed to some phase of the molasses-slow processes of handmaking, which, as we have now pretty much forgotten, is the literal translation of the word "manufacture." Millwork, for a generation and more, remained an adjunct of cottage work as cloth and shoe leather went out for finishing.

As is usually the case when the world is about to shift on its axis, progress sprang from small, abortive beginnings. Benjamin Franklin made discoveries in electricity, but it was a long time before Thomas Edison could harness electricity to the uses of industry. Jacob Perkins of Newburyport made a machine capable of cutting and heading nails in the 1790's, and twenty years before that Jeremiah Wilkinson of Rhode Island had pioneered a device for heading a dozen tacks at once, but it was not until 1825 that a number of men, including Ezekiel Reed of Bridgewater, Massachusetts, finally began to machine tacks and nails in real quantity. As for horseshoe nails, for want of which battles have traditionally been lost, they resisted machine manufacture until 1850, when Silas Putnam of Neponsit, Massacusetts, used a triphammer to form the heads. Putnam's device went begging for a decade, but it caught on just in time to save the day for the Union cavalry in the Civil War.

In bigger things than nails, the first inventor entrepreneurs frequently wound up frustrated and broke. John Fitch of Windsor, Connecticut, escaped from the farm and a dismal apprenticeship in a clockmaker's home to invent a steamboat, but he could not compete with the stagecoach between Philadelphia and Trenton and his enterprise finally failed. Disappointed, he died a drunkard in the West. James Rumsey, a Virginian, put a paddle-wheel boat on the Potomac, and Oliver Evans of Delaware constructed an amphibious monster called *Orukter Amphibolos,* which could run by steam on both land and water and do duty as a dredge. But it was Robert Fulton, as everyone knows, who got credit for making the first commercially practicable steamboat with the *Clermont,* which became an acceptable Hudson River packet some years after the boats of Fitch, Rumsey, and Evans had been retired.

Courtesy the Historical Society of Pennsylvania

Oliver Evans

Brown Brothers

Eli Whitney

In other inventions of Oliver Evans a prescient man might have looked decades ahead to the beginnings of multiple drilling and the Detroit assembly line. When he was twenty-three years old, in what is now Wilmington, Delaware, Evans cut his leg with a scythe and had to spend some time in bed. This was in 1777, in the middle of a war. With nothing to do but think, he designed a machine for making "cards," as the instruments for combing out cotton and wool fibers for spinning were called.

The blacksmiths in Evans' neighborhood considered the card-making machine a "useless gimcrack." But despite the fact that he failed to get his first invention patented, Evans persisted in his gimcracking. Living in wheat-growing country, the ex-farm boy, who had by now taken up storekeeping for a living, was depressed by the amount of backbreaking work that went into milling grain into flour. Millers carried heavy sacks of grain up long flights of stairs at the Brandywine mills to dump their contents into chutes to feed the millstones. Emerging from between the stones, the meal went into a trough, where men attacked it with shovels and loaded it into hoist tubs. Then it was lifted by manpower once more to a loft, where it was unloaded and raked out to cool and dry. Dirt fell into the meal at every point in the operation.

For two years Evans worked on a water-driven sequence of shoveling and lifting devices to change the tedious hand processes of milling into continuous automatic production. His vertical conveyer, an endless belt moving over rollers and carrying hoisting buckets, was worked by the same waterpower that turned the grinding wheel, as was a second and horizontal conveyer that moved grain, meal, and flour from place to place on level ground. Gravity allowed the grain to fall between the cracking and grinding stones and through the "bolting" devices that separated flour from bran. And toothed spokes radiating from a hub that was turned by the mill wheel raked the moist meal until it was dry. Only two men were needed in Evans' mill, one to pour in the wheat from sacks at one end, and another to nail up the barrels of "superfine" flour at the other.

Evans got his mill running in 1787 and obtained monopoly rights to the operation of automated milling equipment from Delaware and Pennsylvania. After 1790 he got federal patents to cover his devices. Bit by bit the millers of the East began to use the Evans machinery, trying the vertical hoist at one time, the automatic raking spokes at another. Before his death Evans had the satisfaction of knowing that his automated mill was being used everywhere in wheat country on both sides of the Alleghenies. He also discovered what other U.S. inventors discovered before and after him, that people would pirate inventions without payment of royalties if nobody bothered to check on them. Oliver's brother and advance agent, Joseph Evans, spent many years of travel gathering evidence of piracy and bringing suits for patent infringement. But whether pirated or legitimately adopted, 1,200 automatic mills were producing some two million barrels of flour a year in states west of the Alleghenies by 1837. Flour milling was our first "automated" business, the precursor of a hundred others to come.

A second point of expansion was textiles, in which the U.S. at first lagged behind Britain. Wishing to keep the benefits of the great textile-manufacturing inventions (Hargreaves' spinning jenny, Arkwright's water-driven spinning frame, Crompton's "mule," and Cartwright's power loom) to themselves, the British had passed laws that prohibited the export of machine designs and even the emigration of any British subject who had had textile-mill experience. To get hold of the English textile know-how, Pennsylvania and other states had offered bounties—in reality bribes to Englishmen to smuggle out the forbidden techniques. In Rhode Island the retired Quaker merchant Moses Brown, using the capital he had garnered in the many Brown ventures from spermaceti candles to the China trade, had backed the firm of Almy & Brown (formed by his son-in-law) in the building of several water-powered cotton-spinning machines. But lacking the precise Arkwright specifications, the devices broke down continuously and there was never any profit in them.

At this point a remarkable young Englishman put in his appearance on Moses Brown's doorstep. He was Samuel Slater, a Derbyshireman who had spent a six-and-a-half-year apprenticeship in the Derwent River mill of Jedediah Strutt, a partner of the great Sir Richard Arkwright himself. Strutt had fancied the young Slater, and had allowed him to experiment with rearrangements of the Arkwright equipment. While still in his mid-teens, Slater had added an important cam device that helped distribute the spun yarn on the spindle more evenly. Working with the Arkwright complication of breaker cards, lap machines, drawing frames, roving frames, bobbin wheels, spinning spindles, and winding reels, Slater photographed the relationships of the equipment in his mind and memorized the key dimensions, and then took off for America dressed as a farm laborer. Arriving in New York, he fell in with the captain of a Providence sailing packet, who told him of the difficulties of Moses Brown. A letter to the Quaker merchant brought Slater a swift reply: "We should be glad to engage thy care so long as they [the defective water-frame spinning devices] can be made profitable

Samuel Slater

to both, and we can agree. I am, for myself and Almy and Brown, thy friend, Moses Brown."

Slater at first tried dutifully to make the old Almy & Brown spinning frames work but soon had to inform his employers that they must begin all over again, if they wished to catch up with the

British Arkwright machines. Using leather and wood for parts wherever possible, and even making shift with corncobs for spindles, Slater and an ironmaster named David Wilkinson set up an entirely new mill for Almy & Brown in an old clothing shop at the falls of the Blackstone River in what is now downtown Pawtucket. At first the new machinery worked no better than the old: a mass of wadded cotton fibers jammed up against the teeth of the finisher carding device. It was not until Slater and master mechanic Sylvanus Brown, another kinsman of Moses, had inspected the slope of the wires used in a hand carder belonging to Sylvanus' wife that a correction could be made. As it turned out, the angle of the carder teeth was the single thing Slater had failed to memorize correctly. A simple but tedious resetting of thousands of wires got the equipment going—and America had its first successful cotton-spinning machine.

Slater built his first mill in 1790, the year in which Rhode Island as the thirteenth ratifying state made the adoption of the Federal Constitution unanimous. Four years later · Eli Whitney patented the cotton gin, which was to supply the textile trade with a plentiful supply of clean raw cotton. For a long time Slater-spun thread went out to cottage weavers for transformation into cloth. Then, in 1814, another remarkable memorizer of English methods, Francis Cabot Lowell of the already famous Boston and Newburyport Lowell family, started weaving cotton threads into finished fabrics by machine processes at Waltham, Massachusetts, where the Charles River moves swiftly enough to provide waterpower. A mathematician without experience in the cotton business, this son of "Old Judge" Lowell and Susanna Cabot had taken himself and his wife (of the old Jackson shipping clan of Newburyport) to Europe in 1810 for a rest. But no Lowells have ever been known to rest for very long, and Francis Cabot's brain remained as busy as ever. For a time his letters to his brother-in-law, Patrick Tracy Jackson, were all about real estate, trading in India, and foreign exchange; but soon the correspondence became concerned with the making of cotton cloth. Abetted by Nathan Appleton, who joined him in Europe in 1811, Francis Lowell forsook art galleries and cathedrals to wander for long hours through the cotton mills of Manchester. He asked questions, took mental notes—and back in Boston, after being captured and detained by a British frigate in the first weeks of the War of 1812, he joined with Patrick Jackson in chartering a company to make cotton fabrics.

This was the beginning of the famous Boston Associates, a group that came to include most of the Lowell clan and their connections (Amorys, Cabots, Higginsons, Jacksons, Russells, Lees, and others of the old trading aristocracy), as well as the new merchant tribe of Lawrences, who were eventually to intermarry with the Lowells to produce a Harvard president, an astronomer, and a cigar-smoking free-verse poetess. But before the "clan" was willing to put much money into the venture, Francis Cabot Lowell had to prove to its cagey members that he was not mad. After raising $100,000 and buying an old paper mill at Waltham, Lowell put his mathematical abilities to work to reproduce—and improve upon—the spinning and weaving processes he had watched in England. Nathaniel Bowditch paid his own mathematician's tribute to Lowell's intricate calculations for the so-called "double speeder," which was mechanically fleshed out at the Waltham mill by the brilliant Paul Moody of Amesbury.

By 1814, at a time when all America was hungry for the cloth it had imported from England before the period of embargoes, non-intercourse, and war, Lowell and Patrick Jackson were ready to card and spin thread and weave cloth all under one roof. Soon the Waltham mill was turning out some thirty miles of cotton cloth in a day and paying 10 to 20 per cent in dividends, and at this point the members of the "clan" started buying shares with a madness all their own. After Francis Cabot Lowell's early death, Jackson, who became the new soul of the enterprise, spent long hours in the acquisition of Merrimack River mill sites as the need for waterpower grew. Out of these sprang the cities of Lowell and Lawrence, and when Slater, too, expanded his operations to include cloth making (he built plants at the Amoskeag development in Manchester, New Hampshire), the U.S. was soon deep in the first textile phase of the industrial revolution.

The pay was at least relatively good at the beginning as the Lowells and Patrick Jackson brought in farm girls to their company-town structures on the Merrimack to work for dowry money; indeed, the English novelist, Anthony Trollope, spoke of Lowell as "the realization of a commercial Utopia" even as late as the 1860's, which was some time after complaints had begun to be uttered against overcrowding and paternalism. Those complaints were to increase as the farm girls were replaced by Irish immigrants. But regardless of arguments over the humanity of employing children and boarding six young farm women to a room, the young U.S., through the remarkable memory feats of Samuel Slater and Francis Cabot Lowell, had caught up with the English in textiles. By 1834 there were six corporations at Lowell operating nineteen mills with 4,000 looms and more than 100,000 spindles. As V. S. Clark says in his *History of Manufactures in the U.S.*, the decade of the 1830's in Lowell was the "most remarkable decade of progress, in a single place and industry, as yet achieved in our manufacturing history."

Meanwhile, other industries were sprouting. Wherever a wheel could be turned or charcoal could be had to fire a forge, some Yankee or Pennsylvania German or Welshman was certain to be at work hammering out machine parts for an entirely new breed of factory designers. Ironworking itself tended to remain a blacksmith's craft, though there were indeed some small iron-rolling mills in America at the beginning of the nineteenth century. The reason for the continued rule of the blacksmith went back to pre-Revolutionary times, when the British had prohibited the flattening and forging of iron for tools and hardware. But the art of metal rolling could hardly be denied for very long to Yankees who were demanding new sinews for new industry.

Curiously, the first impetus to large-scale metalworking in America came not from the blacksmith's shop but from people who had learned their craft in the small world of silversmithing, tinworking, and the alloying of copper with zinc to make brass. It was a silversmith, Paul Revere, famous alike as a "Liberty Boy" patriot and a fashioner of severely beautiful urns and pitchers, who first had the idea of rolling copper in sheets that would be big enough to stretch over roofs and the hulls of ships. Dreaming in his little shop on Boston's Charter Street, Revere—then in his sixties—decided that somebody must provide barnacle-resisting copper bottoms for the young Republic's Navy if the frigates were to be kept sufficiently speedy to catch the Barbary pirates at their insulting work of enslaving U.S. sailormen. Accordingly, the old Liberty Boy put aside his work of making silverware and bought an old powder mill at Canton, not far from Boston on the Neponset River.

To get the proper rolls from England, Revere put up $25,000 of his own savings plus $10,000 the federal government lent him on a promise that he would resheathe the *Constitution's* bottom. Revere learned how to use his new rolls in the course of turning out six thousand feet of sheathing for the dome of Bulfinch's new Massachusetts State House. Copper for the hull of "Old Ironsides" followed in due course.

The venture so pleased the old patriot courier and silversmith that he wrote a poem about it:

> At early morn I take my round,
> Invited first by *hammer's* sound;
> The *Furnace* next; then Roleing-Mill;
> 'Till Breakfast's call'd, my time doth fill . . .
> Not distant far from *Taunton road*
> In *Canton Dale* is my abode. . . .

The italics are Revere's own—and the exultation that runs through the poem is a far cry from the dry irony of Revere's own description of his famous ride on April 18, 1775. Revere never thought his ride amounted to much (his own account of it, stressing his stupidity, is utterly unlike Longfellow's later poetic version) but he was sure his copper "roleing mill" was a truly patriotic contribution. His assessment of the comparative value of the ride and the ability of the Canton mill to provide sheet metal in large quantities may be correct. Ride or no ride, the Minute Men would have assembled anyway. But if it hadn't been for Revere's decision to become America's first big industrialist in metal, the U.S. Navy would not have been ready to take on the British in the War of 1812.

Revere's mill led the way in an industrial breakthrough. In Connecticut, other men contributed to this same development. Well before the Revolution two Irishmen, William Pattison and his brother Edward, had set up as manufacturers of tin kitchenware in a small shop in Berlin, a village a few miles south of Hartford.

Lacking raw materials, the Pattisons imported their tin sheet from Europe. To sell their pots and pans they hired peddlers—the fore-runners of a famous breed that was to make "Yankee notions" known far and wide throughout the American backwoods. In time, Connecticut's pioneer tinworkers became pewter workers and "Britannia ware" workers, alloying the tin variously with lead and antimony. Then, one day in 1802, the Grilley brothers and the Porter brothers of Waterbury on the Naugatuck River took the jump from pewter buttons to brass buttons—and the U.S. brass industry was born.

Though Connecticut had some small copper deposits at Granby and Cheshire, the new Waterbury brass makers had to import most of the copper and zinc for what was soon to become the first in-dustry with an organized system for selling its wares nationally. The Scovills of Waterbury were early experts in annealing copper and zinc to get the proper orange tint that made brass the preferred metal for all sorts of consumer items. They, along with their com-petitors, got their knowledge by paying virtual bribe money to lure British brassworkers to America. It is a Waterbury tradition that British workers were sealed in casks and smuggled out of England.

By the 1840's, the Naugatuck Valley brass makers were turning out vast quantities of pins by new automatic devices and sticking them into papers by use of an automatic sticking machine. Coins for South American governments were struck by Naugatuck Valley dies. When the daguerreotype process was developed, the "valley" made the first U.S. photographic plates; when whale-oil lighting came into fashion, it had a virtual corner on brass lamps. It satis-fied the hunger for hooks and eyes and needles at one extreme, and for huge "spun" brass kettles at the other. Brassware was so profita-ble in those early-nineteenth-century years that Anson G. Phelps, a New York importer of raw copper, betook himself to the Nauga-tuck Valley, founded the town of Ansonia, and started the manu-facturing end of a business that is still with us under the name of Phelps Dodge.

The greatest of all the Connecticut innovators, however, was Eli Whitney, whose exploits in many fields helped shape an entire age. As already noted, his invention of the cotton-cleaning engine, or gin, in the early 1790's was critical to the development of northern textiles. It also turned the American South to the furious exploitation of cotton, and so probably kept the "peculiar institution" of slavery from dying a natural death. But Whitney's towering influence goes well beyond this. He is a key figure in the development of jigs and dies and other machine tools for metalworking. And it was Whitney who started making guns from interchangeable parts and in the process laid the foundation for what was to become the "American system" of mass production.

Whitney was born in 1765 on a small farm in Massachusetts' straggly and sandy Worcester County, which lies between Boston and the fat lowlands of the Connecticut Valley. Hating farm work because of the endless and meagerly productive chores, the young Eli set up a forge in his father's workshop to make penknife blades, nails, and small items for personal use, and presently branched out into making hatpins by drawing steel into fine wire. His youthful fingers knew from the beginning that they had a vocation, but his mind, distracted by provincial ideas of success, did not. For several years Whitney taught school in Massachusetts and Connecticut, and then entered Yale, thinking to become a lawyer. Running out of money after his graduation at the advanced age of twenty-seven, he went south to take on a tutoring job. In Georgia he stopped off at a plantation run by the capable and cultivated Catherine Greene, widow of one of Washington's foremost generals, and heard talk of the difficulty of separating short-staple cotton from its tenacious green seed. (A Negro slave could clean only a pound a day.) Within a few days Whitney's amazing fingers had devised a rough mechanism for forcing the cotton through a series of narrow slits, thus effectively cleaning it. With the gin in mind, Whitney then picked up a business partner, Phineas Miller, a fellow Yale man who was manager of the Greene plantation, and the two set out to make and market the new machine.

Luckily for his own future, Whitney had an endlessly frustrating experience trying to collect royalties on the use of his patent. Everywhere in the South the gin was pirated as cotton production jumped from five million pounds to thirty-five million in seven years; and to pursue the pirates proved more than the effort was worth. The result was a black period in Whitney's life. But after months of terrible strain during which he lost his New Haven machine shop through fire, Whitney came up with another idea that saved his sanity and salved his pride. He had learned something about the construction of machine tools in his efforts to produce cotton gins, and had, presumably, watched the New Haven mint of Abel Buell stamp out identical copper coins. Now Whitney decided to make muskets by constructing in advance a full line of accurately guided tools, and stamping out full mill runs of interchangeable parts.

The idea was epoch-making, though actually it had been anticipated (and dropped) in France by a gunsmith named Le Blanc. In 1798, Whitney got a hearing with U.S. Army officials and obtained a sizable contract. It took him a year to tool his factory, and when the time for delivery of the first 4,000 muskets and equipment came, Whitney had only 500 on hand. At this critical point he put on a demonstration before President John Adams and Thomas Jefferson, then Vice President, in which he disassembled the guns, scrambled all the parts, and put a new batch of weapons together. The demonstration gained him a needed reprieve and the government advanced him most of the $134,000 needed to fulfill his contract.

In 1812, Whitney's success was assured by a second agreement, for 15,000 muskets; and visitors from all over the world began to come to Hamden, Connecticut, to goggle at his tiny factory at the Lake Whitney fall line of the Mill River. Other gunmakers—Simeon North of Middletown and Berlin and, eventually, Sam Colt of Hartford—picked up Whitney's manufacturing ideas. The clockmakers of New Haven and the nearby Naugatuck Valley, seeking mass methods for punching out clock faces, also came to listen and to learn. Whitney's first crude milling machines for chipping and planing metals caught the eye of toolmakers for the textile business. And, presently, a new generation of machinists and inventors emerges in Windsor, Vermont, and in Providence, Rhode Island (home of Brown & Sharpe), to create the machine-tool industry—the "industry that is behind all industry"—which today makes the multiple drills and presses and automated monsters of the modern age.

Thus the vital seed corn of ideas was sown. Yet the pioneer mass-production methods, which appear in startling if primitive clarity in the cotton mills of Slater and Francis Cabot Lowell, the flour mills of Oliver Evans, the brass factories of the Naugatuck, and the gunshops of Eli Whitney and Simeon North, were fated to remain "sleepers" in most manufacturing businesses for some time to come. The industrial revolution in America was still waiting for the national market that had been guaranteed, in legal form at least, by the Constitution. And the market itself was waiting for the magic wand of easy transportation to touch it to life, as Samuel Slater knew when he put $40,000 earned from cotton-thread production into turnpike stock.

The task of the next generation of enterprisers was to break through to the West, to tie America together with roads, canals, and river transportation, and even, perhaps, with the high-pressure steam carriage that Oliver Evans had tinkered with in his later years. Eli Whitney's most important invention—which was nothing less than the invention of a method—could wait its day.

4 Early America Goes Places

Eli Terry shoulders his merchandise.

The turnpikes tap the old Indian trails.

De Witt Clinton's "ditch" creates a canal boom.

"Toot" Fulton opens upriver navigation.

The railroads take over.

THE mystery—and miracle—of early America is that people went to places before there was any way to get there—and took care of their transportation and marketing needs afterward. They followed Boone's old trace to the Cumberland Gap and moved by Indian trails to the open "streets" trampled by the buffalo. They clawed their way over the Alleghenies, following the ridges above the tributaries of the Susquehanna and the Monongahela—and when they couldn't find a way of getting their corn or wheat to market because of its bulk, they distilled it into whisky and shipped it back to civilization by pack horse. Pioneers settled in Marietta and Cincinnati (once called Columbia) on the Ohio River somehow—and once in the West, and presumably "cut off" from their old homes, they made seagoing ships that actually sailed all the way back to the Atlantic by way of the Ohio, the Mississippi, and the Gulf of Mexico. In less exalted fashion they used crude flatboats to get their produce to New Orleans, returning overland by the Natchez Trace, a devious wilderness road where they risked losing the profits of their husbandry to a new breed of land pirate that infested the gloomy woods and canebrakes.

Manifestly, the new world of manufacturing that Eli Whitney had called into being at the turn of the nineteenth century demanded something better than canoes, rutted roads, and trails marked by the tomahawk hackings of the Indians. Mass manufacture was an anomaly—indeed, it was a commercial impossibility—without quick access to market. The dilemma of the manufacturer, using the first crude Whitney assembly-line system, is well illustrated by Eli Terry, the Connecticut clockmaker.

The year is 1803, and Terry, the teacher of a long line of Yankee clockmakers, is already making clocks in his Naugatuck Valley factory for which he has no storage space. With four clocks ready for sale Terry has to tear himself away from his mill, load the clocks into saddlebags, and take off over the hills toward "York State," walking beside his horse because the load is too heavy to permit a passenger. The clocks are offered at $25 each on the instalment plan; when cash is entirely lacking they are "sold" for corn meal, beeswax, sailcloth, or woven cloth, commodities that can be bartered on the way home or passed on to workmen in lieu of cash wages. Four years later Terry has a bigger mill—and has adopted the full Eli Whitney technique of punching out standardized and interchangeable wheels and clock faces. He is now prepared to sell a clock for $5—but he still has no good way of getting his merchandise to the customer.

In modern idiom, that was a hell of a way to run a railroad. Terry, in fact, could have used a railroad—or any other method of smooth and certain transportation. Actually, men like Terry didn't have too long to wait. Although progress may have seemed slow to people of the time, transportation facilities in fact were laid down with startling rapidity between the founding of the federal republic and its near extinction in the Civil War. First came the toll roads, then the canals, then the rise of the river and lake steamers, and then the first railroads, which later generations were to consolidate and merge into huge transcontinental empires; and as the line of civilization pushed West great cities like Cincinnati and Chicago emerged out of prairie and wilderness. Government took a hand in this development, for the American people, though they had resented British mercantilism, were not averse to government help when it came to getting goods to market. However, when

Albert Gallatin, Jefferson's Secretary of the Treasury, proposed a comprehensive system of tax-supported federal waterways, Americans refused to support him. As in Britain, the pertinacity of businessmen seeking a profit contributed significantly to what modern economists choose to call the "public sector" of the economy.

One of the first breakthroughs to the West came in 1792 when a private company got a charter from the Pennsylvania legislature to finance a stone-and-gravel surfaced road from Philadelphia to Lancaster by publicly subscribed stock. Called a turnpike after the old English roads, which had spiked poles that had to be turned to one side to let wagons through at the tollgates, the Lancaster road was an instantaneous financial success from the day of its completion in 1794. Dividends to stockholders on a $465,000 investment ran as high as 15 per cent in some years. The Lancaster Pike connected the smiling "bonnyclabber country" of the Pennsylvania Dutch with the Delaware some sixty miles distant, and tapped the old valley trails that ran southwest into the Shenandoah of Virginia and northeast into the upper Susquehanna region. With twenty-four feet of solid stone in the middle, the new highway went through the Conestoga country, which bred good horses for the pack-train trade and gave its name to the Conestoga wagon, a distinctively American vehicle with a down-and-up sheer from fore to aft that "cradled" cargoes and so kept them from shifting in hilly terrain. Seventy years later variations of the Conestoga known as prairie schooners were still crossing the passes of the Rockies into the Far West.

The success of the Lancaster road touched off a "turnpike fever" that raged for some thirty-five years, sometimes yielding large dividends to investors, sometimes resulting in huge losses, but in the main fulfilling the obvious need of stitching the country together. In New England the Derby Turnpike connected Eli Terry's Naugatuck Valley with the port of New Haven, and paid its investors an average of 5.1 per cent in dividends for a hundred years. Fighting Philadelphia for trade with the West, the fast-growing city of Baltimore took the lead in Maryland in pushing through the Baltimore-Reisterstown Boulevard and the Baltimore-Frederick Turnpike at costs of $10,000 and $8,000 a mile. Baltimore also petitioned the federal government for a national road to the West. But the feeling against nationally supported highways was always active despite western hopes for the "American System" of internal improvements advocated by the Henry Clay-John Quincy Adams wing of the newborn Whig party.

The Cumberland Road, projected by Congress to link the Potomac Valley with the Ohio, was begun in Jefferson's presidency— but the early Democrats, as states'-righters and strict constitutional constructionists, were always of two minds about allocating federal money for it. Jackson actually blocked its maintenance funds, Monroe refused to sanction the collection of tolls along its course, and Madison vetoed Calhoun's so-called "bonus bill," which would have put U.S. Bank charter money into internal improvements. Three Presidents, ten Congresses, and fourteen congressional acts after its beginning, the Cumberland Road with its thirty-foot-wide gravel center on a stone base finally managed to reach Wheeling on the Ohio at a cost of $7 million to $10 million—and by 1852, rebaptized as the National Road, it had penetrated to Illinois. It never reached the Mississippi, for the railroads eventually killed its uses until its comeback in the automobile age as Route 40.

After the "turnpike fever" came a passion for canals. Early short-haul canals paid off handsomely, notably one around the Connecticut River rapids at Holyoke, Massachusetts, into which Amsterdam bankers put capital. A half-million-dollar "ditch" connecting the Merrimack River with Boston Harbor failed to make money, but succeeded in diverting to Massachusetts much of the New Hampshire commerce in lumber, potash, and grain that had originally gone through Portsmouth. As the short-haul ditches succeeded, imaginative and ambitious men dreamed of an all-water route to the West. As early as 1784 an Irish "philosophical adventurer" named Christopher Colles, who is supposed to have constructed the first steam engine in the U.S., had presented a memorial to the New York Assembly on the practicability of canals connecting the Hudson with the Great Lakes.

This idea, which eventually resulted in the Erie Canal, went through many vicissitudes. In 1792 General Philip Schuyler, a Revolutionary hero, and Elkanah Watson, a merchant, pushed the incorporation of the Western Inland Lock Navigation Co., which succeeded in improving the channel of the Mohawk River. For fifteen years scoffers derided those who talked about extending the Mohawk route westward by digging a long connecting ditch from Buffalo to Utica. Shortly before the War of 1812, however, a group of canal commissioners under De Witt Clinton set forth into the western wilderness to have a look at the so-called "water-level" terrain for themselves. Though their main interest was topography, they also had a good look at western economic life. They found

Courtesy the New York Public Library

The Erie Canal at Lockport

Genesee Valley wheat going to Canada; and they very probably heard of Ohio grain and even Kentucky whisky going north by portages to the Cuyahoga and Maumee rivers, at whose mouths (the sites of villages that were to become modern Cleveland and Toledo) Canadian schooners picked up the produce and sent it on its way past New York State to Montreal. Glass from Pittsburgh was also being shipped by Ohio rivers and the Cuyahoga portage to Canadian markets.

In all of this Clinton, as leader of the New York State anti-federalists, sensed a winning political issue. With the conclusion of the War of 1812, "De Witt Clinton's ditch" was finally approved by the New York State legislature, the financing to be done by state bonds without aid from either Washington, D.C., or the new states of Ohio and Indiana. Nobody in the young U.S. really knew how to build solid masonry locks in 1817, but two young surveyors named James Geddes and Benjamin Wright, who had made a joint survey of the canal route in 1811, improvised for themselves in brilliant fashion as they took charge of both the Erie and the Champlain canal projects. Their construction work was so good that it was praised even in Europe. Section by section the Erie came into being as rocks were drilled by hand and blown out of the way by black powder. The digging was done by men with hand shovels. In 1819 the first strip, from Utica to Rome, opened for traffic; by 1825 the whole long "ditch" (together with the connection that linked the Hudson River with Lake Champlain) was completed.

De Witt Clinton was primarily a politician, interested in the digging of his ditch in order to keep control of the Jeffersonian party in New York State. Nevertheless, the memorial he addressed to the state legislature in 1816 is one of the more important American business documents. Everything that Clinton hoped for from the canal was destined to come true. The Erie Canal cost $8 million to build, but it cut freight rates between Albany and Buffalo by 85 per cent. Instead of taking up to a month in transit, goods now moved from New York City to Buffalo in ten days. In 1825, the year of their opening, the Erie and the Champlain canals together earned New York State more than half a million in tolls. Ten years later the canal's width had to be increased from forty to seventy feet, its depth from four to seven feet. Long after the building of the railroads the Erie was still making money; indeed, the peak of its tonnage was not reached until 1880.

The Erie boomed land values in the West and created new manufacturing and processing cities all the way from Utica and Syracuse to Rochester and Buffalo. But its most triumphant creation was modern New York City. New York had passed Philadelphia in population by 1810; and by 1825 it was already more than twice the size of Baltimore, the third city. Its businessmen, led by Jeremiah Thompson, had established the Black Ball Line, the first packet company to run ocean liners to Europe on a regular schedule. They had also developed the so-called "cotton triangle," a system of three-cornered trading which brought cotton in New York ships from Charleston or Savannah to Liverpool, where it was exchanged for British manufactured goods. These, in turn, were carried to New York. Reloading at North and East River docks, the ships would then be off to Charleston again, or maybe to New Orleans. The enterprise of New Yorkers kept the southern cotton planters from developing their own shipping and marketing institutions. But to become truly imperial in a trading sense, however, New York needed more than cotton as an export commodity. The Erie Canal, which brought produce from as far away as the Ohio Valley within two weeks' reach of New York Bay, supplied the answer. Henceforward Cincinnati (or Porkopolis, as it also came to be called) actually had closer physical ties with New York than it had with Baltimore. And the building of Ohio canals connecting the southward-flowing Scioto and Miami rivers with Lake Erie ports completed New York City's call on western products. With a shrewd eye to changing values, John Jacob Astor, who had made his first fortune in the fur trade, transferred much of his wealth into New York City real estate. The Erie Canal helped to boom the fortunes of older landed families in Manhattan, such as the Goelets. And in creating a metropolis the Erie Canal did its part in making the first great department store tycoon, Alexander Turney Stewart, an early millionaire.

The Erie Canal fired the state of Pennsylvania to improve its own water routes to the West. Long before the War of 1812, Pennsylvanians had seen the importance of bringing anthracite coal to market in New York and Philadelphia. To this end they built the Delaware and Hudson Canal, leading from Honesdale in Pennsylvania to the Delaware, and thence to Rondout on the Hudson. A second artery, the Lehigh Canal, designed to supplement slack-water navigation on the Lehigh River, was built by Josiah White of Philadelphia and a group of associated wire manufacturers who had found Mauch Chunk anthracite fuel to their liking. They organized the Lehigh Navigation Co. (capital, $55,000) to build dams and sluices along the river and a connecting nine-mile road to the mines. Later, their two companies were merged as the Lehigh Coal & Navigation Co., and set an important precedent as the first instance of interlocking companies in U.S. business history.

With the Erie Canal open, anguished Pennsylvanians set out to connect Philadelphia and Pittsburgh by water. From Reading on the Schuylkill to Middletown on the Susquehanna the Union Canal had already been pushed without undue trouble. But to drive a lock system along the Juniata River from near Harrisburg to high in the Alleghenies at Hollidaysburg was something else again. The Juniata's drop from head to mouth was greater than that of the whole Erie Canal from Buffalo to Albany. The Pennsylvania canal builders, using state money, succeeded in making the Juniata route navigable. On the other side of the Altoona mountains the Conemaugh, the Kiskiminitas, and the Allegheny rivers were utilized to go from Johnstown to Pittsburgh. But how to get canalboats over the crest of the mountains from Hollidaysburg to Johnstown? There was the rub.

Two men, Sylvester Welch and Moncure Robinson, stepped into the breach with plans for five inclined planes on each side of the Allegheny wall, and the Pennsylvania legislature authorized work to begin on the stupendous project in 1831. Three years later the *Hit or Miss,* a boat owned by Jesse Crisman and captained by a Major Williams, "sailed" from Hollidaysburg to Johnstown by a wheeled cradle over the inclines, with horses providing critical motor power. For a night the *Hit or Miss* rested on the summit of the Alleghenies "like Noah's Ark on Ararat"; then it "descended the next morning into the Valley of the Mississippi, and sailed for St. Louis." The cross-Allegheny projection of the "Main Line"— as the direct western route from Philadelphia to Pittsburgh was known even then—was sufficiently spectacular to please the visiting Charles Dickens, who dropped a rapt section into his *American Notes* about traveling "at a rapid pace along the heights of the mountain in a keen wind" and being dragged up and eased down by stationary engines and by horse, sometimes on rails "laid upon the extreme verge of a giddy precipice."

Some other hardheaded Europeans were less enthusiastic. The crisis of 1837 saw several state repudiations of canal-bond payments, an act that angered British investors in particular. After Pennsylvania's repudiation, Sydney Smith, the wit of the *Edinburgh Review,* remarked that whenever he met a Pennsylvanian at dinner in London he wondered that nobody carved him up and served him in slices to every Englishman present. But even though bonds were repudiated the canals were a boon to businessmen generally. Prior to the canals it cost as much to haul a ton of goods thirty miles by wagon as it did to transport it 3,000 miles by ship across the ocean. Coal mines were useless to iron mines unless they were right next to each other, a proximity normally denied by nature. And at 30 cents a ton-mile, it cost more to haul wheat 200 miles into Philadelphia than it could be sold for in the city at local market prices. The American canals changed all this. They involved high initial capital costs—normally $20,000 to $30,000 per mile. But they brought coal and iron together, and knocked the cost of hauling wheat down to 1 or 2 cents per ton-mile.

The most important function of the trans-Allegheny canals, however, was to provide the vital link between the tidal rivers of the East and the river-and-lake traffic of the surging new West. Here the steamboat took over. *Steamboats Come True* is the way the title of a book about the early inventors of steam-powered river craft has put it—but they never really came true for John Fitch or James Rumsey or William Henry, who couldn't find sufficiently rugged boilers to make their boats commercially successful. It remained for two bitter competitors, Robert "Toot" Fulton of New York and Colonel John Stevens of Hoboken, to prove that riverboats could be sturdy enough to make money over the years.

Fulton, a painter, submarine experimenter, and man of the world, owes his fame, of course, to the successful voyage of the *Clermont* up the Hudson in 1807. In building the *Clermont*, Fulton cadged a Boulton & Watt engine and boiler out of the British, who normally refused to grant export licenses for such things. He also had the good sense to reject steam-operated oars, ducks' feet, and "endless chains" with attached boards, in favor of Nicholas Roosevelt's suggestion that he use paddle wheels. Beyond this Fulton had the enterpriser's instinct for cultivating backing that would be effective in making his enterprise successful. He was a close friend of Chancellor Robert R. Livingston, of the politically powerful New York State Livingstons, and eventually married one of Livingston's cousins. Livingston had seen the potential profits in steamboats and before the turn of the century had actually obtained a state monopoly for operating them on New York waters. Some time before the launching of the *Clermont,* Livingston and Fulton had formed a business partnership. By the end of the War of 1812 the partnership had several boats on the Hudson and others plying between New York and New Brunswick on the Raritan. They also had a Pittsburgh-built boat operating on the lower Mississippi under monopoly rights granted by the Territory of Orleans.

This combination was not destined to hold the field alone, however. In 1804, three years before the *Clermont* made her trial run, Colonel John Stevens and his two sons had launched a twin-screw propeller ship, the *Little Juliana,* built with some British parts, into the waters off Hoboken. Some years later they built a completely American-made ship, the *Phoenix,* and began to compete with the Livingston-Fulton steamers in New York waters. The Livingston-Fulton group fought back and eventually forced Stevens to take the *Phoenix* round Cape May into the Delaware River, where she plied between Philadelphia and Trenton. They also sold a Hudson River franchise to another New Jerseyite, Colonel Aaron Ogden, who had started an independent steam-ferry service between New York and New Jersey.

The man who really broke the Livingston monopoly was a southern planter and duelist, Thomas Gibbons, who began as a partner of Colonel Ogden and then turned violently against him to set up his own service on the New York-Elizabethport run, choosing as his skipper a young Staten Islander, Cornelius Vanderbilt (or Van Derbilt, as he preferred to spell his name).

As skipper, the wily "Corneel" showed endless sagacity and controlled pugnacity in defying what purported to be the law, keeping his "pirate" craft running while Gibbons fought Ogden and the Livingston-Fulton interests in the courts. With Daniel Webster as his counsel, Gibbons finally pushed his case to the Supreme Court; and in 1824, Chief Justice Marshall, in one of the great pioneer majority opinions upholding the interstate-commerce clause of the Constitution, held the Livingston monopoly to be illegal in so far as interstate movement of ships in the coasting trade was concerned. The following year the New York legislature repealed internal monopoly restrictions as they affected the Hudson above the New Jersey line. Thus the rivers of America were potentially freed to all men who could use them, provided they could comply with a growing body of regulations designed to keep boilers from exploding and depositing travelers and cargo over the landscape.

On the Ohio and the Mississippi the steamboat helped create a new civilization and became in time a legend. River navigation in the West called for shallow-draft vessels quite different from those that plied the Hudson. To avoid sand bars they had to ride high on the water and to move over the river as on a "heavy dew," not through it. Just who invented the western riverboat is a matter for controversy. But in devising something to replace the old pole-propelled broadhorn beloved by the "half horse, half alligator" flatboatmen, Henry Shreve, a western Pennsylvanian, made an important contribution when he launched his castle-on-a-raft called the *Washington* in 1816. It was likewise Shreve who devised a floating battering ram or cutting device strung between two boats, which first cleared the Mississippi and its tributaries of snags. Many other small capitalists joined Shreve in the exploitation of western waters: for years most of the steamboats on the great inland rivers were owned by partnerships of two to four men. Wrecks were so frequent owing to constantly shifting channels that the average life of a riverboat was less than five years; and as Mark Twain observed in *Life on the Mississippi,* pilots who knew the rivers quickly became a kind of aristocratic guild. But owing to low building costs profits were large, especially if one found the right captain for picking cargoes and choosing good unloading ports.

The ports themselves rapidly expanded and changed character. In 1810, Cincinnati was a small river town of 2,500 people. In the 1820's its population tripled as it became a slaughtering center known as "Porkopolis," shipping its hams and bacon up and down the Ohio and to the lakes by canal. By 1830, owing in no small measure to the steamboat, Cincinnati had become the "Queen City of the West," second only to New Orleans. Chicago, too, owed its first pre-eminence to water, partly because a canal connected its Lake Michigan shore with the Mississippi River system, and partly because it was the western terminus of the "pathway of the lakes." Thousands of immigrants moved from Buffalo to the lake cities of Detroit, Milwaukee, and Chicago by steamer. And soon the produce that was loaded aboard the new propeller-driven lake freighters—the *Hercules,* the *Samson*—at Chicago, Detroit, and Cleveland made the connecting-to-seaboard links of the Erie Canal and the Welland-St. Lawrence system seem inadequate. Copper and iron ore had been uncovered in northern Michigan and miners were clamoring for transport. As part of the lake traffic system, Chicago was already an important town of 25,000 people in 1847, before a a line of railway had reached it.

Even as, with the clipper ships, the 1850's marked the culmination of the age of sail on the oceans, so they marked the peak of steamboating on western waters. The river steamer went through a period of rococo ornamentation and then settled down into a tradition of stately passenger carriers. The *Yorktown,* for example, had forty private cabins—or twenty-four more than were provided by the *Queen of the West,* the British steamer built for the India trade. At one time there was more steamer tonnage on the western rivers of the U.S. than the British Empire had on all the oceans, and even after the Civil War had ended, riverboats—the *Natchez,* the *Robert E. Lee*—were making new records on the run between New Orleans and St. Louis. Long before the riverboats reached their peak traffic, however, they were doomed by the arrival of the "iron horse," which was preceded, as early as 1826, by the horse-drawn tramway financed by Thomas Handasyd Perkins to carry granite for the construction of the Bunker Hill Monument.

Railroading, like most other things in American business, grew out of small and confused beginnings. Even while operating ships, the redoubtable Colonel John Stevens built a minuscule steam locomotive to run on a small circular track in his Hoboken yard, and obtained a charter to construct a railroad across New Jersey. In 1825, George Stephenson in England proved that his famous "Locomotion No. 1" could pull a ninety-ton train of thirty-four wagons at a speed of ten to twelve miles per hour. Two years later the Delaware & Hudson Canal Co. tried to use a British importation, the *Stourbridge Lion,* on its short "anthracite railroad" to carry coal from the Carbondale mines to the canal itself. The engine proved too heavy for the trestles, which ignominiously collapsed under its weight. In the same year, two Baltimore bankers, Philip Evan Thomas and George Brown, obtained a charter for America's first successful railroad line, the Baltimore & Ohio. They broke ground for their railroad on July 4, 1828. Soon, at a cost of

Courtesy Cooper Union for the Advancement of Science and Art

Peter Cooper

$17,000 per mile, they had thirteen miles of track laid for horse or even sail-car operation.

At this point Peter Cooper, a New York enterpriser, merchant, and philanthropist, came up with a better idea. Working in the B. & O.'s shops, he managed in 1829 to build a small engine, the

Tom Thumb, out of scraps of iron that included pipes adapted from musket barrels, and he was anxious to try it out. He raced the *Tom Thumb* against a stagecoach horse over the track between Baltimore and Ellicott's Mills, losing out at the last minute because of a slipping pulley belt. Even in defeat the demonstration had been made: the *Tom Thumb* had proved that steam could pull a single car around a sharp curve. A year later a New York watchmaker, Phineas Davis, won a $4,000 prize from the B. & O. for an engine capable of pulling fifteen tons at a fifteen-mile-an-hour speed.

The citizens of Baltimore had a truly exalted confidence in their Mr. Thomas, a God-fearing Quaker, and their Mr. Brown. Capital for the new railroad was quickly subscribed. "Public excitement," wrote John Latrobe, the railroad's counsel, whose famous engineer-brother Benjamin was to design the road's viaducts between Baltimore and Washington, "has gone far beyond fever heat and reached the boiling point . . . the possession of stock in any quantity was regarded as provision for old age . . . the excitement in Baltimore roused public attention elsewhere and a railroad mania began to pervade the land."

The B. & O. did well for those who had faith in it. Though the road took four years to reach the Potomac and much longer to cross the Alleghenies, Peter Cooper's investment in shore-front land near the Baltimore terminal eventually brought him a small fortune to add to money he made in glue and gelatin. Taking pay for the land in stock from two Bostonians who formed a company to exploit it, Cooper lived to see the stock rise from $44 to $225 a share. (Some of his money he invested in an iron business that was to make even more fabulous profits by serving the railroads.) It took more than twenty years for the B. & O. to reach Wheeling on the Ohio, but the Chesapeake & Ohio Canal, beaten by railroad efficiency, never got there at all.

Down South, the businessmen of Charleston, South Carolina, were troubled by the fact that Savannah, which had river connection with the West, seemed to be cornering the upcountry trade. Accordingly, they got a charter from the South Carolina legislature for the Charleston & Hamburg Railroad, the first U.S. road actually to be planned from the beginning for the use of steam cars. *The Best Friend of Charleston,* a locomotive made by the West Point

Foundry in New York State, pulled four loaded passenger cars over six miles of completed Charleston & Hamburg track in late 1830. It attained a speed of twenty-one miles an hour. On a subsequent trip the locomotive was buttressed, in its rear, with a flatcar loaded with cotton bales to quell the passengers' fear of an explosion.

The *Tom Thumb* and *The Best Friend of Charleston* were the forerunners of a mighty host. The West Point Foundry went on from its success with *The Best Friend* to make the *De Witt Clinton* and other locomotives for the Mohawk & Hudson Railroad Co., whose line from Albany to Schenectady formed one of the links that were later to be joined into the New York Central. After many disappointments, Colonel John Stevens finally started to build his Camden & Amboy Railroad across New Jersey. He had the luck to use modern-type "T" rails with flanges at the bottom. The flanges were fastened to wooden blocks by hook-headed spikes. The spiked "T" rail was the invention of the Colonel's ingenious son, Robert L. Stevens, who, in default of local rail-rolling mills, had to go to England to have his product made. In the beginning the spike-bearing wooden blocks were laboriously inserted into niches drilled in granite roadbed. Then, suddenly, a cold winter closed the quarries upon which the Camden & Amboy depended. Making the best of the shortage in stone, the Stevenses started spiking the "T" rails directly to wooden crossties. They were surprised when this "temporary" method of tracklaying proved more steady and durable than any other then in use in England or America. The "temporary" method has lasted to the present day.

For a considerable period New York City let other coastal towns take the initiative in railroad building, for it was already linked to the West by the Hudson River, along which Daniel Drew and Commodore Vanderbilt ran their profitable steam packets, and by the Erie Canal. The Erie Canal lobby endeavored to create legislative difficulties for New York State railroad enterprises, even sponsoring a plan to force railways to pay tolls as they passed the canal toll points. When citizens of the upstate cities of Albany, Troy, and Schenectady decided to cut forty miles out of the Erie Canal and Mohawk River routes by building the Mohawk & Hudson Railroad, they were actually forbidden by the first charter to carry freight.

Even after seven separate railroads had established the physical basis for a through line from Albany to Buffalo, no attempt was made to compete with the Erie Canal for long-haul business. The seven roads had different equipment, did not sell through tickets, made no effort to dovetail their schedules, and refused to use common stations. The situation approximated the French economist Bastiat's sarcastic description of a discontinuous railroad, organized to provide superior livings for porters, not to give service to shippers and passengers. The dilatoriness of New York State businessmen in bringing railroads into New York City helped Boston to become one of the more successful railroad terminals. Three different lines made Boston the "hub" of a wheel by linking it with Lowell, Worcester, and Providence; and by throwing an early line over the Berkshires, Bostonians made their own connection with the West.

Despite the anti-railroad propaganda floated by the canal companies, which solemnly warned Congress about the menace to life and limb represented by the spark-belching iron horse, the railroads were soon carrying the more perishable parts of the cargo that had once been entrusted to the waterways. There were still people who questioned the superiority of the rails, and there was, to be sure, plenty of business to be shared by both types of carrier for a long time to come. But eventually the canals were to be relegated to an inferior position, doomed to a mule-gaited trade of hauling such proletarian substances as ice, granite, gravel, limestone, coal, and brick. The iron horse proved itself not only a useful carrier but a profitable one, and money poured into the roads from the eastern cities. Textile and shipping profits went into the early lines radiating out from Boston. In Pennsylvania the Scrantons, owners of iron foundries, invested in the Delaware, Lackawanna & Western, and the anthracite roads were financed by coal-mine owners. The Mohawk & Hudson was financed by New Yorkers, who listed it on the Stock Exchange as early as 1830. The New York money market was utilized by the New Jersey railroad builders; and the Second U.S. Bank took one-quarter of the stock of the Philadelphia & Reading.

The huge wonder of the railroad to our ancestors is summed up in Squire Hawkins' ecstatic outburst to his wife in Mark Twain's and Charles Dudley Warner's *The Gilded Age*. Speaking of the

Tennessee land he is holding for a "speculation" in the pre-Civil War time, the Squire says: "Even you and I will see the day that steamboats will come up that little Turkey River to within twenty miles of this land of ours—and in high water they'll come right *to* it! And this is not all, Nancy—it isn't even half! There's a bigger wonder—the railroad! These worms here have never even heard of it —and when they do they'll not believe in it. But it's another fact. Coaches that fly over the ground twenty miles an hour—heavens and earth, think of that, Nancy! Twenty miles an hour. It makes a man's brain whirl. Some day, when you and I are in our graves, there'll be a railroad stretching hundreds of miles—all the way down from the cities of the Northern States to New Orleans . . . Well, do you know, they've quit burning wood in some places in the Eastern States? And what do you suppose they burn? Coal!"

By 1840, as if to justify Squire Hawkins' ecstasy, there were more than three hundred railway companies in the U.S. and track mileage had risen to about 3,330 miles, drawing abreast of the canals. The rail companies were still a motley collection of enterprises using all manner of gauges. The Erie, which was the first American railroad to provide trunk service from the East to the lakes, had a six-foot gauge; the Camden & Amboy, four feet eleven inches; the South Carolina Railroad, five feet; the B. & O., the standard English gauge based on the old carriage-track width of four feet eight and a half inches. Brakes were still manually operated; and George Pullman had yet to devise his famous "Pioneer A" sleeping car. But even as short lines, the railroads added mightily to what canals and steamboats had done to boost the growth of the western cities. Buffalo, a farm-produce assembly point as early as 1825, and Rochester, which had begun to mill Ohio grain in 1830, benefited from the short lines that preceded the creation of the New York Central. When the Pennsylvania reached Pittsburgh in 1854, almost in a dead heat with the B. & O.'s entry into Wheeling, it helped boom all the Ohio River towns.

As for Chicago, the railroads, coming to it from all points of the compass after 1847, really made it the capital of the new West. Collecting cash in small amounts from farm housewives, William B. Ogden, Chicago's richest booster, built a grain railroad from western Illinois into the city—and within the space of a few years

Chicago had become a world distributing center for western farm crops of all kinds. From the lumber towns of Michigan and Wisconsin, Chicago drew boards and planks and shingles for redistribution to southern Illinois and Indiana; from Missouri and Iowa, it drew beef and pork; from Minnesota, it garnered more grain. The St. Mary's River Ship Canal, built by young Charles T. Harvey (with capital from St. Johnsbury, Vermont, and New York State, as well as Chicago), connected Lake Superior with Lake Huron and gave Chicago access to northern Michigan's iron-ore deposits. And as the city used and transformed and forwarded the raw produce of the frontier, it also drew the finished goods of the East for shipment to the farms. The drummers went out from Chicago, bound for plain and prairie and forest hamlets to the south, the west, and the northwest.

The railroads, which made Chicago, also made the American iron industry, which, besides turning out rails, eventually was to provide the material for such pioneer necessities as the ax, the plow, and the revolver. But even before the U.S. had an iron industry, the western pioneer was necessarily drawing on American factory products made from imported steel. In the seamless web of history, the American frontier and the American factory, with Chicago as the prime binding point, were destined for a time to the closest of working alliances. The East, committed more and more to factory specialization as the years wore on, needed the pioneers' agricultural products. But like so many Huck Finns pursued by the Widow Douglas with the hairbrush, the pioneers couldn't escape the counter-reach of civilization. And business, which moved fast on the heels of the woodsman and the plainsman to the West, was the agent for combing every man's hair.

5 Frontier and Factory

Mr. Astor makes his first fortune in furs for beaver hats.

Down-Easters become the country's first lumber kings.

And the Collinses of Connecticut supply the axes.

Sam Colt mass-produces the great "equalizers" of the American plains.

John Deere's plow and McCormick's reaper put the farmer in business.

THE railroad, which kept many a farmer busy through the winter season cutting cordwood to feed the boilers and the tall belching smokestacks of the iron horse, was perhaps the chief marvel of the pre-Civil War age. But on top of the rapidly spreading transportation system, with its promise of a unique national market, there was piled wonder on wonder. A shrewd historian, Garet Garrett, has spoken of the "breathless generation" of the 1830's and 1840's—the generation to which "happened" the mechanical harvester, the Colt revolver, the sewing machine, the Morse telegraph, the invention of a method for vulcanizing rubber and a hundred other useful devices of both major and minor import. Truly, the period stretching between the presidency of Jackson and the Civil War, which will be examined in this and a subsequent chapter, might justly be called the "Era of the Thousand-and-One Beginnings."

The prop for the new order of prosperity was, of course, the land—acres and acres of it as "manifest destiny" pushed steadily westward. The claims of the seaboard states to territory west of the

Alleghenies had been ceded to the federal government at the very founding of the Republic and thereafter came the Louisiana Purchase, the acquisition of Florida and Texas, the settlement of the Oregon claims with Britain, and the seizure of Mexican lands running all the way to California. As the people moved West this huge public domain was disposed of on easy terms to individuals, making the phrase "a land-office business" synonymous with frenzied merchandising of any sort. Some 28 million acres of public land were offered for sale by the U.S. government in 1834–35 alone, and by 1850 almost half of the U.S. population of 23,200,000 was living west of the Alleghenies. If it hadn't been for a compensating immigration from Europe, the East might have been badly depopulated.

The businesses that were based on the land were still those of a predominantly rural culture, ranging from the well-watered farms in more civilized areas to the crude extractive and exploitative industries such as timbering in territory that was still wilderness. Big planters, moving across the Appalachians with their retinues of slaves, picked up rich bottom land in the states of Alabama and Mississippi at the government price of $1.25 an acre; smaller men, with a slave or two apiece, took up farms farther up the creek. In the states to the north of the Ohio River the frontier was quickly transformed into wheat, corn, and hog farms. The land boom accelerated as towns sprang into being; and speculators who had picked up good street-corner locations even asked for as much as $2,500 for sites that had been plotted as "downtown" lots.

In accordance with the state of the land boom, banks flourished or failed and the currency alternately expanded and contracted. Deep in the frontier woods—so deep that only wildcats could find 'em—state-chartered local banks literally monetized a vacuum, creating vast amounts of paper money by what was tantamount to mere say-so. Flooding back East, the "stumptail" and "red-dog" currency, which the wildcat banks had issued against state bonds and hypothecated acreage priced as the "city lots of the future," forced the more responsible banks to set up a carefully elaborate discount system. Western "currency" was seldom at a par with eastern bank notes. Moreover, there was always a lack of hard money even though Easterners willingly invested in the West.

Yet through all the ups and downs, the price level at the end of the period was more or less what it had been at the beginning. The panic of 1837, which shook out the land speculators, made more farms available to real farmers. And as the triumphs of technology canceled inflations the statistics went up, up, up. By 1860 manufacturing had increased eight times in terms of value and twelve times in terms of volume over 1815. Crop values doubled between 1837 and 1857. In the early part of the century cotton and tobacco were the only big U.S. commodity exports; after the repeal of the Corn Laws in Britain, wheat from the West began to move in some volume in international trade. Cotton textiles expanded even during depressions—and the migrant southern planters piled across the river into Arkansas and Texas to increase their cotton acreage.

During all this period of the pre-Civil War westward push, the frontier and civilization seemed to be profitable reciprocals of each other. The fur trade, which flourished in St. Louis up into the 1830's, was the earliest instance of the way two worlds could work together. To a later muckraking generation, which gloried in such works as Gustavus Myers' *History of the Great American Fortunes*, the biggest fur trader of them all, John Jacob Astor, seemed an evil despoiler of the Indians. But Astor clothed the city people of two continents for thirty years against wintry weather—and his trappers provided a ready market for steel traps produced by the Oneida colony of New York State. If Astor made great profits, it was undeniable that he took the longest of risks. Naturally he worked through some pretty hard-fisted men: one did not toil up rivers and live through northern wilderness winters by practicing a squeamish regard for wild animals—or for the Indian savages who often seemed more treacherous than the very wolves themselves.

Washington Irving, who wrote the history of Astor's fur-trading post of Astoria at the mouth of the Columbia River from firsthand records, captured the feeling of the "way it was" as later writers never could hope to capture it. Mr. Astor's ship, the *Tonquin*, which first planted the community of Fort Astoria, was cruelly set upon by Indians off Vancouver Island. True enough, the captain of the ship, an unpliant fellow who was not loved by Astor's men, invited his own troubles: he had insulted the Indians by rudely unceremonious treatment of their chief, in some first efforts to trade.

But the savagery of the Indians' subsequent assault upon the *Tonquin* was out of all proportion to the insult; in fact, virtually everybody on board was murdered by the screaming red men. The ship itself was presumably blown up by one of its last surviving crew members, who managed to take a hundred Indians to Kingdom Come along with himself. Such was the life of trade in the early far Northwest.

Brown Brothers

John Jacob Astor

Courtesy Colt's Patent Fire Arms Manufacturing Co., Inc.

Samuel Colt

It was almost as chancy a business when it came to pursuing the fur trade across the plains. Far from being presented with an easy opportunity of bribing their way through the country of the Plains Indians by a judicious expenditure of rum, an Astor expedition had to reckon with the implacably hostile Sioux and Blackfeet, whose fur-trading allegiance was to the British companies of Canada. The cry of *"Voilà les Sioux!"* coming from the throats of Canadian *voyageurs* in Mr. Astor's employ was a cry of abject terror, not a happy harbinger of greedy concourse in which innocent red men might be cheated of their winter's catch by an offer of a few glass beads. Even to get horses from friendly Indians, the Astor party had to give good value. It was all gravy to the Indians, who had stolen the horses in the first place.

True enough, John Jacob Astor did not risk his own skin on the plains and mountains of the West. True again, he left a fortune of $20 million, made by nimbly skipping from furs to real estate when peltries threatened to become scarce. Astor's passion for foreclosing mortgages and taking advantage of fine legal points was as unlovely as his enemies have insisted. But Mr. Astor's organizing mind had kept the makers of beaver hats busy for a full generation. He laid

The City of Bangor (circa 1834)

the basis for his fortune by making himself a focus of energies that supplied a commodity in high demand. To a people who regarded the savages, the wild animals, and the very forest itself as things that had to be pushed back if civilized people were to have space for expansion and fields for crops, the fact that the American Fur Co. had fought the British on the northwest frontier as monopoly to monopoly in order to get its way could not have seemed of very great moralistic moment.

Forest and plain had to be conquered—and, luckily, the spoilage of the wilderness that so horrifies modern conservationists was of use to people back home. The hunger for lumber in a period in which the population was almost doubling every twenty years was virtually insatiable. Even before the War of 1812, in places like

Massachusetts, New Jersey, and Maryland, the good close-to-seaboard timber was petering out. But to the north, in Maine (the only place where the American pioneer moved east), there were millions of acres of virgin white pine. The riches on the upper stretches of the Penobscot River attracted the eager attention of William Bingham of Philadelphia, who snapped up two million acres of Maine timberland at a cut-rate price of 12.5 cents an acre. Stewart Holbrook, the historian of the lumber industry, reports that loggers hacked for a century at the Bingham purchase without exhausting it. The land rush in Maine centered on Bangor, which, in the 1830's, became the first of our sawmill boom towns. With saloons on every corner to keep the men from the woods happy at the end of a log drive, Bangor was an anomaly in God-fearing New England. But it became the prototype of a hundred different lumber towns, reaching all the way from Maine to Aberdeen, Washington.

Moving west with the various migrations of the timber kings, Maine men helped staff the logging crews that cut wide swathes through the lake states of Michigan, Wisconsin, and Minnesota and made the leap to the early-twentieth-century empire of Douglas fir in the far Northwest. New men came to the business from time to time—the Shevlins and the Weyerhaeusers of Minnesota being notable examples—but the down-Easters, whether they were Canucks, Swedes, Irish, or Yankees, pioneered all the more difficult arts involved in riding the white-water rivers and breaking the log jams. It was a harum-scarum life in which death was the normal penalty for a single slip—and the business of supplying release (in women, dance halls, and liquor) for lonely loggers who had just come in after a winter in the woods was in itself the source of many a sawmill-town fortune.

To lighten the danger of riding the rivers in the days before the Civil War, a Maine blacksmith named Joseph Peavey invented the lumberman's cant hook, which still bears his name. Characteristically, Joe Peavey disclosed the nature of his invention to a fellow blacksmith during an evening session over a bottle of Medford rum—and soon discovered that someone had stolen his secret and beaten him to Washington with a patent application. Such a minor disillusion couldn't keep the Peavey family out of lumber; at the end of the nineteenth century an Ira Peavey bossed the construction of a conveyer system that was to dump a hundred million feet of Penobscot logs for the Bradstreets of South Gardiner, Maine, into a sluice leading to the Kennebec River, and a Gary Peavey, born and raised to lumbering know-how on the Penobscot, ended his crew-bossing days on Puget Sound after cutting timber in Pennsylvania, another big logging area, and fighting off the Indians who molested his loggers in Minnesota.

In the fullness of time in the 1890's, the elder Robert La Follette, the first Progressive governor of Wisconsin, was to make great political capital assailing the timber barons of Wisconsin for skulduggery in exploiting the state's public domain. But without loggers such as Cadwallader C. Washburn of Maine, who himself became a governor of Wisconsin, the prairie towns and the farm buildings to the south of the lake states would never have been built; and pioneers farther to the west would have gone on living in sod huts. Logging money was to make the school system of Menomonie, in northern Wisconsin, a showpiece for educators who visited it from all over the nation. The loggers' cry was "Let a little light into the swamp!" Slashing a thousand and more miles of white pine without thinking of a replacement, the lumbermen thought they were making new lands available for farms. They could hardly foresee that the acid soil of the cutover lake states was not destined to make good farming country for anyone other than those frugal Northmen, the Swedes and the Finns. To their own generations, lumber kings like Charles Merrill of Maine, who bought his first western forest land along the St. Clair River in Michigan in 1836, or like Charles H. Hackley, who came to Muskegon in 1856 without money and died in 1905 leaving $6 million to his adopted town for culture (including oil paintings), were giants in the same earth that bred the legend of Paul Bunyan's blue ox Babe, whose footprints made the Great Lakes.

Along with the peavey the lumber industry found other ingenious ways to solve its problems. The log boom, a Maine invention designed to channel river-borne timber into the pens of its rightful owners, was still being used in river regions of Michigan in the late 1880's and 1890's by the Tittabawassee Boom Co., a joint concern backed by Saginaw and Bay City lumbermen. In the Far West, lumber had to be dragged to mills over toteroads by "bull-whacking" oxen, or by skidding machines attached to aerial pulleys set high in commanding trees, or by sleds run by donkey engines. Oddly enough, the woodsmen out in the bush, who were quite used to watching the circular saw chew up timber in the mills and who employed two-men Disston crosscuts themselves to cut fallen trunks into pieces, went on using the trusty ax to hew standing timber until the 1880's. It seemed against nature to use a crosscut saw horizontally. For a full half-century some 40,000 axes were needed at any given moment in America to keep the white pine falling— and these axes ordinarily had to be replaced after a month of repeated sharpening. (The woodsmen actually kept the blades honed to the point where they could shave with them on Sundays.)

So, by the law of reciprocity that linked the frontier with the mechanical East in that pre-Civil War period, a little company in Connecticut—the Collins Co. of Collinsville on the Farmington River, which still makes machetes for use on banana and coffee plantations in Central America—grew fat in supplying axes to voracious loggers all the way from Maine to Minnesota. The company was started by Samuel and David Collins, two young brothers who, as storekeepers in Hartford, Connecticut, had been selling British-imported steel to blacksmiths who forged it into ax blades. In an inspired moment David Collins decided that country smithies could not provide enough axes to keep a good store going, either as a supplier of steel or a retailer of finished ware. Accordingly, the Collinses bought an old gristmill on the Farmington and rigged up some machinery to blow air to the forges and to turn the grindstones. This was in 1826, just before the big Maine lumber boom got under way. Two years after the Collinses had turned out their first sharp axes, they were using triphammers to pound the metal into shape. Soon, with the use of huge grindstones from Nova Scotia, they were producing ten axes a day—which was mass production by the standards of those times.

But ten axes a day, or three thousand a year, were not enough to keep the sawmills of Bangor fed with logs, to say nothing of the mills of Williamsport, Pennsylvania, and Saginaw and Bay City, Michigan. The practical physics and chemistry of providing early tool steel that was neither too hard nor too soft resisted short cuts, and the processes never would have been speeded up to the point of supplying the loggers with 40,000 new axes a month if a mechanical genius named Elisha King Root had not appeared at the Collins gates. An ex-bobbin boy from Massachusetts, Root had had some experience with mill machinery. Root devised dies for shaping the hot ax metal and forging machines to supply the groove for inserting the sharp cutting bit into the ax head. Following the ideas of Eli Whitney, Root soon had ax-making fined down to a precision basis, with jigs guiding the ax heads as they were moved into position against the grinding stones. Because of the standardization of their product, the Collinses were able to out-distance all rival ax-makers; they put a trademark on their axes that made them one of the first of our national brands. Collins cutting-edge steel, which had been imported at a cost from Sheffield in England to be fitted into ax heads made out of local New England ores from Salisbury in Connecticut and Great Barrington, Massachusetts, eventually gave way to American Bessemer-made metal, with the iron ore coming all the way from Lake Superior. Up to the time when the crosscut saw, made at the Disston plant in Pennsylvania, began to replace the ax in the woods in the 1880's, the Collins company flourished as ax-maker to a nation. Then, with demand for its pioneer product falling off, it switched to other products. Meanwhile its technological genius, Mr. Root, had moved on to work for another enterpriser, who responded to the law of reciprocity that bound the frontier to the emergent industrial Northeast. We shall meet Mr. Root again, in the Hartford shops of Samuel Colt, whose revolver—the so-called "great equalizer" of the frontier—enabled the American people to conquer the western plains as the Collins ax had helped them conquer the forest.

The story of the push to the Great Plains proper, beyond the 98th meridian which separates watered prairie and woodland from the dry lands that once appeared on the maps as the Great American Desert, is mainly a post-Civil War story. But within the southern limits where the plains curve down through Texas to approach the Gulf of Mexico, Americans were moving out into natural cattle country in the 1830's and the early 1840's.

They were Texans then, living under the Lone Star of the Texas Republic. The "Texians," or "Texicans," had a navy of sorts, and they were also defended by the Rangers, a tough band of men. In the language of a contemporary, the Ranger could "ride like a Mexican, trail like an Indian, shoot like a Tennessean, and fight like a very devil." With headquarters at San Antonio, the Rangers had the twofold job of fighting off the Mexicans, who had never recognized the right of the Texas Republic to secession, and the Comanche Indians. Mounted on horses whose sires had originally been stolen from the Spanish conquistadors, the Comanches were a fearful lot. Where the Rangers would have to dismount to fire their old single-shot flintlocks, which were muzzle-loaded, the Comanches fought with bows and arrows, which they could handle at a full gallop.

Though the Texans had little money to pay for anything (the Rangers sometimes collected their wages in land scrip), they managed, somehow, to get credit for arms in the East. Representatives of several U.S. gunmakers appeared on the Texas scene, among them a salesman named John Fuller who carried a small consignment of weapons from the Patent Arms Manufacturing Co. of Paterson, New Jersey. Fuller had a new type of gun to sell, a breech-loader that carried in a revolving chamber several bullets which might be fired at a clip. Although the Chief Ordnance Officer of the Lone Star Republic turned Fuller down, preferring flintlocks from W. K. Tryon & Co. of Philadelphia, Fuller did get a small order for the revolvers from the Texas navy.

Soon this new kind of weapon was making a name for itself. A Ranger band under the command of John Coffee Hays, for instance, carried the new revolver when it went in search of a Comanche war party in the spring of 1844. The story of what happened has been succinctly told by an eyewitness: "Col. J. C. Hays with fifteen men, fought about 80 Comanche Indians, boldly attacking them upon their own ground, killing and wounding half their number . . . the result of this engagement was such as to intimidate them and enable us to treat with them." The Indians had tried their usual tactics of drawing the Texans' fire before charging them, thinking to catch the palefaces in the interval normally required to reload. They were vastly surprised when each Ranger fired again and again without pause. Years later, when an old Comanche who had been wounded was shown one of the magic revolvers, he said: "Him no good."

The gun the Rangers were using was the Colt revolver in its first primitive guise, the brain child of a remarkable man. Born in Hartford, Connecticut, in 1814, Sam Colt had persistently annoyed the neighbors wherever he lived as a boy by his harum-scarum experiments with black powder. In Ware, Massachusetts, he blew a raft out of a pond during a Fourth of July celebration, and had to be shielded from a soaked and angry crowd by young Elisha King Root, who was one day to become his production genius. On another occasion he blew the windows out of a school building. The proper place for such a boy seemed to be at sea, so Sam was packed off at the age of sixteen on a brig bound for Calcutta. In the Indian Ocean, while watching the helmsman's wheel spin over and catch when a spoke came into line with the desired shift in the brig's direction, the mysterious cross-education that makes for new inventions sparked something in Colt's mind. A whittler, the young Colt soon had a wooden model of a pistol with a revolving cartridge cylinder ready for practice whirls at lining up bullets with a stationary barrel. He got his first patent in England in 1835 (the year before the birth of the Texas Republic), and a year later a Washington patent followed. With a promise of $230,000 in capital, some of which never materialized, Colt founded the Patent Arms Manufacturing Co. in Paterson, New Jersey, the town that had been projected by Alexander Hamilton. Despite the early orders for revolvers from the Texans, the company soon fell into bankruptcy.

What saved Colt was the coming of the Mexican War in 1846 and a hurried trip to New York by Captain Samuel Walker of the Texas Rangers to look for arms. Together the slight, taciturn Texas Ranger and the flamboyantly genial Colt set out on a tour of the New York City gunshops. Everywhere they got the same answer: military volunteers had cleaned the shelves out. Whereupon Walker remarked cryptically that it was just as well. What the Texas Ranger captain wanted from the charming Mr. Colt was a newly designed gun, with a trigger guard and loading attachments that wouldn't come loose in the middle of a fight. The lack of a factory bothered Colt less than the criticism, which he swallowed because he knew that Walker's interest meant his rehabilitation as a manufacturer.

To get around a recalcitrant War Department, Walker appealed directly to President Polk. Colt, who had developed a lordly and convincing manner while lecturing on the "moral" aspects of science as "Dr. Coult of New York, London and Calcutta," promised a thousand "armes" at less than $25 each, a second thousand at $17.50, and "any number thereafter in lots of 1,000 at $15 each." He had no assurance that he could provide the equipment to make the gun, but he had heard of Eli Whitney. And in Whitneyville in Connecticut he found the son of the inventor, Eli Whitney Jr., still in business. Though hesitant at first, the junior Whitney finally agreed to make the guns on a contract basis more favorable to him than to Colt. Colt shrugged off the hard bargain in the best "Dr. Coult" tradition, for in the course of observing the Whitney production methods he had absorbed the information that was soon to make him a millionaire. Within five years he ended his association with Whitney and had his own flourishing establishment in Hartford, where he built the greatest mid-nineteenth-century arms plant in the world. He took his old boyhood friend Elisha King Root away from the nearby Collins ax factory, and together with Root he brought the mass production of interchangeable parts to such perfection that the Colt shop became known far and wide as the school for U.S. manufacturing everywhere. Colt himself was invited to appear in London before a Parliamentary Committee on Small Arms; his machines were adapted by the British to the manufacture of the Enfield rifle; and many years later it was an ex-Colt employee, Henry Leland, who first adapted the Colt mass-production techniques to the making of automobiles (the Cadillac) in Michigan.

Everything conspired to make the Colt venture the first truly great modern manufacturing success. Inventions such as the percussion cap had made the cylinder-firing pistol possible; the conditions of mounted plains warfare rendered a fast-shooting weapon an absolute necessity on the first frontier beyond the tree line. Then, too, the time had come for a quick-on-the-draw personal firearm all through the American West. It was not merely that California and Oregon-bound settlers needed protection against the mounted Plains Indians who lived off the buffalo herds all the way to Canada. Even in mountainous and wooded California itself, where the Gold Rush of '49 had attracted lawless characters from all over the world, there was a seemingly endless market for Hart-ford-made pistols. The profit entries in the accounts of Major Amos Beebe Eaton, a cousin of the Hartford Colts who had an agency for the pistol in California, waxed and waned with the records of gold dust shipped from San Francisco to the East. Between January 24, 1851, and August of 1853, Major Eaton had sold pistols to the value of some $71,000 at a profit of $16,000, half of which went to himself, the rest to his dealers. The market ran out as the mining of western ores became more civilized, but by then Colt had made such a reputation that armies everywhere, including the Yankee army that would shortly be mobilized to fight the Civil War, were clamoring for Colt-manufactured firearms. And the post-Civil War market resulting from the spread of the cattle kingdom was still waiting in the womb of time.

A pioneer in modern employee relations, Colt reduced the work day in his factory from fourteen to ten hours, built one of the first employees' social centers in America, and provided his men with hot water, soap, and towels. Behind this remarkable factory stood the New England machine-tool industry, which had come a long way from Eli Whitney's first dies and jigs. In a dozen small valleys where the streams ran swiftly to supply mill power, Yankee tinkers had been busy devising the light, accurate machine tools that were needed for small precision manufacture. Old England might keep the lead in the invention and development of great boring and shap-ing devices that were necessary for such things as steam engines. But the Yankees were faced with demands for tiny clock parts, for gun components, and for pieces for the new sewing machine; and all this called forth an amazing versatility.

Elisha Root, for instance, not only helped design tools and fix-tures for making the Colt revolver but also added a drop hammer and a horizontal turret lathe to the list. Up the valley of the Con-necticut River, in Windsor, Vermont, F. W. Howe designed vertical and horizontal lathes for the firm of Robbins & Lawrence; and in 1850 this company had the first multi-purpose milling machine ready for sale. Guns machined by Robbins & Lawrence tools cap-tivated the British at the 1851 Crystal Palace Exhibition in London, leading to a British expedition to "Darkest America" to inspect what was then just becoming known as the "American System" in the factories. The British came, saw, were conquered—and when they sailed for home they left an order for 150 machine tools.

Behind the new breed of frontier plainsmen came the farmers, sometimes before the railroads, sometimes after the extension of a railhead into "nowhere." Used to small clearings, the westward-faring husbandmen were often ill equipped both mentally and physically to handle the huge acreage of tough and sticky sods that covered the prairie states, where grass had been growing since the Ice Age. It was not that plows had not already been invented: it was now quite a long time since the New Jersey farmers of Burlington County had rejected neighbor Charles Newbold's cast-iron plow (patented in 1797) out of fear that it would "poison the soil." Thomas Jefferson had worked out the mathematical dimensions of the moldboard plow, but this protean man was so interested in a thousand different things (he also invented the swivel chair and he made what may have been the first American dumb-waiter) that he never got around to manufacturing it. After the War of 1812 Jethro Wood of New York State devised and patented a cast-iron plow that came in three parts, any one of which could be replaced without forcing the farmer to buy a whole new instrument. The Wood plow worked in eastern soils—but cast iron could not be brought to the proper pitch of strength and polish to break and handle the matted prairie grass roots and clinging loams of the West.

Enter, at this time, John Deere, a Vermont-born blacksmith who moved from Grand Detour, Illinois, to Moline in the 1840's, and whose name still graces one of the great agricultural-machinery companies. Deere had noticed that plows improvised by John Lane, a Chicago blacksmith, out of steel saws could cut and turn the toughest earth. (Lane had made the first American steel plow in Rockport, Illinois, as early as 1833.) As scientifically inclined as Thomas Jefferson, Deere worked on the problem of the best mold-board curve for the soils of Illinois and Iowa, and as fast as the problem of getting good steels could be solved, his manufacturing business grew. Later came "soft-center" plows, devised by John Lane's son, in which the ordinary brittle steels were supported by more malleable metals; and in 1855, James Oliver of South Bend, Indiana, came up with a method for chilling the working surface

Cyrus H. McCormick

of a steel casting more quickly than the back supporting sections. The chilled-steel plow had an extraordinarily smooth surface that was not achieved at the cost of excessive brittleness—and on the basis of Mr. Oliver's improvement another great agricultural-machinery company was born to carry its original name far forward into the twentieth century. By the time of the mid-1840's western farmers were hitching two or three plows together and riding them sulky fashion, which took much of the backbreaking tedium out of the job of getting ready for spring sowing. And the sowing itself was made easier when mechanical drills for the planting of wheat came on the market contemporaneously with the sulky plow.

None of this solved the problem of the harvest, which was always a nightmare as the farmers raced against time to cut the wheat before it fell, overripe, to rot in the field. Mower reapers had actually been invented in England and Scotland as early as 1822, but they had run afoul of farm-laborer prejudice and had never come to much. In the early 1830's two Americans, Obed Hussey, a one-eyed Maine Quaker who had gone to live in Cincinnati, and Cyrus Hall McCormick of Rockbridge County in Virginia, were each separately engaged in working on the idea of a reaper. Completing their models virtually neck and neck, the two men got patents embodying somewhat differing principles. The Hussey machine was sturdy and did a good mowing job, and its manufacturing origin in Cincinnati gave its maker an advantage over McCormick's location in Virginia because of the proximity to wheat country. For a while Hussey did better than McCormick, who could find no buyers in his own hilly neighborhood. At this point, however, Hussey made the mistake of moving his production to Baltimore. McCormick, a Scots-Irishman who combined inventive ability with a superb business sense, had meanwhile made a trip through the Middle West, where he saw grain growing in fields that made the Virginia farmsteads of the Shenandoah look like peasants' holdings. Accordingly, as Hussey moved away from the country that most needed the reaper, McCormick pulled up his strong Virginia roots and moved into the territory Hussey had deserted.

Some of McCormick's machines had already preceded him, traveling from Richmond by way of the Atlantic Ocean to New Orleans, and then up the Mississippi. This long haul made the price far too steep for most farmers. The canny McCormick looked over Cleveland, Cincinnati, St. Louis, and Milwaukee for factory sites, and for a time he licensed his production to several manufacturers in Missouri, Illinois, Ohio, and New York. Eventually he took the whole business back into his own hands, narrowing his factory-site choice to Chicago, which he picked because it was at the hub of the new Northwest growing area. Not only was Chicago close to grain country, but it had water access to steel from England and pig iron from Cleveland and to wood from the forests of the lake states. Needing capital to back up his choice of an ugly, mud-streaked frontier village, McCormick tackled Chicago's biggest real-estate operator and former mayor, William Ogden. Ogden put up $25,000 for a half-interest in a partnership, and McCormick was in business in time to manufacture 500 horse-drawn mechanical reapers for the 1848 wheat harvest. Two years later he bought Ogden out for twice the original $25,000.

The time and the place could hardly have been better matched to make McCormick the first great industrialist of the coming "Queen City of the Lakes." In 1848, Chicago was a swamp—it was not until 1855 that engineers started to dredge the malodorous Chicago River and create the fill on which to build a modern city. But even before the big upgrading of the city, the incoming torrents of wheat, entering Chicago by William Ogden's new Galena & Chicago Union Railroad, were already making the swamp the grain-elevator capital of the nation. Into Chicago came young men on their way to farm country—and even while the street levels were being lifted the hotels went on doing business.

To lift the Tremont Hotel to the newly created street level, for example, a bright young man named George M. Pullman assembled 5,000 jackscrews and 1,200 men in the basement and ordered each man to give four jackscrews a half turn on signal. The hotel went up without disturbing the guests in their rooms—a premonition, perhaps, of Mr. Pullman's later career in making it possible for passengers to sleep in comfortable berths while jolting over the rails that led in and out of the many Chicago depots.

While the city was being raised out of the mud of the prairie, the wealth of the whole Northwest kept jumping. But though the population of the new states grew, there were never enough men. When the Gold Rush of '49 was stripping the midwest farms of young workers, the farmers hurried to get the McCormick machines if only to make do without their harvest hands. With a reaper, one man could do the work of ten. By this time McCormick had warehouses throughout the upper Mississippi Valley, ready to trundle out a machine whenever a farmer, facing a harvest without field help, gave a frantic last-minute order for a reaper.

During all this period the reaper kept the farmer in business. In 1853 it enabled McCormick's chosen city to ship some 6 million bushels of wheat; in 1855 the figure had jumped to 16 million. The panic of 1857 barely checked Chicago's development as a wheat market, for in 1859 it was still shipping 16 million bushels. In 1860, on the eve of the Civil War, the figure virtually doubled to 31 million—and in the first year of the war it hit 50 million. The last great jump was accomplished at a time when the sons of Illinois, Wisconsin, Iowa, and Minnesota were marching off to the battlefields, denuding the Northwest of labor as the Gold Rush had never done. Small wonder that Lincoln's Secretary of War Edwin M. Stanton said in 1861 that "without McCormick's invention, I feel the North could not win and that the Union would be dismembered."

Though the really great development of the McCormick company came after the Civil War, McCormick pioneered many modern business practices even before the war had enlarged the market for his machines. He guaranteed his product and allowed farmers to pay on an installment plan that was gaited to harvest conditions. Like the Quakers, he believed in set prices, take it or leave it. The established price for a reaper was $120, $30 down and the remainder within six months. But if the harvest proved disappointing and the farmer lacked the final payment of $90, McCormick would extend the time. By refusing ever to sue a farmer for payment, McCormick built up a great reputation as the farmer's friend throughout the wheat country. Later on, through years of cutthroat battling with his Johnny-come-lately rivals, this reputation was to stand him in good stead. He went on to make binders as well as reapers—and International Harvester, the lineal descendant of the company he founded, still leads in the farm-equipment field today.

As America moved West the McCormick reaper yielded abundant food; the Collins ax contributed to shelter; the Colt revolver was for self-preservation; and the new railroads and steamboats matched the customer with the product or took the pioneering producer where he wanted to go. But these inventions, which shaped life along the frontier, were only a part of the pre-Civil War business story of a Thousand-and-One Beginnings. It was a time and a climate propitious for the small man—and, increasingly, small men were starting things that were to become great.

6 The Pre-Civil War Speedup

A "madman" exploits ice and sawdust.

Charles Goodyear experiments with malodorous "gum elastic."

Sam Morse turns from his easel to electrical circuits.

Farm boy Howe and Isaac Singer thread the sewing machine.

"Household science" flourishes on evaporated milk.

From blacksmith shop to rolling mills.

THE years before the Civil War were politically a time of portent, filled with the alarums that heralded the gathering of the "irrepressible conflict." Looking back on those years, one sees little besides the turmoil of Southerners fighting Free-Soilers over Bleeding Kansas or the rage of the Charleston fire-eaters as they rise to denounce the Abolitionists. Manfully, the gaunt Abe Lincoln debates with the "Little Giant," Stephen A. Douglas; manfully, the great compromiser Dan'l Webster joins with Henry Clay in the futile effort to patch things up and avoid a showdown; and just as manfully the philosopher Ralph Waldo Emerson denounces the godlike Dan'l as a trimmer. So the nation slides toward the abyss past the great milestones of the Dred Scott decision and John Brown's fanatic attempt to steal government arms for a slave rebellion.

When people are living through a period of endemic crisis, however, the "big" problems often seem of less moment than the smaller problems of daily existence. While the political thunderheads were rolling up in that pre-Civil War period, business enterprise continued to sprout from its Thousand-and-One Beginnings in the older seaboard states as well as on the open western frontier. In Philadelphia and in Hartford, Connecticut, men formed companies to insure against fire and marine disaster. In Delaware the du Ponts had developed their black-powder industry—but much of it went quite unmartially to blast rock out of the way for the railroad and canal builders and to uncover new veins of coal in Pennsylvania. In Wall Street, Jacob Little, the first stock-market "bear," devised the art of going short in the market during the depression years after 1837. But others were bucking the trend and shrewder financiers were looking to new inventors and developers. In 1839, William Harnden started an express service that was to become big business; and Wells & Co. shortly extended express delivery to the cities of the new Middle West preparatory to the later push of Wells Fargo across the Great Plains. Men picked at the surface of the land for lead in the Galena region of Illinois, for copper and iron in northern Michigan, for marble and granite in Vermont, and for brownstone in the quarries of the Connecticut Valley. And to make things easier for the financiers, the miners who thronged to California after 1849, either crossing the plains or taking Commodore Vanderbilt's ships to an isthmian portage in Nicaragua, were shortly shipping $50 million in gold to help support new eastern projects.

The Era of a Thousand-and-One Beginnings abounded with other types of pioneers. There was that curious man, Samuel Kier, for instance, who got the idea that "rock oil"—then used only for medicinal purposes—could be used in lamps, and thereby opened the way for the development of petroleum. A character named Benjamin T. Babbitt (whose name later fascinated Sinclair Lewis) built a monster soap factory in New York City, and was so successful in selling his product from brightly colored carts loaded with musicians that he put the word "bandwagon" into the language. Another strange genius, called a madman by his neighbors, was Frederic Tudor, a Boston Yankee who had refused to go to Harvard because it was "a place for loafers." Tudor had the crazy idea that he might pack ice from a pond in Saugus and ship it in sawdust to tropical countries. He actually built a great business transporting natural ice from Massachusetts ponds and Maine rivers to the West Indies and faraway Calcutta. One of the by-products of Tudor's genius was the popularization of ice cream; another was a new market for the ice tong. With people all over the northern part of the nation bidding up the price of ice rights on ponds, many thought that the Tudor Ice Co. would last forever. Practically no one in the whole U.S. population of 23 million noticed it when the Patent Office granted a patent on a cold-air refrigerating machine in 1849 —and, indeed, it was not until the 1880's that the significance of artificial ice—both for home consumption and freight cars—finally began to dawn.

While the railroads pushed westward, the carriage business also flourished—indeed, the horse was the universal equivalent of the internal-combustion engine, and the hay, grain, and feed business filled the place now occupied by the Socony and Texaco dealers. In New Haven, James Brewster built up a nationally famous carriage business and in South Bend, Indiana, the Studebakers made wagons long before they were in automobiles. Thinking, at one point, that the railroad had doomed the horse, Brewster quit carriage making to help finance a railroad between New Haven and Hartford. But he was soon back in his original business when he realized that carriages were more than ever necessary to meet the trains. A Yankee toolmaker's device played an important role in cutting Brewster's costs. In 1818, Thomas Blanchard, working in Springfield, Massachusetts, had invented a profile lathe that was able to follow irregular patterns to make a variety of things from gunstocks to shoe lasts to ax handles. The Blanchard lathe was quickly adapted to the shaping of wheel spokes—and machine-made wheels were shortly rolling a vast variety of stagecoaches, gigs, victorias, cabriolets, surreys, broughams, phaetons, and landaulets over the roads and streets of America. The elliptical multi-laminate spring, patented by Jonathan Mix early in the century, was improved year by year, as were axles, door handles, brass lamps, harness hardware, and upholstery. Meanwhile, two of James Brewster's fellow residents of New Haven came through with two supporting inventions. Ithiel Town, a nationally famous architect, designed a wooden lattice truss bridge that helped road builders everywhere to span creeks and rivers cheaply, and Amasa Goodyear made the first steel-tine pitchfork, which decreased the cost of supplying horses with hay.

Amasa Goodyear's son, Charles, made a far more important breakthrough. A restless, brilliant youth, he began his career as a shopkeeper. But his real heart was in fooling around with elastic "tree latex" from the jungles of the Amazon River, thinking that it would be useful for a rubber life preserver. Soon his rubber experiments became an obsession. To pay his bills he sold the family pitchfork patent, and at one depressed period he even sold his children's schoolbooks. For ten years, many of which he spent in debtors' prison where jailors complaisantly let him work, he patiently mixed various materials with the evil-smelling "gum elastic." He tried magnesia, he tried nitric acid, he tried metals—but no matter what the combination the rubber would crack in cold weather or become an oozy mass on a hot day.

Since rubber always melted with heat, nobody had ever thought to make it durable by combining it with chemicals that might possibly fuse into a tough substance when fired. Mixing his "gum elastic" with sulfur and with lead compounds one day, Charles Goodyear accidentally spilled some of the mess on a hot stove. To his surprise a charring action resulted, leaving a hard rind. Further experiment showed that a durable and useful hard rubber resulted if the charring—or vulcanization—was controlled. A patent followed in 1841. At last Goodyear had the means for making a safe rubber life preserver. More important, however, the L. Candee Co. of New Haven, licensed to use the Goodyear vulcanizing patent, had the basis for a thriving business in providing the nation with rubber overshoes. Raincoats, rubber balls, and tires for carriages, bicycles, and the automobile all followed in due course, and a great city—Akron—was eventually to grow out of the lucky charring on Goodyear's stove.

The "breathless generation" of the 1830's and 1840's, avid for news about the many changes that were taking place around them, offered a great potential market for the first man who could come up with a cheap newspaper. But first, a new press must be designed to replace the old hand-run screw presses similar to the one invented by Gutenberg. The new steam-driven presses made it possible to print some 2,000 impressions within an hour—and Richard March Hoe of New York later improved upon this by making a rotary press capable of an hourly run of 10,000 sheets. Using the new presses, publishers such as Benjamin Henry Day, founder of the New York *Sun,* could sell their papers for a penny and still make money.

The demand for cheap newsprint, combining with the need of businessmen for more effective verbal communication, quickly spurred a search for better methods of papermaking. Even the bark of trees was beaten into a pulp in the effort to obtain paper with-

Courtesy Library of Congress

Samuel F. B. Morse

out resorting to expensive rags—and wood pulp itself (made from wood boiled in caustic alkali at a high temperature) appeared on the scene in the 1850's as Hugh Burgess got the first American patent on a process that had already been developed in England. Earlier the Ames family of Springfield, Massachusetts, pioneered in bringing the processes of papermaking under one capitalistic roof. They had built paper mills by the Connecticut River, and had devised various processes for dressing rags and pulp and for doing away with the old "loft drying" of paper sheets.

The great mutation in business communications came with the invention of the telegraph, the work of a painter, Samuel F. B. Morse, whose father Jedidiah had written the first American geography book. In reality the telegraph could have been made by any-

Courtesy Smithsonian Institution

Elias Howe, Jr.

one, for it consisted of the commercial application of known principles. Actually, the first fruit of Morse's experimentation with sending electric charges over wires was a submarine cable insulated with tar that he sank in New York Harbor in 1842. This led Morse to predict that a cable would someday span the Atlantic—and, indeed, Cyrus Field, bankrolled in part by Peter Cooper of *Tom*

Thumb engine fame, succeeded in laying a momentarily successful cable from Newfoundland to Ireland just before the Civil War. A more durable transatlantic cable came later. At the time of Morse's experiment in New York Harbor it was a foregone conclusion that electrical impulses could be transmitted over wires strung between cities on land—but the problem of raising the capital to buy the necessary wire was a formidable one. Moreover, Morse's original idea was to put the wire safely in underground ditches, which would have involved Herculean labor—and to this end he had enlisted the help of Ezra Cornell, a New York State entrepreneur who had theories about overcoming some of the expenses of digging by utilizing an underground wire-laying machine of his own devising.

In 1843, Morse got an appropriation from Congress to run a test line between Washington and Baltimore. Cornell, finally rejecting ditches as impractical, strung wire from poles and trees, using broken bottle necks as insulators. When in 1844 the magical words, "What hath God wrought," were tapped out in Washington and picked up in Baltimore, it was obvious to the smarter men of the 1840's that brokers and bankers would soon have a medium which would permit them to do business almost anywhere within the hour. And it was also apparent that the railroads would be able to apply new safety concepts to the dispatching of trains.

Morse and his associates raised private capital to organize the Magnetic Telegraph Co., which opened a line between New York and Philadelphia. Soon there were additional stock companies operating different lines between different cities and speeding news of the Mexican War to the eastern newspapers. Western Union, organized in 1856, brought some order out of a welter of small companies. In 1859, going against the advice of Amos Kendall, the old political agent of Andrew Jackson who had become his financial adviser and fellow telegraph capitalist in the 1840's, Morse acquiesced in the formation of the North American Telegraph Association, a near monopoly. Morse lived on well into the post-Civil War period to collect his royalties, a comfortably fixed old man who had come a long way from the near starvation of his early days as an unsuccessful painter and penniless inventor.

With the development of the telegraph, which made national markets and exchanges a reality, the U.S. was approaching the tempo of modern times. There was a sudden speeding up of everything in the years just before the Civil War. With the extension of the market, the corporate form of industry at last commenced to achieve its destined nationwide and even international uses. The exploitation of the sewing machine is a case in point. Beginning as a typical Yankee invention in the mid-1840's, the sewing machine was quickly absorbed into an industrial pattern that anticipated many of the corporate wrinkles of the twentieth century, utilizing everything from dignified advertising to Barnum-like ballyhoo, and from the cross licensing of patents to installment credit organized on an international scale.

The sewing machine completed the textile revolution, which had got off to a grand start in America with Eli Whitney's cotton gin and the spinning and weaving mills of Samuel Slater and Francis Cabot Lowell. For years the transformation of the machine-made textiles into clothes had been for most families a highly laborious process that involved hours of needlework by long-suffering wives. In the 1840's there were some ready-to-wear garments, but they were of the cheapest materials, usually of "shoddy" (as wool cloth woven out of re-used shredded and broken fibers came to be called). Produced primarily for sailors, who would be many nautical miles distant from the sly merchant when the clothing improvidently went to pieces, ready-to-wear suits were manufactured in the crudest sweatshops or by "putting out" the jobs to seamstresses in the country. Those were the days of Thomas Hood's bitter *The Song of the Shirt,* about the woman who, "with eyelids heavy and red," went "Stitch! stitch! stitch!" from dawn to dark, trying to keep body and soul together with her needle. Clearly, the inventor of a workable sewing machine should have been hailed instantly as a great public benefactor by housewives and clothing manufacturers alike.

It was not that easy, as Elias Howe, Jr., a Massachusetts farm boy, was to discover. In 1839, while working in Boston as a machine-shop apprentice, Howe overheard some visitors argue with his employer Ari Davis about the possibility of devising a sewing machine. When Davis insisted the idea was feasible, the visitors scoffed. "Well you do it, Davis, and we'll insure you an independent fortune." This road to riches looked good to Howe who did not know that automation, always and everywhere, has its enemies. As a matter of fact, a Frenchman, Barthélemy Thimonnier, had made a successful machine in 1829, and was already busy with a contract for uniforms for the French Army when a mob, thinking the livelihood of French tailors was at stake, broke in and destroyed his new equipment. Eighty machines in all were wrecked in this savage outburst. Two or three years later, in New York City, a man by the name of Walter Hunt put the eye in the head of a needle and used it to push a thread through cloth to interlock with a second thread carried by a shuttle. This was the true secret of the modern sewing machine—but Mr. Hunt's daughter Caroline felt sorry for the hand sewers who would be put out of business by her father and declined to use the invention in her proposed corset-making establishment. Hunt, who had other projects on the fire (he invented the safety pin, a street-sweeping machine, paper collars, and a repeating rifle), didn't even bother to try for a patent on his machine until it was too late.

Meanwhile Elias Howe blundered ahead, trying to make a machine that would copy the motion of his wife's arm as she sewed for himself and his three children. A double-pointed needle with the eye in the middle didn't work, but Howe was on the trail of Hunt's principle. By 1844 he had hit upon the notion of using two threads to make a stitch that would be interlocked by a shuttle. Impressed by Howe's claims, a friend in the coal and wood business, George Fisher, staked the earnest young man to board and room for his family, provided him with a garret to work in, and advanced him $500 for materials and tools. And in July of 1845, Howe's first practical machine sewed all the seams on two suits of wool cloth.

What followed would have broken almost any man's heart. Racing against the deftest professional seamstresses, Howe's machine won in a classic demonstration at the Quincy Hall Clothing Manufactory in Boston. The inventor got a patent on an improved second machine in 1846, thanks to the expenditure of $2,000 by his benefactor Fisher, but the tailors and garment-makers of America, fearing their employees' displeasure, would have none of it. Faced with a dead loss of the capital he had already advanced, Fisher pulled out of the partnership, and Howe, weary of battering his head against local prejudice, decided to try his luck in England, where he fell on new misfortunes. William Thomas, the agent who had paid £250 for his share of Howe's English rights, kept all the subsequent royalties for himself, making a profit of a million dollars. Meanwhile Howe was so poor he had to pawn his clothes to pay for the cab that took his sick wife to the dock when she decided to go home. He had later to borrow money to reach his wife's bedside in Cambridge, Massachusetts, and was just in time to see her die of consumption. It was a sad homecoming for him in other ways, for while he had been in England his basic idea had been widely copied.

In spite of his mischances, however, the hapless ex-farm boy did have the basic sewing-machine patent; and by 1851 he had managed to interest new partners who were willing to carry on suits for the rapidly spreading infringements. At this point Howe ran up against Isaac Merrit Singer. This singular man, who has been described as "charming but vain, creative but concupiscent, talented but dilatory," had been a wandering journeyman mechanic and a ham actor. He had patented a wood-carving machine, and knew something of basic mechanical movement when he chanced to watch the attempts to repair a primitive sewing machine in a Boston shop in 1850. Completely broke himself (his wood-carving machine had been wrecked in a boiler explosion), Singer got out a pencil and paper. The next day he returned to the shop with a sketch of a machine that rested on a table with the cloth supported horizontally in a position to be guided by the operator. A vertical presser foot held the cloth firmly against the upward lift of the needle. With forty borrowed dollars Singer worked day and night in a shop belonging to other men, sleeping but three or four hours a night and eating only one meal a day. In eleven days he had the Singer sewing machine. At one point it looked as though the thing were a flop, until it flashed upon him that he had forgotten to adjust the tension on the needle thread before trying it.

Bitter patent litigation now broke out between Howe and Singer, who had as his chief lieutenant a bright lawyer and money raiser, Edward Clark, of New York City. Eventually Howe got a favorable decision from the Massachusetts courts assuring his rights to his invention of the eye-pointed needle. The only way, however, that Howe could capitalize on his victory was to collect royalties from

Singer, who in fact, along with a number of others, had taken over the actual business of manufacturing sewing machines. More patent wars developed among the manufacturing companies until finally a patent pool was developed to settle the differences between some of the rivals, which got together in what became known as "the Combination." From the Combination, Howe as well as Singer reaped fortunes. Gradually I. M. Singer & Co. forged ahead, developing a fully matured consumer installment plan, a franchised agency system, and a huge international trade. The Singer name became a byword in Indian huts in the Andes, in jungle hovels in the tropics, and in cabins by northern glaciers.

The lift the housewife got from the sewing machine was part and parcel of a wider change. In Philadelphia, in 1837, Louis Antoine Godey was already publishing *Godey's Lady's Book,* with the remarkable Sarah Josepha Hale as the "Lady Editor." The Lady Editor was annoyed by the menial position of pre-Civil War women and proceeded to put the flattering term "domestic science" into the language. As it turned out, "domestic science" was to make prodigious use of the sewing machine—and around the dress patterns displayed by the women's magazines mass-circulation media were to grow to join the new penny press in the dissemination of information. "Domestic science" also meant the tin can. In 1847 a can-making machine had been invented—and later, with 240 cans passing through a crimping machine in a minute, gold and silver miners in California and Colorado and explorers in the Far North shared garden peas or Maine lobster meat with the housewife all year round. In 1856 Gail Borden devised the process for evaporating milk and putting it into a can—a foreshadowing of the day when Elsie the Cow, one of Madison Avenue's more engaging creations, would impress the principles of "domestic science" on her skittish offspring.

Meanwhile, as early as the 1850's, the sewing machine had been used to do the stitching on shoe uppers. But in the Massachusetts shoe towns—Lynn, Haverhill, Marblehead—and in Hartford and Philadelphia, the business of matching soles and uppers was still being farmed out to household workers. A successful shoe-pegging machine had been invented in 1833, but hand sewers and peggers threatened boycott and mayhem. Even after the prejudice against machine pegging had evaporated, as shoe manufacturers pirated the various mechanical pegging devices there wasn't much money in them. By the time a manufacturer had paid for the eternal litigation his pegging profits had vanished. Consequently, when Lyman R. Blake in South Abingdon, Massachusetts, managed to do the heavy work of sewing soles to uppers mechanically, the industry was ready for his invention.

Ironically, the Blake invention, patented in 1858, became known as the "McKay Sewing Machine"—so called because Gordon McKay, an engineer, bought Blake out for cash and a royalty that was to total $70,000. (Eventually, through patent renewal, Blake got far more money.) McKay had the financial resources to fight patent suits—and he also had the will and the skill to adapt Blake's machinery to large-scale operations. He helped devise special machines to melt the wax on thread as it passed through heavy leather, and he substituted steam-driven factories for the old piecework system that had been in force ever since Ebenezer Breed, the Quaker, had started the wholesale shoe business in Lynn in the eighteenth century.

McKay refused to sell his machines outright, preferring to lease them and to collect royalties on every pair of shoes made. As a bonus, the client who leased a McKay machine got a small part of the McKay company capital stock. As patents ran out, McKay kept picking up other inventions: he was, at one time, a partner of Charles Goodyear Jr., the son of the inventor of vulcanized rubber. In time the so-called "Goodyear welt" was to become synonymous with quality shoemaking, and when S. V. A. Hunter, secretary-treasurer of the company, suggested that the welt be advertised as "better than" hand sewing, an important mercantile slogan was born. Out of the McKay industrial leasing and various mergers United Shoe Machinery was eventually created—and so low did this company keep its royalties that it encountered little organized opposition for a long period.

The growing industrialization of the nation in the forties and fifties argued the necessity of an iron and steel industry. But here the U.S. lagged for years behind Britain, partly because the British government in the eighteenth century had tried to hold the Americans down. Much of the colonists' pig iron was in fact exported to the mother country. Later, utilizing new processes for puddling and rolling invented by Henry Cort in the 1780's, the British mills established a long lead time in the unfolding industrial revolution. So even in the middle of the nineteenth century American ax-makers, sewing-machine makers, and railroad builders were still dependent on British sources for good iron.

Nevertheless, the U.S. had the makings and the tradition for creating an industry. The first iron works, at Falling Creek in Virginia, was destroyed by Indians in 1622, ending "a good project." So, properly speaking, the Iron Age in America goes back to the New England Puritans, who had their small blast furnaces for the production of metal needed in pots, skillets, and andirons. America's first important iron master, John Winthrop Jr., the son of the first governor of the pioneer Massachusetts Bay Colony, had a real modern enterpriser's flair; he built an early salt works for evaporating sea water to obtain the preservative that enabled New England to establish its first fishing industry. When the swamps in back of Lynn showed the color of bog iron in the water, Winthrop raised a thousand pounds in England and returned to Massachusetts with workmen and equipment to set up blast furnaces and a refinery forge. The result was the famous Saugus works—and a production of iron amounting to some eight tons a week by 1648. Later Winthrop started an iron business in Connecticut, whither he had gone to become governor of Massachusetts' daughter-colony.

The industry created by the junior Winthrop in New England, by the Dutch in Monmouth County, New Jersey, by Colonel Alexander Spotswood in Virginia above the falls of the Rappahannock, and by the remarkable Leonard family at several places, was small-time stuff; at first, it provided barely enough metal for use in blacksmiths' shops. Nevertheless, it pointed the way for some ambitious schemes. Spotswood himself, after resigning as lieutenant governor of Virginia in 1723, built an early American air furnace near Fredericksburg, where he used bituminous coal for smelter operations. In Salisbury, Connecticut, local ores put the Green Mountain Boy Ethan Allen temporarily into the iron business—and caused Litchfield County villagers to dream that their town might some day become the Birmingham of America. Using Salisbury iron, Philip Livingston started a forge and foundry business across the border in New York. The Quakers of Philadelphia formed early joint stock companies to build forges and furnaces in the Reading region; and in New Jersey, where there were small amounts of really good ore in the mountains near the New York line, an ambitious German named Peter Hasenclever, using London capital, splurged way beyond his credit in setting up a huge complex of furnaces and mines for something variously called the London Company or the American Iron Company.

Hasenclever went broke and was discharged by his irate stockholders; but a Scotsman, Robert Erskine, took over the enterprise in 1771 and made something of Hasenclever's pioneering. He found that Hasenclever had provided him with many valuable "firsts"— furnaces whose inside walls were made of durable slate, forges whose hammers were operated by strong overshot waterwheels, and artificially dammed reservoirs to provide a continuity of water power in dry months. Adding some wrinkles of his own, such as the country's first magnetic ore separator (an oak drum fitted out with magnets), Erskine put the American Iron Company in shape in time to provide iron for Washington's armies. Washington himself thought so much of Erskine that he made him his chief engineer and map-maker, appointing him as official geographer to the Continental Army.

In all that pertained to the extraction of ores from bogs and pockets and small seams, and the subsequent melting and shaping of the mined ore into pig iron, the early American iron industry was first-rate. But the colonists always had to reckon with the British government's refusal to countenance a local iron fabricating industry. J. Leander Bishop speaks eloquently of the "dexterity of Americans in the manufacture of scythes, axes, nails, etc.," but "the flood of foreign iron . . . at the close of the war" kept American production from growing rapidly. Aside from a few slitting mills which provided iron for nails and other close-to-home building items, there was nothing much of a real iron manufacturing business in the America of the late eighteenth and early nineteenth centuries.

What gave impetus to developing something better was the coming of the railroads. When Peter Cooper started work on his first locomotive, the *Tom Thumb,* in Baltimore he found a dearth of fabricated iron pipe, and in fact built his engine largely from scrap.

It was thus borne in on him that iron manufacturing might make him some money to add to what he was getting out of his glue and gelatin business. Throughout the 1830's and the early 1840's, Cooper, a public-spirited gentleman, was busy with a hundred projects, from public-school education to the organization of the Croton River water supply for Manhattan Island. But he also found time to build an iron foundry on Thirty-third Street, near Third Avenue, in New York City, where he experimented further with using anthracite coal instead of charcoal in the smelting of the ore. At the same time he put his profits from glue into railroad securities. The New York iron foundry was too far away from coal and iron sources to be a profitable producer of iron for railroads, and Cooper, who believed in supporting his investments, meditated the transfer of his mill equipment to the valley of the Delaware.

He might have done nothing about this if he had not had an able son, Edward, who had demonstrated inventive and mechanical talents as a boy. Edward, in turn, had an even more able friend, Abram S. Hewitt, who ultimately married Peter Cooper's daughter. Though he had a prejudice against partnerships, Peter Cooper yielded to the point of becoming a silent partner with his son and son-in-law-to-be in a new mill at Trenton, New Jersey. Hewitt, who had transcendent organizing and merchandising ability, took hold of the selling while Edward Cooper remained in the shop—and within a year the new mill had a contract with the Stevens' Camden & Amboy Railroad for replacing unsatisfactory English rails. The Camden & Amboy contract, which yielded $180,000 in cash, posed many problems, both of mill technology and of raw-material supply. Edward Cooper had to learn from scratch how to roll Robert L. Stevens' T-rail, with its flanged bottom. But inside of a year he was producing the rails, and contracts with the Hudson River Railroad, the New York & Harlem, and the Rutland & Burlington followed. In 1848 the Trenton mills paid a dividend of 20 per cent.

Eastern iron posed problems for rail-makers, whose early rail tops splintered easily. Hewitt, whose avocation it was to tramp the forested hills of the upper New Jersey counties, found himself looking into the old shafts of abandoned colonial mines in search of an iron that would be "close-grained and tenacious." He found such ore in the disused Andover mine, which had once been in the possession of William Penn's family. Purchased in 1847 for less than $10,000, the Andover mine yielded two strains of ore, red hematite and blue magnetite, which, when combined, made a particularly tough iron rail. It was not until Lake Superior ore became plentiful after the Civil War that anybody could compete with Andover and other eastern ores for durable iron rails. In the sixties the Andover ores played out—but for a generation they kept Trenton competitive with Pennsylvania and Ohio mills for leadership in producing iron for the rapidly expanding American railroad grid.

The making of rails was a chancy business, for the British kept expanding their own production for export, and the Democratic party, which often bested the Whigs for control of the American government during the forties and fifties, refused to yield to the New Jersey and Pennsylvania iron-masters in the matter of a high tariff. In 1851 and 1852, when 4,400 miles of railway were built in the U.S. between the seaboard and the Mississippi, there was plenty of rail business for the Trenton mills at $55 and $60 and even $70 a ton. The British, who were busy manufacturing rails for western Europe, Russia, South America, India, and Australia, posed no problem until the middle fifties. Then, suddenly, the new mills and the newly discovered iron deposits of Yorkshire started flooding the market with cheap British rails—and disaster stared American rail-makers in the face.

Characteristically, Hewitt saved Trenton not by wasting too much time crying for a tariff but by turning to other uses for his iron. In the fifties the new telegraph millionaire, Ezra Cornell, started substituting galvanized iron wire for copper in his telegraph lines. In 1852 Hewitt was able to announce that Trenton had made virtually all the telegraph wire that had been strung in the two preceding years. Another man who turned to the Trenton Iron Co. for his iron was John A. Roebling, a genius from Germany who had persuaded the builders of the inclined planes that lifted the canal boats over the Alleghenies to substitute iron cables for the constantly fraying hawsers of Kentucky hemp. In 1846 Roebling put a suspension bridge of wire rope across the Monongahela to Pittsburgh. Needing a better supply of wire than he could get in the Pittsburgh area, Roebling made a deal with Cooper and Hewitt, and ultimately he built his own plant next door to their mills. When Roebling took over an unfinished suspension bridge at the Niagara gorge in 1850, the Trenton mills furnished him with quantities of wire sufficient to spin the cables for 800 feet of bridgework. In 1855 a test train weighing 340 tons traveled over the bridge, held aloft by good Andover iron cable. Meanwhile, in New York, Peter Cooper demonstrated one of the by-product uses of philanthropy. He had been buying plots of land at Fourth Avenue near Astor Place, planning to build a workingman's institute—Cooper Union—when he had assembled an entire block. A stone structure with ponderous arches and pillars seemed ridiculous to Cooper—but nobody, in 1852, had yet succeeded in rolling a structural iron beam capable of bearing the weight of a huge building.

To roll flanged beams, the Trenton mills experimented with something known as a three-high mill capable of turning out girders that were twenty and twenty-five feet long and seven inches deep. The girders went into the first construction work at Cooper Union. A year later the offices of Harper & Brothers, the greatest publishing company in the U.S., burned down. Abram Hewitt, with an order from the Harper company for a fireproof building in his hand, promptly suspended work on Cooper Union until he had provided enough beams for a new seven-story structure able to support the heaviest Harper presses. With money gained from the Harper exploit, Peter Cooper then proceeded to complete Cooper Union. Meanwhile, in his little notebook, he figured that he had become a millionaire; the builder of the *Tom Thumb* engine estimated his net worth in 1856 at $1,106,000.

Throughout most of the fifties the Trenton mills prospered, making iron rails for the fabulously successful Illinois Central, and they were also taxed to capacity during the Civil War. Nevertheless, even before the war Trenton was giving ground to new competition. In 1856 Henry Bessemer in England had patented a process that blew cold air through molten iron to make a high-quality steel. But New Jersey ores lacked the purity needed for making Bessemer wrought iron or steel in the days before chemists were able to take such elements as phosphorus out of inferior ore. The ores of Michigan and Minnesota were to prove far more suited to the Bessemer process. Even before these ores were fully exploited, mills had begun to sprout beyond the Alleghenies. When the new Pennsylvania Railroad, pushing toward Ohio, went into the market for rails, it tended to favor the Cambria Iron Works of Johnstown, Pennsylvania, where the redoubtable and beloved John Fritz, later the soul of Bethlehem's armor-plate manufacture, had built a three-high rail mill very much like the one the Trenton mills had pioneered for structural beams. By the time of the Civil War, Cambria was turning out 20,000 tons of pig a year.

Farther to the west the firm of Jones & Laughlin's was already pioneering the cold rolling of iron. Andrew Carnegie, a Pennsylvania Railroad employee, had not yet gone into the iron business, but his partner-to-be, a first-rate blacksmith named Andrew Kloman, was busy forging railroad-car axles before 1859. A Westerner, Isaac Meason, was puddling and rolling flat iron bars in Pittsburgh as early as 1819; Dr. Peter Shoenberger's Juniata Works in Pittsburgh made bar iron, sheet iron, boiler plate, and nails as early as 1824; and in 1839 one of the largest pre-Civil War integrated companies, the Great Western Iron Co., was started in western Pennsylvania with an investment of $500,000. Later capitalized for a million as Brady's Bend Iron Co., it mined its own coal, ore, limestone, and fire clay, made its own coke, and ran four blast furnaces to feed its rolling mills.

Along with this expansion in production came new ideas and inventions. The real genius of the pre-Civil War period was the unappreciated William Kelly, who worked at Eddyville, Kentucky, on the Cumberland River. Kelly anticipated the Bessemer process as early as 1847, and used it to some extent in the making of boiler plate. The story goes that his wife, thinking him crazy to be blowing cold air through iron when the idea was to burn out the impurities, had him examined by a doctor. After listening to Kelly, the doctor decided that everyone else in the iron business was crazy and Kelly alone was sane. It seemed perfectly plausible that the oxygen in cold air, blown into iron, would unite with carbon impurities and so purge the metal. When Kelly, in later years, heard that the Englishman Bessemer had got an American patent for the Eddyville "pneumatic" process, he proved his own prior discovery to the Patent Office and so obtained a patent for himself. Bessemer, however, patented his own distinctive converter not only in Britain but also in the U.S.

Because of the confusion in the Bessemer and Kelly patent situation and the paucity of good ore for the conversion process, the Civil War was destined to be fought without Bessemer steel. But the northern iron industry that had been built up in the forties and fifties was prepared for the struggle if only because the Confederacy had the sketchiest of iron-making resources. The weight of metal the North was able to bring to bear on the issue was sufficient to prove crucial.

So, too, was the morale deriving from the intangibles. In a civilization that was fast becoming used to machines, slavery must have seemed more and more futile as well as morally intolerable. Even the "domestic science" of the period protested against it: the housewife who had been at least partially liberated from drudgery by the sewing machine and the tin can must have been more content to view the slave as an anachronism.

When Seward, Lincoln's great rival for Republican party leadership, called it the "irrepressible conflict," he was indulging in the same sort of easy rhetoric that made the phrase "manifest destiny" come so patly from his tongue. But behind the rhetoric there was the reality: the northern business system and the southern slave system had become increasingly incompatible. Whether sectional differences could have been settled by peaceful means is a moot question. But when the crunch of war actually came, northern industry had its implacable contribution to make.

7 The Civil War and Its Aftermath

The illusions that led to Fort Sumter.

Machine-reaped wheat feeds the North.

The Tredegar Works rolls armor plate for the South's iron-clads.

Supersalesman Jay Cooke hawks war bonds.

Four shopkeepers create a continental market.

Just before the onset of the Civil War, William Tecumseh Sherman, a transplanted Ohioan then serving as superintendent of a military academy in Louisiana, addressed a somber warning to a southern friend. "You people speak so lightly of war," he said. "You don't know what you are talking about. . . . You mistake . . . the people of the North. They are a peaceable people, but an earnest people and will fight too. . . . Besides, where are your men and appliances of war to contend against them? The northern people not only greatly outnumber the whites at the South, but they are a mechanical people with manufactures of every kind, while you are only agriculturists—a sparse population covering a large extent of territory, and in all its history no nation of mere agriculturists ever made successful war against a nation of mechanics. . . . The North can make a steam engine, locomotive or railway car; hardly a yard of cloth or a pair of shoes can you make. You are rushing into war with one of the most powerful, ingeniously mechanical and determined people on earth—right at your doors. You are bound to fail. . . ."

The future conqueror of Atlanta, always a prescient man, had looked below the surface. He was not the first prophet to warn the South: years before, Langdon Cheves of South Carolina, who had preceded Nicholas Biddle as head of the second Bank of the United States, had warned Calhoun against playing with the idea of secession. But the South had not listened to Cheves, and it was not disposed to listen to Sherman.

One reason for the South's obduracy was that it had been used to having its way. Up to the very election of Lincoln as a minority president in 1860 it had almost invariably got what it wanted politically. Its representatives in Washington were skilled—and it had consistently been able to fall back on a close working accord with western agricultural interests. The old Cotton Kingdom and the steadily expanding corn-and-cattle-raising West had always, with the short-lived exception of the 1828 Tariff of Abominations, combined to defeat the northern millowners' desire for a really strong protective tariff. Working in concert, the South and the newest western states had made it possible throughout the forties and the fifties for squatters to take up land cheaply and pay for it out of production. In the matter of a railroad to the Pacific, the new West would have liked to see San Francisco directly linked to Chicago or St. Louis. But it did not seriously object when all immediate action on this project was stymied by southern politicians like Jefferson Davis, who wanted to be sure that a transcontinental road would, if subsidized by Congress, begin in cotton territory in Louisiana and reach the Pacific by way of Texas.

There was, however, a febrile quality in the late fifties to the South's hopes of holding the West forever as its political ally. The weight of immigration into new western territories was from the North—and prospective wheatgrowers from Germany or Scandinavia, with the new McCormick machinery at their disposal, wanted neither slaves nor any competition from slave labor. Though the South made an abortive fight for "bleeding Kansas," it could not muster enough slaveholders who were willing to attempt to settle in western territory where cotton would not grow. And even the Southwest threatened to elude the Southerners' grasp. Though the South's domain had been vastly enlarged by the entry of Texas into the Union, the subsequent Mexican War, undertaken to satisfy

Texas border grievances, had not resulted in the acquisition of further lands that were really adapted to slaveholding. The new territories of New Mexico and Utah permitted slavery, but as Daniel Webster had predicted, virtually no Southerners took their slaves there. Brigham Young, the Mormon leader, though not theoretically opposed to slaveholding, told Horace Greeley that Utah could not afford slaves.

Thus right up to the outbreak of the Civil War the slave system was still highly concentrated in the open Delta and river-bottom regions, and its operation there was in turn highly concentrated in relatively few hands. In 1850 there were some 1,800,000 blacks in the South as compared to 2,100,000 whites, which would have theoretically permitted three or four slaves per family. But the profits created by the blacks were channeled into the coffers of the three or four thousand families that received three-fourths of the returns from southern exports. A thousand great families shared in an income of $50 million a year; the remaining 660,000 southern families divided $60 million a year. To keep pace with expanding opportunities, the richer planters kept plowing their profits into the purchase of new field hands, whose value was compounded every time a slave reproduced himself. The owner of a hundred slaves might conservatively estimate his wealth at upwards of $100,000 in the 1850's. A prime field hand brought $1,500 and more in the palmiest days of cotton culture—and the old tobacco states of the upper South shared in the new prosperity by becoming slave breeders. Planters lived well and variously, dipping snuff, attending barbecues, visiting town on court days, traveling by carriage for great distances to visit their kin, feuding and dueling when they were angered, reading Greek and Latin classics (and the beloved Waverly novels of Sir Walter Scott) in their libraries, and listening to the new theorists of "Greek democracy" expound the virtues of a republic reared on the backs of an inferior class.

Yet this well-being was also in a way febrile: though the laws of genetics seemed to guarantee a permanently expanding wealth, the profits of cotton culture mysteriously disappeared from the southern banks. In 1850 cotton and other southern crops sold for $120 million—yet total bank deposits in the South amounted to only $20 million. In 1860, when southern crops were valued at $200 million for the year, the banks contained less than $30 million on deposit. The reason, as historian William E. Dodd explains it, is that southern plantation earnings were eaten up by tariffs, freights, commissions, and profits that the planters had to pay on northern manufactured goods. Moreover, the possession of slaves was in itself a sink for capital. In the North, where workers owned their own bodies and took care of their own adolescents and aged, labor actually cost much less for its maintenance and support—and there was no need for any deployment of funds to catch a worker in the first place. The South, putting its money into slaves, never seemed to have a margin to build the mills and factories that might have saved the planters from paying commission and freightage and tariff charges to northern and European exporters. The North, on the other hand, using its capital for other purposes than buying tool users, steadily increased its stocks of machinery; it had something solid, something tangible, to show for its capital expenditures. Indeed, as early as 1846 Daniel R. Goodlow of North Carolina argued the case that if southern field hands were hired on a contract basis, capital would be freed to flow into labor-saving improvements.

But, though Goodlow had his partisans, it became increasingly unhealthy even to offer a speculative criticism of the Cotton Kingdom's business system. In a rousing document written and published in the fifties by a North Carolinian named Hinton Rowan Helper, the South's delusion should have been made plain. Helper noted that the value of northern manufactures was some nine times that of southern crops of all kinds, and his statistics indicated that the North had a virtual monopoly on industrial capital because the South had been tying up its profits in human beings who would have been there to work the plantation economy whether they were slave or free. Even the hay crop of the North, so Helper insisted, was worth more than the whole cotton production of the South. But far from convincing his fellow Southerners, Helper was regarded as a turncoat by them.

So it fell that the South had a wholly false sense of confidence when the first fateful shots were fired at Fort Sumter. Curiously enough in retrospect, the North for its part at first underrated its own powers. In New York, businessmen took seriously the rebel prediction that the withdrawal of southern trade from northern markets would "make grass grow" in Manhattan's streets, and the first developments of the war seemed to confirm their fear. During 1861, the first year of the war, business in the North was so bad that 12,000 commercial establishments failed—which actually exceeded the number of failures in the panic year of 1857 by some 2,000. In the first three months of 1862 the failures continued, with 1,000 firms collapsing.

Slowly, however, the North and the naturally pro-Union West began to realize that together they possessed sufficient economic strength to crush the South and meanwhile continue "business as usual." The incredible thing about the years stretching from 1862 to 1865 is that even the luxury trades expanded: in the North there was more horse racing, more grand opera, more theatre-going, more traveling circuses, more summer vacationing at Saratoga and Cape May, more splurging on fashions, more money spent at Tiffany's for jewelry, and more purchases of camel-hair shawls at A. T. Stewart's big New York department store than ever before. To be sure, the luxury trades floated on a frothy inflation but beneath the inflation was a solid agricultural and industrial base.

The first big economic victory of the war was the clothing and feeding of the troops. Surprisingly, the loss of cotton from the South was quickly taken in stride by the clothing industry, which had been moving into the factory by virtue of the industrial harnessing of Howe's and Singer's sewing machines. What the clothing industry did was to switch to wool. During the war the annual production of wool jumped from 40 million pounds to 140 million—and the number of sheep from 16 million to 32 million. As one historian has put it, "almost all New England became a sheep pasture"—and New England's cotton mills either lost their supremacy for the moment to the new wool factories or adapted their own processes to the use of a heavier fiber. Thanks to Army contracts, New England woolen mills paid dividends of 10 to 40 per cent during the war years. Nor did the manufacturers who stuck to cotton suffer unduly: as supplies of raw cotton began to trickle in with the capture of southern territory, the high prices offered for cotton thread and fabrics brought continuing profits. The great new cotton-thread mills of Willimantic, Connecticut, which were set up in the lee of a new tariff levied on English thread, were a creation of the Civil War.

The ready-to-wear clothing industry, which took the cloth from New England and New York mills and turned it into uniforms for the Army, was largely the creation of immigrant German Jews who had left their homeland after the suppression of the liberal uprisings of 1848. They had no feeling against the new Howe and Singer machines, for as nascent capitalists they represented a new order of business. Situated largely in Boston, New York, Philadelphia, and Cincinnati, the ready-to-wear clothing business was not only taking care of a million soldiers by 1864, it was also providing clothes for civilians in ever increasing quantities. And the shoe industry of Massachusetts, using the new machines supplied by Gordon McKay, provided shoes for both Army and civilians on a mass basis. The application of steam power to both textile and shoe factories, increasing throughout the Civil War period, provided a pattern for all types of manufacturing industry in the years to come.

The feeding of the Army turned at first on the ability of the western farmers to substitute McCormick reapers and other new mechanical equipment for their sons who had responded to "Father Abraham's" call for soldiers. But it was not only mechanization that saved the day for the Union in the matter of food. The truth is that there was a great increase in the working farm population even while the slaughter at Gettysburg, Chattanooga, Cold Harbor, and other sanguinary fields was snuffing out a half-million young lives. Thousands of immigrants from Europe, landing in New York, moved on west to take up land in Illinois, Wisconsin, and Iowa. During the first two and one-half years of the new Homestead Act, signed in 1862 by Lincoln, 2,500,000 acres of land were parceled out to settlers for merely nominal entry fees, the whole amounting to some 15,000 new farms of 160 acres each. As men from the war-torn border states straggled north to join immigrant Germans and Scandinavians in availing themselves of peaceful acres, the Boys in Blue who left the farm regions were hardly missed at all in any aggregate sense. Indeed, there were so many prospective farmers that the western states found no difficulty in disposing of lands which had been granted by the federal government for the support of agricultural colleges—and a single railroad, the Illinois Central, which had received 2,600,000 acres as a federal bounty for building a north-south line which vastly facilitated Union troop movements, sold off more than 800,000 acres during five years of the struggle.

Far from having to worry about an agricultural stringency, the embattled Union had a crop surplus on its hands almost from the beginning. As luck would have it, the Civil War coincided with three years of disastrous crop failure in England, and with one year of failure throughout the whole of Europe. Where the South had counted on the hunger of Manchester's mills for cotton to bring England into the war on the Confederate side, it was actually King Wheat, not King Cotton, that was destined to control the course of events. The American farmer profited egregiously during those years as the Great Lakes steamers, competing with the railroads for the traffic, actually cut the rates on grain. Indeed, it would not be until the wheat farmer had moved to the high plains, far from the alternative of water transport, that agricultural carrying charges would become a prime issue in U.S. politics.

With cattle and hogs, the war shifted the packing business in the West, centralizing it for a full century to come. Previous to 1860, Cincinnati, Louisville, and St. Louis had all packed meat products for southward disposal by water route and railroad. But with the Mississippi virtually closed, Chicago quickly became the single great focus for those with cattle and hogs to sell. In a single wartime year Chicago's meat-packing capacity doubled, with eight new large packing plants and a number of small ones rising in what had been a swamp. Just before Grant started his drive through the Wilderness on Richmond, Philip D. Armour sold pork short—and in ninety days made a killing of over $1 million, which was to set him up as the first of the great national meat-packing barons. Even before Armour had entered the packing business the new railroads converging on Chicago got together to establish the Union Stockyards, a 300-acre development that cost $1,500,000 to build and could handle 10,000 head of cattle and 100,000 hogs in pens at a single time.

Throughout the entire West, and even in the East, a population multiplied by displaced Border State "neutrals" and the immigrants who thronged through New York City's Castle Garden to take advantage of wartime wages carried on a score of activities that were sometimes only distantly related to the war. As we shall see, the Pennsylvania oil industry really got its start in the war years. In Michigan, the Saginaw valley became a great producer of salt brine. The lure of the western mining camps was one of the greater attractions—the Civil War years witnessed the prodigious development of the Comstock silver and gold deposits in Nevada, where George Hearst, the father of William Randolph Hearst, mined ore that was worth $2,200 a ton. The territory of Colorado, which had contained some 30,000 people in 1860, tripled in population by 1864 as prospectors and their camp followers poured in after the tapping of the Gregory silver lode. In Idaho and Montana there were great gold strikes which, after the notorious Plummer gang of robbers had been cleaned out of the territory, helped compensate for the decline of the California mining industry. In Utah, where the disciplined Mormons stuck to such prosaic occupations as farming, shopkeeping and carriage making, some unlooked-for profits were made by supplying the miners by stagecoach lines running north to Montana and by cutting telegraph poles for the new wires that were crisscrossing western territory. Meanwhile, throughout the entire war period, what amounted to a "continuous caravan" of emigrants crossed the ferry at Omaha, Nebraska, in good weather. Besides the hundreds of converts to Mormonism, the endless caravan included a vast and restless floating population that wanted to get away from war on any excuse. Indeed, at one point the wartime governor of Iowa had to forbid anyone leaving his state until after the federal draft of troops had been completed.

Despite the distractions of the West and draft riots in New York City, the Union managed to raise a decisive army. And in the matter of armament the industrial power of the North also proved decisive even though it commenced the struggle with only enough saltpeter available to provide the powder for a few battles. The du Pont powder mills along the Brandywine River in Delaware, which had been started in Jefferson's day, had been growing slowly, producing black powder for guns and for mine blasting in California and elsewhere. Despite the fact that it was in vulnerable territory (at one time a Confederate force reached to within fifty miles of Wilmington), the du Pont works quickly became a mainstay of the Union forces. Traveling to London in the autumn of 1861, Lammot du Pont secretly rounded up enough brokers to buy large amounts of saltpeter in England. The British, favoring the Confederacy, tied up Lammot du Pont's shipments for a period—but in 1862 the saltpeter reached America in time to flush the dangerously low Union

The du Pont powder works on the Brandywine

military cupboard. Before the war was over the du Ponts had made four million pounds of powder for the government, selling the whole at a price of nearly $1 million.

The interrelated gun and iron industries were less well prepared than the du Ponts in powder and curiously enough made less progress during the fighting than might have been expected. At the outset of the war old weapons such as the discarded Hall carbine were hauled out of storage and sold to the Army, thus giving rise to the legend that the young financier J. P. Morgan (who put up some money to finance one small deal) had consciously unloaded "defective" rifles on the government. But the carbines that figured in the

Morgan-financed episode were probably as good as any to be had in the pinch. Though Colt had already popularized his breech-loading six-cylinder revolver, which was used throughout the war as a side arm, the War Department refused to sanction the new Spencer breech-loading "magazine gun" for more than limited use until the very last year of the war. The hand-cranked Gatling gun, which could fire hundreds of shots a minute, did not find its way into battle until 1864. Fortunately for the North, the South was no more enterprising in its use of the available new ordnance: if Lee had had a breechloader at Gettysburg, the result might have been different.

In iron, the standoff in the Bessemer-Kelly patent situation made it impossible for the northern armies to avail themselves of weapons made out of steel. To get the secrets of good gun metal, Abram Hewitt of the Trenton mills was sent to England, where he met with official rebuffs. But, presumably by good detective work among Staffordshire workmen who favored the Union cause, Hewitt came home with the needed knowledge. His company did well enough by the government throughout the war to enable the northern forces to win once Lincoln had found some able generals. On one hurry call from President Lincoln, the Trenton mills, aided by a considerable amount of what would now be termed subcontracting, produced thirty mortar beds—or heavy gun carriages—within three weeks. The mortar beds served Grant well in his campaign to open the Mississippi. When the War Department delayed in reimbursing Hewitt for the expenditure of $21,000 on the mortar contract, Lincoln remarked to Secretary of War Stanton, "Do you suppose that if I should write on that bill, '*Pay this bill now,*' the Treasury would make settlement?" The bill was paid with Lincoln's request at the bottom of it.

War production involved the Trenton mills and their subcontractors—E. Abbott & Son of Baltimore, Cornell of New York, the Phoenix Iron Works of Phoenixville, Pennsylvania—in a production battle with the Tredegar Iron Works of Richmond, Virginia, where a West Pointer, Joseph Reid Anderson, operated locomotive shops, a cannon foundry, and a rolling mill. It was to protect the Tredegar Works as much as anything else that Lee and Jackson based all their strategy on the defense of Richmond. With the use of slave labor, Tredegar produced the plates that the Confederate government used on the first ironclad, the *Merrimac*, which struck terror into the North when she made her first depredations against Union shipping off Hampton Roads, Virginia. The answer to the *Merrimac* was John Ericsson's cheesebox-on-a-raft, the *Monitor*, financed by J. W. Griswold and J. A. Winslow, crucible-steel makers of Troy, New York, and armored by a consortium consisting of the Griswold & Winslow Co. and the Canton Rolling Mill of Horace Abbott in Baltimore. After the *Monitor*, using a powerful new du Pont powder, had dispelled the threat of the *Merrimac*, northern ironclads continued to play a part in blockading southern ports and forcing southern harbors. But the Bethlehem Iron Co., which was to become the nation's leading specialist in rolling armor, got under way barely in time to become a Civil War producer. Bethlehem's energetic ironmaster John Fritz did his bit for the Union cause by providing for the restoration of iron rails that the retreating Confederate soldiers had twisted around trees as they fell back toward Atlanta. Beyond the railheads the Union armies used the heavy-wheeled wagons that were making the Studebaker brothers of South Bend, Indiana, into "big business."

In its over-all effect the war vastly changed the nature of American industry, bringing forward new men and new methods of organization. It also profoundly changed the ground rules under which business operated, inevitably strengthening the role of the federal government. The change was most noticeable in finance, where the Administration faced problems that made those of the War of 1812 seem picayune. At the beginning the North had no idea of the expenses that were to be involved in four long years of bloody destruction, and Lincoln's Secretary of the Treasury Salmon P. Chase felt his way somewhat cautiously, turning first to the banks of New York, Boston, and Philadelphia for the $320 million initially needed to transform a nucleus of 20,000 Indian fighters into a national army. The banks had enough for a one-shot loan— but since there had not been a national banking system since Jackson's day, and since depreciating "wildcat" state bank notes were still the main source of funds in many places, Chase couldn't look indefinitely for help from professional money marts. It took a once amended National Bank Act, and a prohibitive 10 per cent tax on state-chartered bank-note issues, to create a real national banking system—and this was not finally achieved until 1866, too late to help Chase in his predicament.

The cost of the war and its immediate aftermath came to some $4 billion by 1869, not including interest on the debt and pensions. To meet the bill the government turned hopefully to taxation. The Morrill Tariff of 1861 lifted average rates to 25 per cent (increased to 47 per cent by 1864); a tax on incomes was levied at 3 per cent in 1861 and raised to 10 per cent on incomes over $5,000 at the war's end; and a tax on sales of industrial products in all stages of manufacture was instituted at rates running up to 6 per cent of value. The tariff proved disappointing (its tendency was to shut out goods completely); the income tax was to yield only $347 million before it was dropped in 1872; and the industrial-sales levy was minimized by businessmen by the simple device of putting separate manufacturing processes (spinning, weaving, dyeing, and so on) under one corporate roof, which left only a final product to be taxed.

Unable to pay for the war out of taxation and borrowing at the banks, the government resorted to two other expedients. The first was the issue of some $400 million in greenbacks—federal "wild-cat" money, which had only the printing press behind it; the second was the sale of government bonds directly to the people—the "five-twenties," "ten-forties," and so on. The greenbacks stimulated trade at the cost of inflation, and their value fluctuated in accordance with the progress of the military campaigns (a greenback dollar was worth as little as 39 cents in gold after the failure of Grant's drive on Richmond in 1864). Eventually the greenbacks were to pay out at 100 cents on the gold dollar with the resumption of specie payments in 1879.

As for the bond issues, the government hired a handsome, bearded man, Jay Cooke of Philadelphia, to put them over in two great loan drives. Just looking at him people believed in Cooke; they willingly parted with their greenbacks for bonds (thus counteracting some of the inflation), and they dug deep into hidden stocks of hard coin to help the government in its extremity. A person of infinite resource, Cooke reached into every nook and cranny of the North and West to uncover buyers. His sub-agents

Courtesy the Historical Society of Pennsylvania

Jay Cooke

used posters and broadsides and popular songs; they importuned people in hotels and trains; they invaded newspaper offices and insisted on editorials as well as the more usual forms of journalistic publicity. With such Barnum techniques, Cooke managed, at one point, to market $600 million in bonds in 180 days. The 1862 "five-twenties" series (maturing in from five to twenty years), a $500-million loan that the banks and bankers would not touch, was oversubscribed by $11 million, with Cooke selling bonds at so furious a pace to individuals that the Register of the Treasury could not sign them fast enough to keep up with the drive.

But it was not just in finance that the role of the central government changed. Well before the "stillness at Appomattox" it was apparent that government as a compromise between regions would never again flourish in the same terms as those envisaged by Jefferson, Madison, and John C. Calhoun. With the Southerners absent from Washington during the war years, the new-born Republican party was in the saddle; and the "radicals" of the party—notably grim old Thaddeus Stevens of Pennsylvania in the House of Representatives and the implacable Charles Sumner of Massachusetts in the Senate—were resolved to make the new alignments permanent by voting perpetual disfranchisement for any Southerner who had supported the rebellion. Despite the tradition of Lincoln's humanity, and despite the magnanimous behavior of Ulysses S. Grant at Appomattox toward the conquered Robert E. Lee, the South was to be treated through three presidential terms as a conquered province. Without power to affect the issue in Congress, the Southerners could do nothing to prevent the passage of the Fourteenth and Fifteenth amendments, which put civil rights under national as well as state protection, quite in defiance of the old Bill of Rights. Incidental to the business of making the South an occupied territory, the language of the Fourteenth Amendment extended the national government's protection to the business corporation as a legally defined "person." This, whether by chance or design, was to have an importance for business that was not remarked upon at the time: for better or worse, it was to exempt interstate corporations, notably the new railroads, from much local regulation.

Beyond these political changes, the Republicans became early committed to a new economic program that originated in what would today be called "postwar planning." The Republican blueprint called for a permanent fusion of the various private-interest groups that had responded to Lincoln's call to arms. The essence of the blueprint was "something for everybody" with federal subsidy as the essential lever. The Republican party has sometimes been referred to as the stalwart champion of an absolutely pure Adam Smith type of individualism. This is wide of the mark. It can be more logically maintained that the Republicans were the first to succeed in instituting that canny balance of subsidies that Henry Clay had praised as the American System in the palmy days of the Whig party. The old slogan "Vote Yourself a Farm" was quickly fleshed out by the passage of the Homestead Act. (So much for the settler in Minnesota and Nebraska.) The Morrill Tariff, which was amended upward in 1862 and 1864, gave manufacturers a protection they had long been seeking, with special favors being doled out to the masters of iron and steel. (So much for the Northeast and for the booming centers of coal and iron production in the valleys of western Pennsylvania and eastern Ohio.) As for labor, it figured less extensively in the Republican "plan"—and many workers were to fear the new proposals for bringing immigrants from Europe to America under actual working contract. But the tariff, so it was argued, would enable manufacturers to pay a high wage; and free lands in the prairie and plains regions were there to constitute a safety valve for immigrant pressure on the labor market.

Too much can be made, of course, of this Republican system of subsidies and tariffs in developing the country. The subsidies to special interests were, in fact, peanuts when compared to the new torrents of wealth that non-subsidized individuals were shortly to bring into being in the postwar years. Yet in one critical area subsidies were to have far-reaching repercussions—namely, on railroad building. During the war years the northern railroad system had served the armies well but had not greatly expanded. The passage of the Union Pacific Railroad Act in 1862, however, opened new opportunities for transcontinental lines, which were presently to link both oceans together even while the eastern-seaboard states and the Deep South were painfully recovering from the war itself.

In accordance with the railroad legislation, the Union Pacific was to build westward from a point in Nebraska and the Central Pacific was to go eastward from California with a guarantee of $16,000 a mile for plains country, $48,000 for mountain country, and $32,000 for inter-mountain stretches. In addition to the cash, each railroad was to get large grants of land along the rights-of-way. The four ex-storekeepers who had got in on the ground floor of the Central Pacific, Collis P. Huntington, Leland Stanford, Mark Hopkins, and Charles Crocker, quickly devised a means of channeling much of the subsidy money into their own pockets, setting up dummy construction companies that (in effect) paid themselves huge building fees at the taxpayers' expense. The proprietors of the Union Pacific were also on two sides of the construction bargain, subletting their building contracts to their own creature, the oddly named Crédit Mobilier of America, which paid them some $50 million in profits.

The Crédit Mobilier has been defended as a useful buffer device for building a road through howling wilderness that was populated by fierce Indians who followed the buffalo. The price of iron rails was high in the sixties; wood for crossties had to be packed in from eastern forest lands that were far away; and there was no way of calculating gains in advance, no assurance that the railroad could originate much freight. In the light of such uncertainty, the new railroad entrepreneurs felt justified in limiting their risks. Nevertheless, the bribery of Congressmen that figured in the creation of the Crédit Mobilier constituted skulduggery even in an age that was inclined to overlook the corner-cutting "smart" men considered to be an inevitable part of smart business. But the skulduggery, which touched depths of rascality, was accompanied by engineering feats that gave the West "men to match its mountains." Despite all the seaminess, splendor was there.

The man who had surveyed the route over the California Sierra for the Central Pacific and who had stirred the federal government into the subsidizing action, Theodore (or "Crazy") Judah, did not live to see how well he had plotted the future; he died of yellow fever contracted in Panama while going east on business. But Charlie Crocker, a mountainous figure of a man who could not endure office work, took over where Judah left off. When the white laborers he hired deserted him to seek their fortunes in the silver diggings of Nevada's Comstock Lode, Crocker looked at his servant, a frail but perdurable Chinese named Ah Ling. It flashed across Crocker's mind that maybe here was his answer for manpower; after all, it was men like Ah Ling who had built the Great Wall of China. Though Californians scoffed, Crocker rounded up whole crews of 110-pound Orientals in San Francisco and Sacramento and sent them along "Crazy" Judah's route into the Sierra fastnesses. There, working on a diet of rice and cuttle-fish, they swung out over gorges to chip ledges from the sides of the sheer granite cliffs. They drilled the great Summit Tunnel by hand, completing it in September of 1867 without benefit of the newly invented steam-driven drills that Leland Stanford, a confirmed gadget-lover, tried unsuccessfully to bring to Crocker's attention. From this point on it took Crocker less than two years to lay his ties and rails across Nevada and Utah, where he met the westward-going Union Pacific (built largely by Irish immigrants) at Promontory Point by the Great Salt Lake for the famous Golden Spike ceremony of May 10, 1869. Crocker's construction prodigies had been matched by the Union Pacific's ex-Army engineer, General Grenville Dodge, who actually laid temporary tracks on beds of ice and snow during the blizzard-swept winter of 1868 to comply with the technicalities required to push his right-of-way across the Wasatch Mountains before Crocker's Chinese could get there.

Once the transcontinental system had been built, an entranced nation was confronted with the problem of finding some immediate use for it. The High Plains through which the Union Pacific passed were still the undisputed domain of savages. In Utah there was the Mormon theocracy, but Brigham Young, though he was himself an astute businessman, had set his community up on a more or less self-sustaining basis. The main hope of the Central and Union Pacific owners was that a transcontinental line would cut the time required to travel from Europe to the Far East, but this hope went glimmering when the Suez Canal, completed in 1869, offered faster transportation and cheaper rates. The Wells Fargo Express Co., the California, Pioneer, and Overland Stage companies, and the Pacific Mail Steamship Co. had opposed the building of the Central Pacific on the ground that it represented unfair (because uneconomic) competition—and at the time few could "prove" that they were wrong.

Quite fortuitously, it was a more modest railroad venture, the Kansas Pacific, which had reached into mid-Kansas only in the

The meeting of the Central Pacific and Union Pacific railroads

1860's, that first showed how a western road could originate freight. The original proprietors of the Kansas Pacific had no idea of how they were going to earn enough from their road to live on. But in the South, far off in the strip of Texas between the Nueces and the Rio Grande, cattle had multiplied during the Civil War. The Texans, who had learned how to protect their herds from the Apaches and Comanches by use of the horse and the Colt revolver, tried to find buyers for their stock in Missouri in the first days after the Civil War, only to discover that war-hardened border ruffians made it impossible to move their herds with any safety past the Ozark Mountain country, where men used to the open plains could be ambushed. It was at this point that a business strategist from Illinois, a cattle buyer named Joseph G. McCoy, looked at the map. Journeying in 1867 to Abilene, Kansas, a "small, dead place, consisting of about one dozen log huts . . . four-fifths of which were covered with dirt for roofing," McCoy brought with him enough lumber from Hannibal, Missouri, to build pens and loading chutes for cattle. He then sent a scout to the South to intercept Texans who were hoping somehow to get past the border ruffians to a market in Sedalia or St. Louis. The first Texas drover that his scout encountered felt, McCoy said, that "it was almost too good to be believed" that "someone was about to afford a Texan . . . any other reception than outrage and robbery." The Texans came in force over the open plains to Abilene, first of the cow towns—and from this time forward it was Chicago, which was at the other end of McCoy's rail connections, that got the swiftly growing cattle business as the whole area of the High Plains became the new Cattle Kingdom. (St. Louis lost out when the president of the Missouri Pacific threw McCoy out of his office.) The fact that cattle money was the first northern money to move south of the Mason-Dixon Line after the Civil War has prompted historian Walter Prescott Webb to ask, "Who can say that Abilene was less significant than Appomattox?" Or, as the historian might have asked, "Who can say that the Kansas Pacific was less significant than the Central and Union Pacifics?"

Even with cattle, however, the immediate post-Civil War surge of railroad building through the empty country west of the 98th meridian led to a temporary setback. The basic unsoundness of trying to build on the Republican wartime blueprint too far, too fast, became obvious in the panic of 1873. Here all the Civil War subsidy and inflation chickens came home to roost. Between 1865 and 1873 much of the war-engendered capital—the greenbacks, the credit reared on the structure of the bond issues—had been siphoned off into the West as other railroad builders tried to match the feats of the Union and Central Pacific construction gangs. In 1873 eastern and middle-western railroads were yielding 5 and 6 per cent dividends on some 35,000 miles of road representing a capital account of $1.9 billion. The western rail system, with 36,000 miles of newly built road representing almost as much investment capital, was earning just a little over 2 per cent when things were still booming. The minute there was a downturn in business, the western roads were vulnerable. As old Cornelius Vanderbilt had put it, "Building railroads from nowhere to nowhere at public expense is not a legitimate business."

Ironically, it was Jay Cooke, the hero of the government's Civil War bond-marketing exploits, who was the immediate (though hardly the basic) cause of the 1873 collapse. Used to the flourish of great affairs, Cooke had sought to repeat his Civil War financial feats by undertaking to market the securities of the Northern Pacific Railroad. Projected as a line that would link the shores of Lake Superior with the Columbia River region, the Northern Pacific was a grand idea. (Eventually the Northwest would be able to support two transcontinental railroads, the Northern Pacific and Jim Hill's Great Northern, the latter to be built without subsidy.) But in 1873 the money available for railroad investment was getting thin—and the Northern Pacific had no immediate earning prospects. The Franco-Prussian War had dried up capital markets abroad, and the plain people of the U.S., though they still trusted the look of probity on Cooke's face, couldn't digest the bonds he offered at home. Since the resources of his bank were pledged to the Northern Pacific's success, Cooke failed. The magic of the Civil War financier had run out. And with his failure, collapses were touched off everywhere.

It was all a mistake born of incredible enthusiasm stoked to no small degree by the war-engendered greenbacks. But if it was a mistake, it was one of those fruitful errors that are destined to have highly constructive consequences. Like Mount Everest, the west-going railroad system was "there," and it made such cities as Denver, Cheyenne, Helena, Portland, Seattle, Albuquerque, Salt Lake City, Kansas City, Minneapolis, and St. Paul into great and prospering communities. It also drew the attention of people to far horizons at a time when the agonies of war desolation and reconstruction were still fresh and dividing North and South. The new continental railroad grid was to complete the underpinnings needed for a national market, thus ushering in the reality of modern America.

8 The Gilded Age

Dan'l Drew and Jim Fisk wreck the Erie.

Commodore Vanderbilt cuts the Central's time to Chicago.

Drake strikes the crude and Rockefeller turns up his nose at wildcatting.

Then with Flagler and Harkness he builds a tin-pot refinery into the "Original Trust."

Carnegie teams up with a Prussian blacksmith and forges the structure that becomes U.S. Steel.

THE PANIC year of 1873 marked the height—or the trough—of the Gilded Age, so-called in the satirical novel that Mark Twain and his Hartford neighbor, Charles Dudley Warner (known as Deadly Warning to some of his contemporaries), wrote in collaboration. The Twain-Warner story, which catches a period in the clear aspic of comic overstatement, is a compendium of all the more dubious business practices of its time: it tells how a hilariously fantastic booster, Colonel Beriah Sellers, puts his best brains to work luring a railroad into laying tracks from "nowhere to nowhere" in order to make a real-estate killing out of the Missouri mudhole of Stone's Landing; and the scene of its Washington chapters is scarcely changed at all from the reality of stock-distribution scandals that in the Crédit Mobilier case reached as high as the vice presidency.

True enough, *The Gilded Age* is not wholly devoted to satirizing business; it has for its hero a quite legitimate enterpriser, a sound and honorable young engineer named Philip Sterling who ensures

140

himself a fortune by mastering the subject of geology and actually mining Pennsylvania coal without benefit of lobby or subsidy. But who is Sterling to compete for attention against the flamboyance of Colonel Sellers? What could he do to build an image of industrial probity in the "General Grant" period of scroll-saw architecture, convoluted walnut furniture, flickering gas jets, and brass spittoons? The very atmosphere of the Gilded Age—built on smoky coal and disfigured by the first fumbling attempts of architects to learn the true uses and limitations of strange new building materials (the country was departing from the age of wood)—makes us all too willing to believe the worst of the period that has been variously referred to as "the era of brass knuckles" and "the time of the great barbecue." So ingrained has the folklore become that William Allen White has suggested in all solemnity that the men of the seventies cultivated beards for no better reason than to hide their naked shame.

And, indeed, the age had its shameful aspects. There was nothing very secret, however, about the contemptuous piracy practiced by the stock gamblers of the late sixties and seventies. Giving no quarter to each other, the rascals of the stock market conducted their raids with such brazen humor ("Nothing is lost save honor," said one of them) that the backward-looking writer in a more circumspect age is stopped in his tracks and looks for nothing else. So it is that we know far more today about the picturesque skulduggeries of Daniel Drew, Jim Fisk, Jay Gould, and other market highbinders of that type than we do about the creative accomplishments of men to whom these stock gamblers were anathema. One forgets, if one ever knew, that the vampirish Jay Gould, who made money by sucking many an enterprise dry, was too much even for the parvenu Vanderbilts, who refused to invite him to their social affairs. This despite the fact that Gould was a builder in Cornelius Vanderbilt's own image in at least a few of the enterprises he bought into, such as Western Union and the Union Pacific Railroad.

That the age had its pushing qualities was admitted by a brother novelist of Mark Twain, William Dean Howells. But Howells, as a social historian, forebore to be comic about what he glimpsed around him; he knew that "push" was an inevitable part of a life of lusty change. Speaking of the Boston business scene, which he knew at first hand, he wrote: "Before 'Appomattox' the banker and merchant appeared upon State Street, the business center, about ten in the morning, conventionally dressed, precise in movement and habituated to archaic methods. Within six months after the fall of the Confederacy the financial centers of the 'Hub,' vitalized by the inflow of new and very red blood, had taken on the aspect which is familiar to this generation. Everything that interfered with serviceable activity was set aside. Tall hats and long coats disappeared. . . . New names appeared at the head of great industrial enterprises. Boys who had gone to the War as junior officers had brought back honorable titles which vouched for responsibility, character, and daring. . . . You can't, if you will, hold down a Captain, a Colonel . . . who has earned and won the admiration of the public, and who has tested his worth." As for Howells' own fictional businessman and colonel, the self-made paint manufacturer Silas Lapham, he is, though a trifle coarse by Brahmin standards, a thoroughly likable and honest fellow. Since Howells was not an inventive novelist, somebody must have sat for the portrait.

If Howells had been writing of post–Civil War New York City, the center of the new Kingdom of Push, he might have mused upon the fading of such old families as Beekmans, Rhinelanders, and Brevoorts from the active business scene. As Burton J. Hendrick, our pioneer historian of the Age of Big Business, has pointed out, the U.S. was to hear less and less henceforward from landlord millionaires like William B. Astor (worth $6 million), or James Lenox ($3 million). The old New York merchant aristocracy— William Aspinwall ($4 million from shipping), John Haggerty ($1 million from auctioneering), Japhet Bishop ($600,000 in hardware), William L. Coggeswell ($500,000 as a wine importer) —was on its way to superannuated respectability. A. T. Stewart, who had made $2 million in dry goods, and Phineas T. Barnum ($800,000 from exhibiting Jumbo and Tom Thumb and acting as impresario for singer Jenny Lind) would still manage to stir others to emulation, but in the coming age the word "merchant prince" had an increasingly archaic ring.

In the swift change from old to new, one representative of the pre-Civil War order managed not only to survive the shift but to dominate it. Quite in line with the ethics of his age, the New York Central's Cornelius Vanderbilt did not scruple to use even the most outright trickery to get control of properties he wanted. Legislators, to him, were holdup men who had to be bribed to keep them from selling out to his opponents, who in most cases hap-

Cornelius Vanderbilt

pened to be Fisk, Drew and Gould, the pirates of the Erie Railroad "ring." But the old Commodore was no vulture; and when he owned something he worked relentlessly at its physical improvement, provided, of course, that he intended to keep it.

Way back in 1833, when he was a young steamboat man, the Commodore had been injured in a railroad accident in New Jersey. He disliked railroads, and thought to have little to do with them. At the age of sixty-nine, however, sensing that his beloved river steamboats had seen their best days, the Commodore swallowed his distaste for the Iron Horse and decided to become a railroad man.

Taking some of the $20 million he had made on the rivers and oceans, he quietly bought up the shares of the Harlem Railroad running out of New York City and the Hudson River Railroad leading north to East Albany. This gave him a right-of-way all along the east bank of the Hudson, with terminal facilities right in the heart of Manhattan Island. Later, using guile to depress the shares of the New York Central, which ran between Albany and Buffalo (the wily Commodore had publicly announced his discovery of an ancient law on the statute books that made it illegal to deliver his own Hudson River Railroad passengers to the Central's depot across a bridge at Albany), the old ex-ferryman from Staten Island got control of the Central at a price he could afford. Stock control of the Canada Southern, the Lake Shore, and the Michigan Central eventually followed—and the first important integration of east-west systems was thereby accomplished.

A lusty and superstitious fellow, Vanderbilt took a thirty-year-old second wife at the age of seventy-five, bickered with his children (ten out of thirteen survived both his tempers and his death), summoned up the ghost of the dead Jim Fisk to get advice on stock manipulation (it must have been good, for when Vanderbilt himself died in 1877 he was worth some $100 million), and proposed that a large monument should be reared in New York's Central Park to commemorate the two greatest Americans, George Washington and Cornelius Vanderbilt. But amid all his egotistical cavortings the Commodore relaid the Central's tracks from New York to Chicago with new steel rails, built strong steel bridges, threw away the picturesque pre-Civil War Iron Horses in favor of a drabber but more efficient type of locomotive, and cut the time of the New York–Chicago run from fifty hours to twenty-four. Whether the Commodore's son, William H. Vanderbilt, ever actually said, "The public be damned!" is a point still disputed by historians. But on one thing there can be no dispute: the public was served by the new trains on the Commodore's New York–Chicago tracks. If Cornelius was a robber baron, the country needed more like him. Old "Corneel" may have watered the Central's stock. But as fast as he watered it he solidified it—and the worst that can be said about him is that he was a shrewd capitalizer of future earnings.

Meanwhile, to the south of the territory covered by the ring-ridden Erie and the well-managed New York Central, the Pennsylvania system was built up in the sixties and the seventies under the wise and circumspect direction of J. Edgar Thomson. If Thomson was not averse to turning a quick deal to his own private advantage on occasion, he kept this aspect of his character quite apart from his rigorously ethical concern for the Pennsylvania's economic health. In 1859 the Pennsylvania consisted largely of the Main Line from Philadelphia to Pittsburgh—but within ten short years Thomson had expanded the system until it comprised nearly a thousand miles in the state of Pennsylvania itself and (by virtue of leasing the Pittsburgh, Fort Wayne & Chicago line) had reached the shores of Lake Michigan. Not satisfied with the single terminus of Chicago in the West, Thomson formed a holding company to acquire other lines, notably the Cleveland & Pittsburgh Railroad and the so-called "Pan Handle" route, which linked Pittsburgh with both Cincinnati and St. Louis. Thomson's management ended in 1874, but he passed on to his successor, Thomas A. Scott (who was, incidentally, Andrew Carnegie's friend and boss), a property quite capable of weathering the long depression that began in 1873. To quote John Moody, the Pennsylvania "was the first American railroad to lay steel rails and the first to lay Bessemer rails; it was the first to put the steel firebox under the locomotive boiler; it was the first to use the air brake and the block signal system; it was the first to use in its shops the overhead crane"—and from 1859 to the end of the nineteenth century (and after) it never skipped a dividend. Moreover, unlike its great competitor for freight originating in the new Pittsburgh area, the Baltimore & Ohio Railroad (which in times of stress paid dividends out of capital), the Pennsylvania paid all its dividends out of earnings, with the stockholders themselves keeping a tight rein on management.

The records of both the New York Central and the Pennsylvania were in marked contrast to that of the Erie, whose mulcting by Drew, Fisk, and Gould is often cited as "typical" of Gilded Age railroading. And few post-Civil War railroads were as badly served as the pre-Civil War New York and New Haven Railroad, whose president—Robert Schuyler—issued 17,752 shares of unauthorized stock and sold them to his own brokerage house before skipping the country.

For decades after the Civil War the railroads were to remain the greatest business of the nation, and even as late as 1898, as Bernard M. Baruch was to note, "something like 60 per cent of the securities listed on the Big Board were of railroads." (By 1914 they had declined to less than 40 per cent of the Stock Exchange listings, by 1925 to 17 per cent, and by 1957 to 13 per cent.) For better or worse, the railroads became implicated with the pioneer giant

Courtesy the Library of Congress

Andrew Carnegie

corporations in other fields—with Western Union (for it was along their rights-of-way that telegraph lines were strung), with Andrew Carnegie's successive steel companies (the Pennsylvania was such a good customer of Carnegie's that he named a big mill after the railroad's J. Edgar Thomson), and with Rockefeller's Standard Oil through tank car manipulation and the notorious rebate system.

The first big "trust" was the Standard Oil Co., which grew so fast and with such seeming disregard for popular criticism of its tactics that it found itself a prime political target from the 1870's until the time of its dissolution into a number of component companies by the Supreme Court in 1911. Just why the first industrial giant should have been so hated is a mystery if the question is tackled from the standpoint of the consumer. Buyers always liked the company's product—they proved it by rushing to substitute petroleum kerosene for the old coal-oil and whale-oil illuminants. And buyers did not have any particular reason to complain of Standard's pricing policy: not only did kerosene cost less than the older fluids, but it had to meet the competition of the Welsbach gas burner and Mr. Edison's carbon-filament electric-light bulb. Standard Oil could not have imposed a lighting monopoly even if it had tried.

If the consumer had no real quarrel with Standard Oil, however, other producers had. Standard offended a nation's traditional competitive ethics—and the company made itself thoroughly hated by people who never bothered to square their liking for the products of mass production with the fact of big enterprise itself. In his main objective—which was to achieve what the economists were soon to be calling "economies of scale"—the youthful John D. Rockefeller was right. But his very zealotry provoked fear: a people who were used to small regional businesses could not understand Rockefeller's passion for nipping off all the buds on the rosebush of oil so that his own American Beauty Rose, the Standard, could grow to absolute perfection. Besides the zealotry, which seemed inhuman, there was the Rockefeller secrecy. In pursuing his objective, with muffled footfalls and sudden blows in the dark, the silent little man from Cleveland seemed to have come out of the Sicily that spawned the Mafia.

Curiously, the "monster" who provoked such spasms of fear was, in actuality, a very simple person. As the son of old Bill Rockefeller, a genial cancer quack from upstate New York, John D. was bent on becoming what his father was not. He lived simply (he never owned a yacht or a race horse), he followed his mother in reading the Bible, he was generous with his money (notably to the Baptist University of Chicago) even before the pioneer public-relations counselor Ivy Lee convinced him that he should be ostentatious about his benefactions, his family life would have been worthy of emulation anywhere, and wherever he could he

John D. Rockefeller

bought out competitors on generous terms in preference to squeez-
ing them into the dust. As for the oil business, which was stupidly
wasteful when Rockefeller first decided to make it his vocation,
it was, through his orderly approach to things, eventually to learn
much that was of value to itself.

In 1860, John D. Rockefeller, then a twenty-year-old junior partner in the Cleveland commission firm of Clark & Rockefeller, visited Pennsylvania's Venango County, where the first drilled oil well had yielded its black wealth the year before. He came as the agent for Cleveland businessmen who had been impressed with the young merchant's sobriety and his ability to judge a balance sheet. What the businessmen wanted was some guidance to investment possibilities in a region that had brought the bonanza feeling far closer to the East than it had ever been before.

What Rockefeller found when he got to the Oil Creek region of Venango was enough to fill his fastidious soul with acute distaste. Oil, in that last pre-Civil War year, was a raffish, up-and-down business, and had been so from the very start. It had had its origins in medical quackery as white men, posing as Indian doctors, put the skimmings from Pennsylvania creeks into eight-ounce bottles and hawked them as a sure cure for "cholera morbus, liver complaint, bronchitis, and consumption." Using by-product oil from salt wells, the greatest of the "Seneca oil" Barnums, Doc Samuel Kier, had made a big enterprise of selling the stuff as "medicine" long before anyone had thought of drilling a well directly to get at it.

The transformation of Pennsylvania "rock oil" into an illuminant dates from a day in the 1850's when George H. Bissell of New York took a specimen to Yale's professor of chemistry, the younger Benjamin Silliman, and asked him to analyze it in his laboratory. In a scientific classic, Silliman reported that "rock oil" could be refined into a better illuminant than oil squeezed from coal tar, cannel coal, asphalt, or "albertite" bituminous rock, all of which went under the generic name of coal oil. But how to get the oil out of the earth? Bissell had seen a picture of a salt-well derrick on a Kier Seneca oil advertisement but he had not acted on it. One of Bissell's associates, the New Haven banker James Townsend, was the man of action who dispatched a New Haven Railroad conductor named Colonel E. L. Drake (he had a free railroad pass) to Titusville in Venango County with instructions to dig a well directly into oil-bearing strata. Using a salt-well driller's tools, Drake made his soon-to-be-famous strike in 1859. Despite the distractions of the Civil War the Oil Creek region of Pennsylvania took off from a standing start and by 1869 was producing 4,800,000 barrels yearly. Meanwhile the price of crude oil zoomed and plummeted crazily as the race between new wells and new oil uses went first one way and then another.

Watching the boom-bust careers of well drillers as they wild-catted, the young John D. Rockefeller decided that the producing end of oil was nothing in which a sane man should invest his funds. His advice to the Cleveland businessmen was to keep out of the oil country; refining was obviously a much safer thing. He himself returned home to put a few thousand dollars into a small refinery run by a man named Samuel Andrews, who seemed to have better refining methods than others in the business. When the new firm of Rockefeller & Andrews promised to be far more profitable than the commission-merchant business, Rockefeller lost no time in transferring his eggs to a single basket. The pious, orderly young man quickly took on new partners, men who had capital and a knowledge of refining; and with every enlargement of the business the unit cost of producing and marketing a gallon of kerosene was decreased.

Under its various names (it had become Rockefeller, Andrews & Flagler by 1868), the Rockefeller company pushed its integration forward, backward, and sidewise, making its own barrels in its own cooperage plants, shipping its products in large quantities, and plowing most of the profits back into the business. By 1870 Rockefeller and his partners were doing about a fifth of all the refining in the Cleveland area. The partners celebrated their success by organizing the Standard Oil Co. of Ohio, with Rockefeller taking 2,667 shares of the new stock and Henry M. Flagler, Samuel Andrews, S. D. Harkness, and brother William Rockefeller taking 1,333 shares each.

Standard of Ohio was advantageously placed to weather the fall in prices that came with the seventies; and with the bankruptcy of many marginal concerns it would in any event have achieved a continually expanding share of the business of providing a growing country with kerosene. But this was not enough for Rockefeller, who dreamed of bringing permanent stability to his appallingly chaotic trade. He hated what he called the "idiotic, senseless destruction," "the wasteful conditions" of competition. By convincing his fellow Clevelanders of the advantages of combination, Rockefeller, in the first two years after the formation of Standard of Ohio, had managed to absorb all but five out of a total of some twenty-five local refineries. He pressed on to take in the largest refineries in Pittsburgh, Baltimore, Philadelphia, and New York, buying up distressed competitors in the depression years of 1873 and after.

It was the fact that nobody seemed able to resist Rockefeller when he really decided he wanted a company that scared the life out of refiners who wished to remain independent. In defending his

Courtesy the Cleveland Picture Collection, Cleveland Public Library

Cleveland refineries of the Standard Oil Company of Ohio

methods of "persuasion," Rockefeller put it this way in later years: "Every refiner in the country was invited to become a member of the Standard Oil Company . . . The Standard . . . turned to them with confidence and said: 'We will take your burdens, we will utilize your ability, we will give you representation; we will all unite together and build a substantial structure on the basis of co-operation.' " But to the 1870's, this sort of explanation was just so much soft soap. To bring recalcitrants into line, something more than an offer to assume "burdens" was employed. For example, when Rockefeller tried to move in on the refiners of

the western Pennsylvania oil region itself, where he was regarded
as a usurper and an outsider, he found that deviousness was the
only solution to his problem. Deaf to his pleas for "co-operation
and conservation," the Titusville operators hung him in effigy
and sought to band against him. By 1875, John D. Archbold, a
local refiner who had opposed Standard, had succeeded in putting
some twenty-five of the Titusville independents into a big combination—the Acme Oil Co.—which would presumably be able to
compete with Standard on its own terms. The curses and lamenta-
tions in Titusville were loud when it was subsequently disclosed
that Acme had secretly become a Standard Oil subsidiary.

Beyond such manipulations, Rockefeller invoked a still more
dread device for forcing his opponents to join with him "or else."
This device has gone into the history books as the South Improvement Co. To the end of his life Rockefeller insisted that he did not
start the South Improvement Co. himself. Even so, Rockefeller, his
brother William, Henry Flagler, and others high up in Standard
of Ohio owned 900 of the South Improvement Co.'s 2,000 shares.
The working control of South Improvement was theirs.

One South Improvement Co. proposition was to exact rebates
running up to 50 per cent of the carrying charges on all of its oil
transported by the Pennsylvania, the Erie, and the New York
Central. This was quite in line with the conventional railroad
practice of the day. Virtually all manufacturers of the time considered it quite legitimate to get special discounts for bulk shipments and for a guarantee of a steady flow of business. It was an
"economy of scale." But the South Improvement contract contained something that went far beyond the rebate. It read: "The
party of the second part [i.e., the railroad] will pay to the party of
the first part [the South Improvement Co.] . . . on all oil transported for others, drawbacks." The word "drawback" signified that
out of the regular freight rates paid by South Improvement's competitors a fourth to a half would be handed over by the railroad to Rockefeller and his mates. Even to the moral code of 1872 this seemed
sheer industrial murder. When the Oil City *Derrick* printed a list
of the South Improvement Co.'s directors under a caption, "Behold
'the Anaconda' in all his hideous deformity," righteous indignation
swept the oil fields and flamed out toward the state capitals of

Pennsylvania and New York. And when the newspapers ferreted out the South Improvement contract and published it, the frightened railroads quickly promised that all future oil shipments would be on a basis of equality for everybody.

In response to the angry clamor, the Pennsylvania legislature revoked the South Improvement Co.'s charter in April of 1872— and that particular adventure in exacting special tribute from a common carrier to throttle competition was at an end. But Rockefeller had already used the tacit threat of the South Improvement contract to bring the Cleveland refiners into his combination—and these eggs, once scrambled, remained an inextricable part of the dish. Moreover, Rockefeller's resolve to "stabilize" the oil market by eliminating competition remained inexorable, and the Standard empire continued to grow. It was "common knowledge" to the oilmen of the eighties that Standard had a firm grip on some 90 per cent of the refining business. It also controlled all the major pipelines, and all the oil cars on the Pennsylvania Railroad. Its tank-car control was to increase through its domination of the Union Tank Line, called Rockefeller's "secret weapon" by Albert Z. Carr.

How had all this been accomplished? The enabling trick was the "trust," an ingenious legal device that had been cooked up by a young Pennsylvania lawyer named Samuel C. T. Dodd. Dodd had first come to Rockefeller's notice as a vigorous opponent of the South Improvement Co. Asked to become the Standard Oil lawyer at a time when his voice was failing and incapacitating him for courtroom work, the young Pennsylvanian took the job with the understanding that he would keep the company within the law in all future attempts to bring stability to oil marketing. Dodd knew, of course, that property could be turned over to "trustees": it was done every day by people who wished to pass on their estates to wards and minor children with some continuing provision for wise control. Why not, so Dodd argued, why not adapt this ancient device to the peculiar circumstances of the oil business? Why not let the less able oilmen put their properties in "trust," with Standard Oil management acting as custodian?

The first Standard Oil trust was a small committee of nine men headed by Rockefeller himself and Flagler. To this committee of nine the owners of a wide variety of oil companies had surrendered their stock certificates and voting rights, receiving in exchange "trust" certificates that entitled them to dividends pro rata on general earnings. The committee took it upon itself to settle all questions relating to price and volume over an area of several states.

The "trust" form of organization necessarily imposed a "line and staff" administration on Standard Oil, and from the line-and-staff idea there sprouted many of the modern techniques of combining "bigness" with efficiency. The management of operations under the trust agreement had necessarily to be delegated to the executives of the individual corporations. But the top committee kept control of planning and policy functions. Committees of specialists advised the executive committee. Uniform accounting and reporting were adopted, functional committees set standards of performance, and the drive to cut costs and to realize "economies of scale" was pushed by top executives who traveled throughout Standard's empire.

The Standard Oil Co. of Ohio was eventually outlawed, in 1892, by the Ohio State Supreme Court. By this time, however, the sovereign state of New Jersey had rewritten its corporation law to permit companies chartered at Trenton to own stock in other corporations. Under a holding-company dispensation, the newly incorporated Standard Oil of New Jersey simply took over where the old Dodd-devised "trust" had left off. Jersey Standard was the *de facto* boss unit in a new combination created by shuffling some ninety companies into twenty.

The story of how John D. Rockefeller brought industrial "bigness" to America has been told so often from the "monopoly" angle that two big points bearing on his success have been quite obscured. The first point is that the silent little man from Cleveland was perhaps the nineteenth century's most able competitor. The second point is that Standard, though it had 90 per cent of the refining capacity at its monopolistic peak, was unable to keep competition from returning to the field as the twentieth century approached.

As a competitor Rockefeller was positively savage, and Standard became known, whether truthfully or not, as the company that "cut to kill." But price cutting was not the whole of the story. Rockefeller was the first really to push research, hiring a German chemist named Herman Frasch, who showed him how to refine a marketable product from the sulfurous crude "skunk oil" of the new Lima-Indiana field, the first to be opened up outside the Appalachian district. And in overseas markets Standard was the leader in providing "oil for the lamps of China."

For all the fearsome Rockefeller power, however, other men fought him and remained in business. The Pews of Sun Oil, a company that got its start in Ohio in the mid-eighties, built up a compact and powerful rival organization. Lewis Emery Jr., who hated the whole Rockefeller tribe, built two pipelines (one for refined oil, one for crude) from the Pennsylvania fields to the Delaware River for his Pure Oil Co., and, unlike other pipeline builders, kept his creation out of Rockefeller hands. The emergence of these companies proved that Standard Oil could be fought right on Rockefeller's own home grounds. Then, after 1901, the year in which a Yugoslav immigrant named Anthony Luchich—or Lucas—pounded his drill deep into a salt dome at Spindletop on the Gulf Coast of Texas and opened up a geyser of oil that caught fire and burned for days, the Rockefellers could no more dominate oil than King Canute could dominate the tides. Two Pittsburghers, John H. Galey and Colonel J. M. Guffey, had backed Lucas financially, and when they in turn ran out of money, Guffey went hat in hand with the Spindletop prize to the Mellons. No strangers to oil (a Mellon had once built a pipeline and had unloaded it on Rockefeller at a profit of $2 million), the Mellons liked the prospects. The result was the Mellon-backed J. M. Guffey Petroleum Co., the forerunner of Gulf Oil. This time the Mellons, who kept 40 per cent of Guffey for themselves, had no intention of selling out to Rockefeller.

Standard tried to operate in Texas through the Waters, Pierce Oil Co., a southwestern marketing concern, but it was too late to head off the newcomers. Soon the Texas Co.—the forerunner of Texaco—was in the field. Gulf and Texas moved quickly into the new gasoline market at a time when Standard was still pretty much committed by its technological investment to kerosene. The rise of the new independents was accomplished some years before the Supreme Court invoked the Sherman Act of 1890 to force the dissolution of the Standard Oil holding company into its constituent parts. This occurred in 1911. When he heard of the Supreme Court decision, the elder J. P. Morgan growled that it would take more than a court order to force Rockefeller to compete against himself. But the Rockefeller companies were already competing against many new companies, both in Texas and in the new mid-continent, California, and Illinois fields. Moreover, Standard had already been challenged overseas by the Royal Dutch/Shell combination and by the Nobels in the Russian Caucasus. It was nature and the inexorable workings of the market, not the Supreme Court, that had brought about the end of the dominance of the first great American "trust."

A second road to bigness in the late nineteenth century was followed by the Carnegie Steel Co., which grew from a small west Pennsylvania axle forge run by two Prussian immigrants, the Kloman brothers, to become the major unit in the formation of J. P. Morgan's United States Steel Corp. in 1901. Andrew Carnegie was merely one among many steel-company men before the 1873 depression; he was not even among the first to exploit the new Bessemer-Kelly process of blowing cold air through molten iron to make a superior grade of metal. But Carnegie had a genius for riding hard times—and with every depression his organization gained in strength.

An immigrant boy from Dunfermline, Scotland, where his father, a hand weaver, had been displaced by the new machine looms, Andy Carnegie was used to adversity. Instead of crying about the sad fate of his family, the young Scot, transplanted to Pennsylvania, cheerfully set to work at the age of thirteen as a $1.20-a-week bobbin boy in a cotton mill. Given an opportunity to keep the books of the mill because he wrote a "fair hand," Andy, with three other boys of his Allegheny City neighborhood, walked into Pittsburgh all through one winter to be tutored in the mysteries of double entry, which was his substitute for a high-school education in mathematics.

The habit of biting off more than he was immediately compelled to chew persisted. When he quit his cotton-mill job to become a telegraph messenger boy he became a kibitzer of the Morse operators, learned their code, and got away with handling an important message without authorization. Installed as a Western Union operator on his own account, he ingratiated himself with Tom Scott, the superintendent of the Pennsylvania Railroad's new Pittsburgh division, by giving special attention to his messages. Scott liked the "little white-haired Scotch devil" and put him on the railroad payroll as his private operator at $35 a month. When a railroad accident tied up traffic one day in Scott's absence, Andy broke the rules all over again and got things running by issuing "train orders" in his boss's name.

Instead of firing Andy as he should have for an incredible breach of railroad discipline, Scott was entranced by the boy's nerve. He began to throw investment opportunities Carnegie's way. Borrowing money from a bank, Carnegie took a one-eighth share in the Woodruff Sleeping Car Co.—and, fortuitously or not, Woodruff was soon building more and more sleepers for the Pennsylvania. During the Civil War the wide-awake Andy helped Scott co-ordinate the railroad and telegraph services of the War Department. He kept his eyes and ears open for investment opportunities so well that, in 1863, he was able to record an annual income of $47,860, with only $2,400 coming from his railroad salary. The biggest chunk of dividends—$17,868—came from the Columbia Oil Company, into which he had bought with his sleeping-car profits.

Carnegie's memorandum of income for 1863 mentions $4,250 through "T.M.C. from Kloman," and $7,500 from J. L. Piper and Aaron Shiffler, manufacturers of iron railway bridges. "Kloman" was, of course, the maker of an excellent railroad-car axle, and the "T.M.C." who is so cryptically mentioned was Thomas M. Carnegie, Andy's brother. Andy had joined the Kloman and the Piper and Shiffler iron companies as a sleeping partner, presumably in order to keep his dual connection with the Pennsylvania and two of its suppliers from becoming the subject of gossip.

Carnegie first took an active part in the Kloman axle company by accident, when he tried to mediate a quarrel between the suspicious Andrew Kloman and a partner. This air of casual adventitiousness seemed to set the tone for Carnegie's connection with the iron-and-steel business for years to come. Yet underneath the apparent negligence there was a definite pattern to everything the young capitalist did after he finally quit the Pennsylvania Railroad in 1865. By indirection Carnegie went swiftly to his goal. He set up an office in New York, not as a steelman but as a bond broker. He spent much of his time in travel, cultivating literary men, philosophers, English royalty, and U.S. Senators who were in a position to grant him a high steel tariff. Somehow, though no one could quite fathom the process, his control of the various steel companies in which he was so distantly interested always seemed to increase.

Indignant historians, put off by Carnegie's colossal vanity in taking credit from others, have endlessly reiterated that it was Andrew Kloman who really built up the firm of Kloman & Phipps in the Civil War period; that it was William Coleman, the father-in-law of the younger brother, Thomas M. Carnegie, who first proposed that a Carnegie enterprise—the Edgar Thomson mill—be set up to make steel rails at Braddock, Pennsylvania, by the new Bessemer process; that it was Captain Bill Jones, a refugee from the Cambria Iron Works at Johnstown, who supplied the managerial ability that made the Edgar Thomson mill so profitable; that it was the relatively late newcomer Henry Clay Frick, owner of the rich Connellsville coke fields, who persuaded the Carnegie organization to become a tight vertical trust, commanding its own sources of coke and iron ore as well as its mills; that it was the hardboiled Frick, once again, who took on the unpleasant task of breaking the hold of the Amalgamated Association of Iron and Steel Workers at the Homestead mill when Carnegie was hiding in Scotland from the consequences of having written that the great law of the workingman was "Thou shalt not take thy neighbor's job."

All of the allegations that Carnegie grew rich on the labors and ingenuity of men who knew considerably more about steel than he did are perfectly true. But if it hadn't been for Andy Carnegie's peculiar character there would have been no glue to hold the whole vast enterprise together in those years when the Bessemer process was displacing the old puddling processes only to give way in turn to the great open-hearth furnaces of the modern mill. In this whole development Carnegie exhibited a unique talent for moving in and taking control when the time was ripe. In 1871 he scoffed when William Coleman and Thomas Carnegie proposed entry into the Bessemer field. Running off to Europe on a bond-selling expedition for an Iowa railroad, Carnegie left Coleman and brother Thomas to dig up capital for their new enterprise as best they could; he, Andy, would have nothing to do with it. Though the Bessemer patent situation had long since been straightened out, and though good Bessemer rails were already being made at Cambria and in Chicago, Andy thought an investment in Bessemer converters would be "pioneering." And his rule, often stated, was that "pioneering don't pay."

But while Carnegie was wandering around Europe, two things happened. First of all, he managed to dispose of $6 million of the railroad bonds, which gave him a profit of $150,000 that he had to invest somewhere. Second, he discovered that the British believed in the Bessemer rail; indeed, they delighted to point to one particular piece of Bessemer track that had been doing business on the Midland Railway at Derby for fifteen years and was still far from needing replacement. Sailing quickly for home, Carnegie offered to put all of his European commissions into Coleman's and Thomas Carnegie's venture. This sum was more than enough to give Andy belated command of the Edgar Thomson project. By 1878, when the Carnegie enterprises were recapitalized, Carnegie had 59 per cent of the stock in his own hands.

Another remote control coup of Carnegie's was responsible for bringing the greatest steel man of the age, Captain Bill Jones, into the Edgar Thomson management. Loafing in New York, Carnegie picked up some gossip about a labor dispute at Cambria which, obscurely, seemed to involve the company's operating bosses. Knowing that Cambria had had a long experience with the Bessemer process, Carnegie hastened to Pittsburgh with the suggestion that the heads of the Cambria departments be hired to run the Edgar Thomson. This is what brought Jones into the Carnegie organization. And along with Jones came a whole corps of trained Bessemer men.

By such intelligent opportunism Carnegie dominated his industry even though he knew little of the technical details of steelmaking. His chronic absence from Pittsburgh gave him all the more opportunity to sell Pittsburgh's products; he was, as Burton Hendrick has pointed out, "perhaps the greatest commercial traveler this country has ever known." When it was to his advantage to do so, the opportunistic Carnegie entered steel price and production pools. When the advantage ran out, however, he was the first to quit. He absorbed the Duquesne Steel Co. after spreading what today would be termed commercial libel against it. He forced his partners to sign an "ironclad" agreement that they would return their stock to the company at book value if, by any chance, they proposed either to retire or resign. He kept the steel tariff as high as he could for as long as he could, and if a railroad would give him a rebate he was not averse to accepting it. But none of these things really accounted for the basic profitability of the Carnegie enterprises. What counted was that Carnegie kept the organization on its toes: the cost of production was constantly lowered by men whom Carnegie often set at each other's throats to make new records. Young men like Charlie Schwab—the "young geniuses" of Carnegie's verbal adulation— were generously rewarded for enterprise, acquiring partnerships by acquiring stock they paid for on easy terms out of earnings. Whenever a depression came, Carnegie bought out his rivals, ending up in the nineties with a completely integrated company that owned or leased its Mesabi ore beds, its limestone and coke sources, its Great Lakes freighters, its docks and railroad lines, and its great mills at Braddock, Homestead, Duquesne, and Beaver Falls. Despite a fierce quarrel with Frick, and despite his inability to tolerate anybody near the throne very long, Carnegie could still truly suggest for his epitaph, "Here lies the man who knew how to get around him men who were cleverer than himself."

The proof of the Carnegie pudding was in the eating. Profits, which had been at the rate of $2 million per year in the early eighties, had jumped to $5 million in 1890, and had risen to $40 million by 1900. This immense profitability derived from the fact that Carnegie had a grip on the bulk of crude-steel production in the U.S. Even so, his position was not entirely impregnable. For one thing, the Chicago steel area, where Captain Eber B. Ward had rolled Bessemer rails as early as 1865, was producing ingots, and in the late nineties this production increased with the organization of the Federal Steel Co. More seriously, Carnegie found himself harassed by the creation of wire, tube, tinplate, bridge-making, and other fabricating companies which threatened to build basic-ingot capacity in preference to buying from Carnegie mills. If

Carnegie had been a younger man he might have met this threat head-on by building his own fabricating facilities. But he felt drained after his quarrel with Frick, and besides he had always had an ambition to retire with honor and become a great philanthropist. "The man who dies . . . rich," he had once written, "dies disgraced."

What allowed Carnegie to fulfill his philanthropic ambitions (and still die rich) was the intervention of powerful outside financial forces. The investment banker, J. P. Morgan, who had been busy consolidating the nation's railroads, began toward the turn of the century to fix his attention on the steel business, and the outlines of a new Goliath, which was to become U.S. Steel, were already taking shadowy shape in his mind. Obviously the Carnegie properties were crucial to such an enterprise. One evening late in 1900, at a famous dinner at the University Club in New York City, Carnegie's man, Charles Schwab, painted such a glowing picture to Morgan of the future of steel that Morgan asked him to name a price for the Carnegie mills. Whether Carnegie consciously set out to bait Morgan is still argued by the historians of steel. In any event, a deal quickly followed in which Carnegie received $492 million in U.S. Steel bonds and stocks in exchange for all of his properties. He himself took $225 million in 5 per cent gold bonds; the rest of the exchange went to his "young geniuses."

As had happened with the Standard Oil empire, the formation of U.S. Steel in 1901 invited the most bitter public attack against monopoly—an attack that was to continue through the beginnings of the new century and has recently been renewed by the Kennedy administration. Actually, as events turned out, this new colossus of steel was to prove as vulnerable to market forces as the Standard Oil trust. In its early years U.S. Steel had 65 per cent of the market; this was to dwindle to 45 per cent in 1914 and 30 per cent today. This would hardly have surprised Carnegie, who wrote: "Whenever consolidations . . . or syndicates, or Trusts, endeavor to circumvent . . . [competition] it always has been found that after the collision there is nothing left of the panaceas, while the great laws [of the market] continue to grind out their consequences as before. . . ." But at the time of the creation of U.S. Steel, things looked different. A vast and concentrated command over money had put U.S. Steel together. Where had the money come from? Who was this J. P. Morgan anyway and what were his real powers? As Andy Carnegie, the master builder, stepped down and retired to Skibo Castle in his native Scotland, these were the questions the American people wanted to have answered.

9 The Rise of the Money Power

Trustification sears the public.

"Jupiter" Morgan reorganizes the rails.

He collides with Gould and Harriman.

He pours Rockefeller's Mesabi ore into U.S. Steel's furnaces.

He glares down the Pujo investigation.

WHEN the U.S. Steel Corporation was put together in 1901, the impact on public opinion was swift and almost physically tangible. Expressing the prevalent consensus of horror, President Arthur Twining Hadley of Yale remarked that if public sentiment would not regulate such monster businesses, there would be "an emperor in Washington within twenty-five years."

U.S. Steel was indeed a monster to a nation whose older citizens still recalled the days when iron and the village blacksmith had been almost synonymous terms. Capitalized at $1.5 billion, "the Corporation" added to Andrew Carnegie's ingot-producing mills a formidable majority of the nation's most important steel-fabricating companies. What whipped up public apprehension still more was the fact that the financier J. P. Morgan had not only linked all these properties together, but by a final coup had brought John D. Rockefeller's Mesabi ore fields, the richest in the world, into his seemingly stock-watered combination. President Hadley had discerned his forthcoming American "emperor" at some distance

163

around the corner. But even as Hadley spoke, Finley Peter Dunne's "Mr. Dooley" voiced the popular opinion that the king was already on the throne in all but name. "James," said Mr. Dooley in his impersonation of Morgan, "call up the Czar an' th' Pope an' th' Sultan an' th' Impror Willum, and tell thim we won't need their services afther nex' week."

John Pierpont Morgan, the conjurer of U.S. Steel, was then sixty-four years old, and did not have another quarter century to live. But to the public he had suddenly taken on a mythic quality. Nicknamed "Jupiter" (he was also to be called Pierpontifex Maximus), he was a great burly figure with a huge red nose and startling eyes that nobody ever quite dared to stare down. His growl was like thunder; his word in his own community was taken to be law. In the long Indian summer of his later life, when he turned some of his prodigious energies to collecting, his house at Prince's Gate in London and his home and adjacent library at Madison Avenue and Thirty-sixth Street in New York City became stuffed with a king's ransom in paintings, ceramics, glass, textiles, sculptures, illuminated manuscripts, and first editions. His movements, whether large or small, had the stateliness of a royal progression: his yacht, the *Corsair,* dominated the fleet wherever the New York Yacht Club anchored; he had a special riverboat constructed to take him up the Nile; he spent part of each year contemplating eternal objects in the Eternal City of Rome; and when he attended conventions of his beloved Episcopal Church as a lay delegate (he was senior warden of St. George's in Manhattan), it was as if the chief lord temporal of the realm had decided to hobnob with ecclesiastical peers among the lords spiritual.

This pomp and circumstance flowed out of the earnings of a banking business, J. P. Morgan & Co., which, located at the famous "corner" of Broad and Wall streets in New York, seemed to be the arbiter of the nation's economic destiny. For one thing, Morgan acted as a kind of private Securities and Exchange Commission: stocks and bonds that he sponsored, he let it be known, could be trusted. For another thing, he served as a kind of private Federal Reserve System, even bailing the U.S. Treasury out at a stiff price when, in the depression year of 1895, it ran short of gold. Finally, as arbiter of the economic decisions of great railroads, Morgan essayed the role of a private Interstate Commerce Commission. In all of these roles the great Pierpontifex Maximus symbolized the new and rising "money power" of Wall Street, which had grown out of a few relatively small specialty banking houses such as Moses Taylor's City Bank, J. & W. Seligman & Co., and Kuhn, Loeb, among others. In the beginning these houses had simply financed imports such as sugar and copper or exports such as cotton and had dealt in government bonds. But by the turn of the century they were in just about everything. Seeking outlet for their funds and energies, they had become bone and marrow of the scary "trustification" of American business.

Well before the formation of U.S. Steel there were big trusts like the American Sugar Refining Co. and the American Tobacco Co., with capitalizations running into the hundreds of millions. And there were little trusts like those in the hide and leather or the chicle industry, where mere millions seemed the co-ordinating factor. Some of these trusts had been created by promoters with a legal knowledge of how to pyramid small companies into big ones by an exchange of paper securities; and as paper-created pyramids they represented no great initial dependence on the "money power." But "Wall Street"—meaning men like Morgan—was behind enough of the new combinations to give many of the 1901 generation the creeps. Despite the fact that the Sherman Antitrust Act had been passed in 1890, people thought they saw "restraint of trade" sprouting up everywhere.

Fears for the future were further abetted by old political and social enmities that refused to die. The farm-border Populists, who had carried the banner for Free Silver in the Bryan campaign of 1896, had popularized the idea that Wall Street was oppressing the hinterlands by nailing the country to a "cross of gold." American labor, though somewhat mollified when President McKinley promised the "full dinner pail," nevertheless was still smarting from its defeats in the Homestead strike of 1892 and the Pullman strike of 1894. Many a businessman who had sought refuge from competition in "pools" such as the early whisky and cordage trusts was disillusioned when price fixing broke down and sent marginal producers to the wall. The grousing on all sides was magnified into predictions of Red Revolution whenever labor violence occurred.

Nobody, to judge by the decibel register of the era, liked the late nineteenth century—and it was easy to distrust its projection into the first "Morganization" activities of the twentieth.

Some of the fears of the power of Wall Street and the trusts were well founded. Others were grossly exaggerated and, most understandably, lacked perspective. In the first place, the "money power" had not achieved its "take-off" position by grinding the faces of the poor. In the long span of the post-Civil War period—i.e., from 1865 to 1890—hourly wages rose by nearly two-thirds, and, with the continual fall in the price level, real wages did considerably better than that. Between 1865 and 1897 savings-bank assets rose from $243 million to $2 billion—and this money, by the nature of things, went into local, not Wall Street, enterprise. Moreover, despite Morgan and Rockefeller, small business continued to dominate the landscape in the years between Appomattox and the nineties. As Thomas Cochran has pointed out, firms of all types increased twice as fast as the population between 1860 and 1890—and only a corporal's guard among them were big. There were some 750,000 business firms in 1880; by 1890 the number had jumped to 1,100,000, and this proliferation has continued to the present day.

Looking back from the vantage point of the present, moreover, it is clear that, after all, the influence of Wall Street on business was far more creative than the Populists and later the muckrakers supposed. Many of the new "giant" combinations such as the American Can Co., the International Paper Co., and the U.S. Rubber Co. made economic sense; indeed, as precursors of the modern corporate era, they were the pioneers of the age of mass production and low competitive pricing that lay just over the horizon. What the bankers did for many a company was to prevent speculators from milking it dry: the great Morgan contribution was to force managers to look to long-term rather than short-term profitability. Finally, it was men like Morgan, Schiff, the Seligmans, and the Drexels who brought European capital into American enterprises and thereby gave U.S. business important international connections. These connections, plus the bankers' strong support of the gold standard, drew down the wrath of "progressive" and Populist critics of the day. The fact remains that it was Wall Street, not

Courtesy the New York Genealogical and Biographical Society

J. P. Morgan

Main Street, which first discerned the potential of a widening Atlantic community.

J. P. Morgan himself—nicknamed "Pip" in his youth—was a peculiar product of this greater Atlantic world. Born in Hartford, Connecticut, which was already taking shape as the great Yankee insurance capital, he came naturally by his feeling that business, as well as life, should be protected against the hazards of indiscreet plunging. The strains that went into the tough amalgam of his character were diverse, but all of them made for self-assurance. His maternal grandfather, the Reverend John Pierpont, pastor of the Hollis Street Unitarian Church in Boston, had defiantly resigned his pulpit rather than keep mum on the issue of slavery, which he detested. His paternal grandfather, Joseph Morgan, a stalwart Yankee businessman, had made the reputation of the Aetna Fire Insurance Company when he raised enough money to enable it to pay its losses in the disastrous New York City fire of 1835. In addition to such resolute grandparents, J. P. Morgan had the advantage of a spacious upbringing. His earliest life was spent in Hartford and in Boston, where his father, Junius Spencer Morgan, was engaged in the dry goods business. As the "best business man in Boston," Junius soon commended himself to George Peabody, the Massachusetts-born merchant banker who had emigrated to London in order to specialize in the lucrative financing of Anglo-American trade. Asked to become Peabody's partner in 1854, Junius took his own family abroad. The young "Pip" Morgan, after a period at the Cheshire Academy in Connecticut, was deposited at Fayal in the Azores for a short period because of his lagging health; then he was sent on to Vevey in Switzerland before entering the German university of Göttingen, where he distinguished himself in mathematics.

Two years of Göttingen were enough for the self-assured young man. So, from Germany, "Pip" took his mathematical facility to London, where his father was already the chief executive in Peabody & Co. Becoming an expert in arbitrage—or foreign exchange dealings—the young Morgan was sent to New York a few years before the Civil War to act as his father's eyes and ears. Early in his American career "Pip" was taken in by the sharpie who on the eve of the first campaigns of the Civil War had gotten hold of a big stack of Hall carbines which had previously been rejected as unfit for use by the Army. The facts would seem to be incontestable that Morgan knew nothing about guns, and that he carried the sharpie for $20,000, pending a resale of the carbines, as a routine matter of turning over his capital. Later Morgan teamed up with a second questionable character to manipulate the gold market.

Whether these actions should be characterized as legitimate, or whether they were ordinary youthful mistakes of a profession that had not yet discovered the virtues of *noblesse oblige,* Morgan swiftly put such operations behind him. Discovering the necessity of basing all decisions on "character," the fledgling international financier matured rapidly as a gentleman who believed in living by a gentleman's code, and was among the first to take the view that an investment banker must guarantee the long-term solvency of his underwritings. Soon he formed a partnership with Charles H. Dabney, an accountant, doing a big business in foreign exchange and also maintaining close and profitable connection with his father, Junius Morgan, in London. With that connection as a lever, Pierpont in 1871 teamed up with the Philadelphia Drexels to form Drexel, Morgan & Co. with New York offices at 23 Wall.

The first successes of Drexel, Morgan were in the field of competing for the placement of U.S. government bonds, a business that had hitherto been monopolized by the German-Jewish bond dealers of Frankfurt and their American agents and by Philadelphia's own Jay Cooke. The failure of Cooke inevitably lightened the competition for Drexel, Morgan, but the daring exploit of J. S. Morgan of London, who successfully organized a syndicate to float a French loan of 250 million francs in the middle of the Franco-Prussian War, was what brought the greatest *réclame* to the Morgan name. Henceforward young Pierpont was able to use his father's reputation in bidding for all manner of American business. When, after the collapse of Cooke, the Drexel, Morgan firm successfully disposed of a large share of $750 million in U.S. bonds in a great refunding operation that was signally aided by J. S. Morgan in London, it was accepted as proof that America had been "reopened" to British investors.

If it was one thing to sell U.S. government securities in London, it was quite another thing in the 1870's to rehabilitate the name of American railroad stock in English eyes. Britons who had invested heavily in the Erie Railroad had taken a particularly hard shellacking. When he was still the junior partner in Dabney, Morgan & Co., the young Pierpont had run athwart Jim Fisk and Jay Gould, scoundrels of the so-called Erie Ring. Some of the Fisk-Gould operations were technically within the law, for in a period in which corporation officers were not compelled to make public record of their purchases and sales of company stock it was not considered amiss to take secret advantage of inside knowledge. But there was considerably more to the ring's depredations than getting in and out of the market before the public could know what was up. When the ring needed stock to support its operations, it simply voted itself bonds from the Erie treasury and "converted" them into stock by literally operating a printing press. So it was that the Erie became known as the "harlot of the rails" or the "scarlet woman of Wall Street." The $60 million of "pure water" that the thieves of the ring pumped into the capitalization of their long-suffering railroad within the short span of eight years was enough to give all U.S. railroad securities a bad name with foreign investors.

Morgan tangled with the Erie Ring when President Joseph A. Ramsey of the Albany & Susquehanna Railroad asked for his aid in a fight to keep Jay Gould from using strong-arm tactics to unseat the legitimate directors of the company in a rigged proxy fight. The history of the "Susquehanna War" of 1869 is somewhat clouded by legend: in one of the stories Morgan has been described as standing guard at the top of the steps leading to the meeting room and tossing Jim Fisk and a retinue of hired gangsters bodily downstairs, where they were left to pick up their phony proxies and depart. The story is certainly apocryphal, but Morgan did use his influence to help Ramsey out—and the raucous behavior of Gould and Fisk was surely not lost upon him. Prior to the directors' meeting their thugs had tried to steal the rolling stock of the railroad, and the feud was all over the newspapers as locomotives operated by the contending groups collided in the struggle for control of a key tunnel between Binghamton and Albany.

It was his brush with Gould and Fisk, among other things, that made Morgan decide in the seventies that some kind of order must be imposed on the American railroads before he would undertake to put British investors into the most tempting of American speculations. He had traveled to the Pacific coast by Pullman from Chicago, crossing the Great Plains through antelope herds and Pawnee Indian braves, and he had presumably learned something thereby about the long-term potential of railroad travel. When William H. Vanderbilt, son of the old Commodore, came to him for help in disposing of part of his New York Central stock, Morgan could see an opportunity to get into the railroad picture with both feet; but he insisted on naming his conditions.

At the time of Vanderbilt's visit to Morgan, which came in 1879, two years after the old Commodore's death, there was a vast hue and cry about "one-man rule" of the Central. Possessing 87 per cent of the Central's stock, and lacking his father's stomach for a fight, young William H. decided for prudential reasons to cut back his ownership of the Central to a point where his interest would be not quite equal to half the number of outstanding shares. Morgan offered to dispose of 150,000 shares of the Central stock to overseas purchasers in private sales at $120 a share, with an option of taking 100,000 more shares at the same price—a deal that proved highly profitable. But in return for helping Vanderbilt out, Morgan insisted that he be given a seat on the Central's board as the holder of proxies for English purchasers who trusted his judgment. This marked Morgan's emergence as a positive force in the railroad field. It meant that henceforward there would be no tampering with Central stock, no use of the railroad's funds to forward the private fortunes of insiders. It was also the first venture by an important American investment banker into the sort of thing that has been called "finance capitalism," and significantly it was undertaken with the long-term good of the property in mind. Old Cornelius Vanderbilt, who would certainly have disapproved of his son's timidity, would have understood Morgan's motives.

As the years passed Morgan threw his influence against what seemed to him suicidal rate wars, and also sought to prevent the railroads from needlessly duplicating facilities in order to blackmail each other. In 1885, for instance, the Pennsylvania, seeking to discommode the New York Central with something more than a $1 "immigrant rate" to Chicago, started buying the bonds of the half-bankrupt West Shore Railroad running on the west bank of the Hudson from northern New Jersey to Albany. Worried lest the Pennsylvania should steal its traffic from right under its nose, the Central, in turn, started work on something known as the South Pennsylvania Railroad, which was to go from the Susquehanna River to Andrew Carnegie's mill sidings in the Pittsburgh region. None of this duplication made sense to Morgan, for it promised a mutual financial ruin of both the Central and the Pennsylvania roads, with no long-term benefit to shippers or passengers, who needed solvent railroads to provide them with good service over the decades.

Even Morgan lacked the financial power to force President George B. Roberts of the Pennsylvania to make peace. Moreover, since his own partners, the Drexels of Philadelphia, had helped finance the Pennsylvania in the past, Morgan had qualms about trying to impose himself on the Central's great rival by way of stock purchases and a vicious proxy struggle. Lacking the power to dictate through money, Morgan turned to moral suasion and finally managed to arrange a conference on his yacht, the *Corsair*. Steaming up the Hudson in pleasant circumstances, the compelling "Jupiter" of Wall Street talked the situation out with Roberts and Frank Thomson of the Pennsylvania, and Chauncey Depew, the witty president of the Central. By the time the *Corsair* had returned to the Jersey City docks Morgan had a promise from Roberts to call off the war. The Pennsylvania agreed to let the West Shore tracks go to the Central, and in return Vanderbilt and Depew were to abandon the half-completed South Pennsylvania project to weeds, moss, and sumac. Years later, the automobile public was to get an unlooked-for dividend from the whole business when the South Pennsylvania's old embankments and tunnels were utilized by the new Pennsylvania Turnpike.

The success that Morgan achieved on the deck of the *Corsair* advertised him as the appropriate doctor for sick concerns. First the Philadelphia & Reading, which had a big English stock interest, came to him; next the Baltimore & Ohio; then the Chesapeake & Ohio. In the relatively flush days of the 1880's Morgan was able to organize syndicates capable of drumming up enough new capital to put these ailing roads on their financial feet. When the depression of the nineties brought more railroads—the Erie, the Northern Pacific, the Norfolk & Western, and the group of southern railroads organized under the direction of the Richmond Terminal—to the edge of collapse, Morgan had the money, the prestige, and the experience to undertake reorganizations right and left. He put the Southern Railroad together out of the ruins of the Richmond Terminal properties; he devised a "voting trust" to save the British bondholders of the Erie; he brought the Northern Pacific out of its state of shock; he set the Hocking Valley up, and the Lehigh, and the Central of Georgia; and, though he did not maintain control of the Baltimore & Ohio, or get a dominating position in the Santa Fe, his influence continued to help both of these roads.

The Morgan method, worked out in detail by his partner, Charles H. Coster, was to scale down the fixed liabilities of a company until it could meet its interest payments even in the worst of circumstances. Bondholders were persuaded to take bonds of lesser yield, or to exchange their bonds for stock. Stockholders were assessed for new working capital. Finally, new stock was issued pro rata to enable the railroad owners to recoup in good times what they had given up to save the day in the emergency. Sometimes this drastic medicine backfired by creating a plethora of stock that could not be held to high value in depression periods. But for a time it made "Morgan roads" safe for investors, for Morgan kept his representatives on the reorganized boards to see that no shenanigans took place to run down the properties.

During the eighties and well into the nineties, Morgan had the help of a really first-class staff. There was Egisto P. Fabbri, who, before his breakdown in 1884, kept Morgan in touch with what Thomas Edison, the inventor, was doing to justify Drexel, Morgan's first imaginative venture outside the railroad or government-bond field. There were J. Hood Wright, Charles H. Godfrey, George S. Bowdoin and, finally, the shrewd Coster himself, a man who eventually killed himself by overwork as a director of some sixty corporations. In his railroad reorganizations Morgan had the counsel of lawyer Francis Lynde Stetson, known as the Morgan "Attorney General," and Samuel Spencer, a professional railroad man who became head of the Southern Railway. And Morgan's good friend, George F. Baker of the First National Bank of New York, was always ready to lend a helping hand in creating a voting trust or raising necessary capital.

The methods employed by Morgan and his men were copied widely as the depression of the nineties fostered a widespread reorganization and merger movement in most industries. In putting little companies, often rickety, together into bigger and usually safer ones, a new breed of promoter made good use of the New

Jersey holding-company law of 1889, which had been drawn up according to specifications supplied by a shrewd corporation lawyer, James B. Dill. The New Jersey law permitted corporations to buy and hold stock in other companies, and since the prospective earnings of combinations were capitalized without regard to the actual cost of existing plant, the law became known shortly as the "millionaire mill." James B. Duke put together the great American Tobacco Co., which in turn grew into the even bigger Consolidated Tobacco Co.; the Moore brothers of Chicago merged match companies and biscuit companies; Henry O. Havemeyer transformed the old-style sugar trust into the $50-million holding company called the American Sugar Refining Co.; and Thomas Fortune Ryan, a Horatio Alger-type Irishman from Virginia, parlayed a shell corporation he cheerfully called "the great tin box" into a utilities fortune of more than $200 million.

Morgan himself disapproved of many of the slicker deals of financiers outside his own circle, for they often depended on what he regarded as unsound shuffling of "other people's money." (He didn't like, for example, what Ryan and others did with insurance-company money fed by way of trust-company deposits into industrial combinations.) Because of his fetish for providing safety for his clients, Morgan let more than one tempting opportunity go by. Even in his own favorite railroad field there were things he didn't dare try. When the Union Pacific, faced with the necessity of paying off its huge thirty-year-old debt to the U.S. government, became a candidate for reorganization in 1895, Morgan looked the property over and gave it up as a hopeless job. This was the cue for Jacob Schiff of Kuhn, Loeb & Co. to take a hand in the railroad reorganization game. Getting an explicit go-ahead from Morgan, Schiff tinkered for a year with plans for the Union Pacific. But everywhere he encountered a hidden opposition. Thinking that Morgan might be behind it, Schiff called on the great man a second time. No, said Morgan, he had nothing to do with the opposition—but he might be able to find out who had organized it. The name Morgan eventually turned up was that of Edward H. Harriman, a shrewd and able man whom Morgan detested as a "two-dollar broker." Harriman had already cut his railroad eyeteeth as one of the powers behind the successful Illinois Central—and when Morgan uncovered his trail he was well on the way toward getting stock control of the Union Pacific.

Instead of fighting Harriman, Schiff—and Kuhn, Loeb—proceeded to make common cause with him. But since the Union Pacific had to raise $45 million for repayment to the federal government, it needed more cash than either Harriman or Schiff could drum up. Accordingly, James Stillman—who had become head of Moses Taylor's old City Bank—was invited to join the Union Pacific reorganization committee.

The City money was no ordinary banking money; it also happened to be Rockefeller money. The dour and ironically named "Sunny Jim" Stillman, a personal friend of John D.'s gregarious brother William, had managed to attract the mounting profits of Standard Oil to the City's coffers. Thus the City, soon to be rebaptized the National City, became known as the "Standard Oil Bank" —and thus, also, Standard Oil became allied with Harriman and Schiff in the reorganization of the Union Pacific. Under Harriman's wise rebuilding program the Union Pacific began, in true Rockefeller fashion, to function almost as a bank in itself. Within a decade after the reorganization the road had a billion and a half of capital within its own system—and controlled $2 billion invested outside itself.

The Harriman-Schiff-Stillman-Rockefeller feat in making a vast financial power out of the Union Pacific was the first event to serve notice on the country that all American finance had become polarized between two figures, J. P. Morgan and John D. Rockefeller. Henceforward the American railroad grid was pretty much divided between "Morgan roads" and "Rockefeller roads." The two huge aggregates of capital necessarily began to impinge on each other. The one-eyed James J. Hill, the great railroad tycoon of the Northwest, had gravitated into the Morgan system; he not only ran his own Great Northern but he had also functioned as Morgan's ally in refinancing the bankrupt Northern Pacific and placing it with his own railroad in a common "community of interest." Like Harriman's Union Pacific, the Morgan-Hill Great Northern and Northern Pacific alliance needed a feeder route from the trans-Mississippi country into Chicago. The Chicago, Burlington & Quincy, a road that tapped rich territories wherever it went between Chicago and

The old Stock Exchange

Minnesota and Chicago and Denver, was the prize both Rockefeller-Harriman and Morgan-Hill coveted—and a battle was joined in 1901 that was shortly to shake Wall Street to its foundations.

Harriman didn't succeed in getting the Burlington, which was bought by Morgan and Hill for the Northern Pacific. But Harriman had an even bolder design: he proposed through his Schiff and Stillman-Rockefeller money alliances to buy quietly into the Morgan-Hill Northern Pacific itself until he had majority control of its common and preferred stock. This would give him a truly spectacular control of the Chicago, Burlington & Quincy—and also confer upon the Union Pacific alliance a vast competitive power in Jim Hill's and Morgan's pre-empted Northwest region itself.

When J. P. Morgan, belatedly, discovered what Harriman was up to, the contest for available Northern Pacific stock sent shares up to a high of $1,000. Brokerage houses that had sold the stock short were faced with ruin, and as a result almost every other stock in Wall Street plummeted. At this point the principals in the fight, scared by the tempest they had unleashed, decided to call the battle off. They let the shorts settle at $150 a share—and Harriman joined the Northern Pacific board. The Northern Securities Co., subsequently organized by Morgan to exercise stock control of the Northern Pacific, the Great Northern, and the Burlington, was broken up in 1904 by Theodore Roosevelt's trustbusters—but the country as a whole was not particularly reassured. The fact that Morgan and the Rockefeller-Harriman interests could join forces may have promised "stabilization." But in the trust-busting temper of the times a prospective "stabilization" under two allied giants was something to be feared almost as much as unremitting warfare.

The coalescence of big money in the railroad field was frightening enough. But the formation of U.S. Steel in 1901, piling Pelion on Ossa, seemed worse for several reasons. To begin with, it was a trustification in good part of companies that were already trusts. The initial impetus to steel trustification had come in the Chicago area, where Judge Elbert H. Gary had turned his expert legal knowledge to the task of putting little steel companies together into big ones. Gary could get along with anyone and, as events were to prove, he had an excellent public-relations touch. Teaming up with John W. "Bet-a-Million" Gates, a flashy barbed-wire salesman, Gary created the American Steel & Wire Co., and the "wire trust" was followed by other combinations: the National Tube Co., the Moore brothers' American Tin Plate Co., the American Bridge Co., and finally the Federal Steel Co., which was fashioned by Gary with Morgan money out of Illinois Steel and some smaller concerns. This marked Morgan's first really important venture into "industrials"—and when Federal Steel proved extremely profitable in the flush days after the Spanish-American War, it whetted the great man's appetite for more.

Judge Elbert H. Gary

Once Morgan had been baited or intellectually persuaded into accepting the idea that all the smaller steel trusts could be put together with the Carnegie properties into U.S. Steel, it was a question of mobilizing capital on a scale that had never before been dreamed of. The syndicate that was organized to float the issue of U.S. Steel stock included some three hundred participants. Besides J. P.

Morgan & Co., there were the First National Bank of New York, the New York Security & Trust Co., and Kidder, Peabody of Boston. And there were rich men and daring promoters by the score—the Moore brothers of Chicago, William B. Leeds, Daniel G. Reid, and many others. One by one they were herded into line by Judge Gary, Morgan's trusted agent who was persuaded to quit his Chicago law practice and take over as chairman of U.S. Steel. "Bet-a-Million" Gates tried to hold Morgan up for the stock of the American Steel & Wire Co. but was finally prevailed upon to surrender his properties for a sum that was within reason.

If this had been all that there was to U.S. Steel, the fright caused by its creation might not have been so pronounced. But the final shiver of apprehension was provided when Rockefeller wealth turned up as an integral part of the great combination.

John D. Rockefeller had picked up the rich Mesabi ore deposits in the nineties when the Merritt brothers of Minnesota, lacking capital for exploitation, had been unable to hold on to their great discovery. When Gary suggested to Morgan that the Mesabi ore must be made a part of U.S. Steel, Morgan demurred; he didn't like John D. Rockefeller, and wished to have no part in dealing with the man. But U.S. Steel without Mesabi would have been extremely vulnerable. Gary's calm logic persuaded Morgan to swallow his prejudices and a price was extracted from Rockefeller. It was more than Gary had originally been prepared to pay, but Morgan, who always refused to haggle, accepted it without blinking. Possession of the Mesabi gave U.S. Steel a source of ore that was to last through two world wars—and it put "Rockefeller influence," representing Rockefeller stock, on the U.S. Steel board. Thus the two great titans —Morgan and Rockefeller—were united not only in the field of railroad domination but in the steel trust that would presumably be virtually the whole source of metal for railroads and all other big industry.

The spectacle of U.S. Steel and the Northern Securities Co., which were created at virtually the same time, was too much for a country that looked back to small-scale business with an acute nostalgia. And when the muckraking journalists began to issue forth in full cry in the years after 1903, the alarm about a prospective "benevolent feudalism" (socialist W. J. Ghent's ironic phrase for it) under an alliance of money barons trickled down into every hamlet in the land. The journalistic din, which was augmented year by year, pointed to "trusts" everywhere. In 1904, John Moody listed as "greater industrial trusts" the Amalgamated Copper Co. ($175-million capitalization), the "smelter trust" (American Smelting & Refining, $201-million capitalization), the American Sugar Refin-

Courtesy the New York Public Library

"The Castaway" by Frederick Opper

ing Co. ($145 million), the Consolidated Tobacco Co. (150 plants and $502-million capitalization, which included Duke's American Tobacco Co.), and the International Mercantile Marine Co. ($170 million). These were in addition to Morgan's U.S. Steel and Rockefeller's Standard Oil. Moreover, there were lesser "trusts" everywhere—the American Hide & Leather Co. controlled $32 million in assets, the Atlas Portland Cement Co. dominated a Pennsylvania area in cement, du Pont (with forty plants and $50-million capitalization) was the transcendent power in manufacturing explosives, Otis represented $12 million in elevator factories, and so it went. The Pullman Palace Car Co. had 85 per cent of its market; the "bobbin and shuttle trust" made 90 per cent of its type of product. And there were the so-called "natural monopoly" trusts—the American Telephone & Telegraph Co., the street-traction companies, and the new gas and electricity companies, all of which depended on politically granted franchises.

The coalescing of power was further intensified by the phenomenon of "interlocking directorates." As spread on the record by crusading lawyer-authors such as Louis Brandeis (later a Supreme Court Justice) and by the muckraking magazines, the Morgan–Rockefeller–George F. Baker crisscross was everywhere. Morgan, of course, ran his own private bank—but he was also a big stockholder and director in Baker's First National Bank. Two of the newest Morgan partners—Thomas F. Lamont and H. P. Davison— had been First National vice presidents, and they remained as First National directors. The First National, in turn, was associated with Morgan in the control of the Guaranty Trust Co. Baker and Baker men appeared with Morgan or with Morgan men on the directorates of the New York, New Haven & Hartford Railroad Co., the Pullman company, the new International Harvester Co., the Reading Railroad, the Baldwin Locomotive Works, the American Telephone & Telegraph Co., the Mutual Life Insurance Co., and so forth and so on. The National City Bank–Rockefeller interests got in on the crisscross by being associated with Morgan and/or Baker in the Bankers Trust, the Guaranty Trust, the Astor Trust, the National Bank of Commerce, the Chase National Bank, the Equitable Life, the Adams Express Co., numerous anthracite-coal carriers of Pennsylvania and New Jersey, the International Mercantile Marine Co., and a whole host of railroads. As for Jacob Schiff of Kuhn, Loeb, he too was represented on a number of Morgan-Baker-Rockefeller boards.

To fears that all this interlocking control would snuff out competition was added long-standing popular discontent with the country's whole monetary system, which Wall Street also seemed to control to its own interest. After the 1870's the country's gold supply failed to keep pace with the growth of industry, thus leading to periods of extreme monetary stringency that benefited the bankers but all too often forced the little businessman to the wall. The passage of the Bland-Allison Act of 1878 and the succeeding Sherman Silver Purchase Act of 1890 put the U.S. temporarily on a limited bi-metallic standard, to the joy of the Populists, but this in turn gave rise to a new problem: how to keep the market ratio of gold and silver from disastrous fluctuation. The fortuitous discovery of new sources of gold in Alaska and Australia and the introduction in South Africa of a cheap, more efficient method of extraction (the famous cyanide process) expanded the gold supply in the late nineties and, with an enlarged gold base, McKinley finally put the nation on the full gold standard in 1900 despite the outcries of the silverites and Bryan. But the U.S. was not yet out of the woods, and in 1907 there occurred a disastrous panic with widespread bank failures.

Morgan met this situation by forming an impromptu committee of New York bankers and, working from his Madison Avenue library, hastily assembled a central pool of capital to stem the tide. His cool nerve in the crisis—and his famous order to his banker associates to sign on the dotted line no matter what their overstrained commitments—saved the country from disaster, but his bold act simply raised the further question: how come that a private banker and not the government itself should be the arbiter of national solvency or insolvency? This question, plus the allied one of "trustification," boiled to a head in the famous Pujo Committee investigation of 1912–13. Through endless hours on the congressional stand the aging Morgan glared at inquisitive government counsel and defended both the powers of the bankers and their manifold activities.

In the matter of money and credit he had a far better case than his critics at the time assumed. It was all very well to charge that in the panic years of 1895 and 1907 the bankers had overstepped their normal functions. But if they had not held the money system together, who would have? The fact was that ever since Jacksonian times the U.S. government had lacked the authority to mobilize the country's monetary reserves in adequate fashion. And the further fact was that the centralization of credit, begun privately by men like Morgan, set a precedent for a more rational solution of the problem by the passage of the Federal Reserve Act in 1913. This act (which set up twelve private regional Reserve banks, heading up in a politically appointed Reserve board in Washington) gave the country the liquidity it needed—perhaps in retrospect too much liquidity—and was a vast improvement over Morgan's *ad hoc* credit pools. It is notable, however, that private bankers played a large role in the Fed's formation. First proposed in embryo by Paul M. Warburg of Kuhn, Loeb, it received powerful support from Morgan's partner, Henry P. Davison, as well as Frank A. Vanderlip of Stillman's National City Bank. And Morgan himself, who died just nine months before the creation of the new structure, would hardly have contested its desirability.

What of the other charge of the Pujo investigators that Morgan and his associates had ruined the country through trustification? Certainly it could not be laughed off, for the record showed that policy-making decisions in 100 leading U.S. companies were strongly influenced by a tight group of commercial, trust, and investment banks, which, in turn, depended on Standard Oil and Morgan resources of $2 billion in capital. Yet when all is said, the Pujo Committee claimed too much in its attacks on the "old order." Nobody could gainsay the fact that the Morgan and Rockefeller banking interests had enormous power, or that the trusts and the new giant corporations replaced so-called "perfect competition" in many industries with the "workable" competition we know today. Yet, as noted in the previous chapter, Standard Oil was unable to prevent the rise of Gulf, Sun Oil, and Texaco, and U.S. Steel's dominant position was likewise to give way to the inroads of Bethlehem, Republic, and Jones & Laughlin, to say nothing of smaller but competitively important companies like Inland Steel, Armco, and National Steel. Moreover, if the country, in 1913, had been truly in the grip of the New York "money power," such industries as automobiles, aluminum, the moving pictures, chemicals, rubber, sulfur extraction, and the western oils would never have been born. A Morgan partner, George Perkins, advised against putting money into automobiles—but Ford as well as Durant of General Motors got the money they needed from other sources. The Mellons of Pittsburgh financed Charles Martin Hall's ingenious electrolytic method of obtaining aluminum from an oxide existing in a common form of clay. A lone speculator, Bernard Baruch, lured the Guggenheims into backing the Jackling method for processing low-grade copper ores. Baruch also offered Morgan a part of the sulfur industry—and when Morgan turned him down with the statement that he "never gambled," the cagey Baruch went ahead successfully on his own.

Ideas were to remain as important as money—and ideas had a way of generating their own funds from a combination of regional capital and internal expansion. Though the banker needed the inventor, the inventor could—and frequently did—manage to make do without the banker. Indeed, a single inventor alone, Thomas A. Edison, was enough to give the lie to the more inflated claims of the Pujo Committee. Edison used banking money at times—but he generated far greater aggregates of capital than he ever borrowed. Money was money—but even amid all the clamor about "trusts" the free lance with the idea and the determination was still supreme.

10 The Age of Edison

Alexander Graham Bell flabbergasts Brazil's emperor.

Edison clears the telephone's voice.

The light bulb wakes up the American city.

And the streetcar jounces toward suburbia.

From kinetograph to Warner Brothers.

The "Edison effect" leads to electronics.

Long before he was ready to jump from his railroad reorganizations to the financing of "industrials," John Pierpont Morgan allowed himself to be beguiled by a patent lawyer, Grosvenor Lowrey, who told him marvelous tales of a New Jersey "wizard" who was about to do wonders with the mysterious force of electricity. Though he doubtless knew as little as most men of the time about the workings of Ohm's law of electrical resistance, Morgan, who trusted Lowrey, managed to dig up a few dollars to help support the inventor in his tinkering with filaments for an electric light bulb. It was thus that Thomas A. Edison got some of the funds that enabled him to crash through with the invention of the first practical electric bulb in 1879. Edison was not always to depend on bankers, whom he affected to scorn, but Wall Street, through Morgan, shares at least a little of the credit for enabling the electrical revolution to get off the ground.

To most financiers of the late nineteenth century, however, the strange new force seemed little more than a fascinating toy. The power potential of electricity had been foreshadowed as early as

185

1831, when the great English physicist Michael Faraday whirled a magnetic core around a wire, thus hitting on the principle of the dynamo. But for years public attention centered on the building of great empires in oil, steel, railroads, sugar refining, and banking, and few even suspected that the silent force from the dynamo would transform the whole of modern life. This force finally broke in upon the harsh realities of steam-driven America like a magician from another planet, replacing the whacking, noisy mechanical belts in the factories, changing city life beyond recognition, and laying the basis for a decentralization of motor power that was to play its own part in breaking up the tight industrial conglomerations of the era of the trusts.

In its unfolding, the electrical revolution plays hob with the neat sequence of U.S. business history, since it began in the mid-nineteenth century and is still busy putting forth its manifold shoots. Out of Edison's little light bulb and the dynamo there grew the whole vast complex of privately owned electric utilities—Consolidated Edison, Pacific Gas & Electric, Southern California Edison, Commonwealth Edison, etc.—an industry with assets of over $45 billion. To provide equipment for the utilities there arose manufacturing giants like General Electric and Westinghouse, which now make everything from ponderous turbines on down through household refrigerators to toasters and solder pots; and it is Westinghouse and Otis elevators that have made the modern skyscraper possible. Even the typewriter, which Christopher Sholes of Milwaukee *thought* he was inventing to make braille-like characters for the use of blind people, is now run by electric current. And to all this must be added the rise of the Radio Corporation of America, the proliferation of broadcasting and television stations, and the rest of the electronic revolution, which not only has brought in automation but also will one day soon allow the communication companies, notably A.T. & T., to commercialize the bounce of human voices off the sky itself.

So many of the electrical era's ramifications flow from the "Wizard of Menlo Park" that it can be called the Age of Edison without doing violence to the truth. Yet Edison, who was born in 1847 and died in 1931, built on the work of others, and in the development of early communication by electricity he actually played a tangen-

Courtesy Edison Laboratory National Monument

Thomas A. Edison

tial, although critical, role. It was Samuel F. B. Morse, as we have seen, who, taking off from the work of the American physicist Joseph Henry, first perfected the telegraph and set the stage for the emergence of the Western Union Telegraph Co. In 1861 this company pushed its lines across the continent well ahead of the railroad —and the Plains Indians, persuaded by linesmen that electrical messages were nothing less than the voice of the Great Spirit, left the transcontinental wires alone. Awesome as the Western Union service was to others besides the Indians, it was at first limited by the fact that the traffic over any given line was severely restricted—

a defect that men of the time hoped to overcome by the development of the "harmonic telegraph," a device for sending several pitches over a wire simultaneously.

It was while tinkering to solve the problem of simultaneous messages that the second great figure of the electrical era, Alexander Graham Bell, came on stage. A Scottish student of phonetics, Bell had made a providential recovery from tuberculosis in the clear air of Canada. Daring the climate of rainy Boston, whither he had been invited by the board of education, he took over the teaching of deaf-mutes in a local school. It so happened that two Boston capitalists, Gardiner G. Hubbard and Thomas Sanders, each had a deaf child. Impressed by Bell's personality, the two capitalists not only sent their children to him for help (he was later to marry deaf Mabel Hubbard) but also decided to back him in the race to beat Western Union in devising a usable harmonic telegraph. Living in Sanders' mother's home, Bell went to work with electromagnets and diaphragms in the attempt to vary musical pitches over a telegraph line in such a way that they would not interfere with each other. But in the back of his mind was something else: he wanted to "make metal talk."

Bell's notion was that if he varied spoken words in intensity close to a sensitive diaphragm, the corresponding variations in air density could be turned into electrical impulses that would emerge at the other end of a wire to be transformed by electromagnetic vibration back into human speech. In conducting his experiments he was operating pretty much in the dark: he was even reported as vibrating the ear of a corpse in front of an electrical circuit. Serendipity —or discovery by accident—eventually led him to his goal. Working on receivers in one room while his assistant, Thomas A. Watson, was testing transmitter ideas in another, Bell heard something promising come over the wire. Rushing in upon Watson, he shouted, "What did you do?" Watson hadn't done anything more than pluck a piece of vibrating wire that lay close to the magnetized telegraph circuit that led from his room to Bell's. But this time the make-and-break points of a transmitter spring had become accidentally welded together—and a noise that was tantalizingly close to human speech had emerged at Bell's end of the fused circuit. Further experimenting with the transmitter turned the noise into authentic words, and a year later Bell's primitive telephone was on exhibition at the Centennial Exposition of 1876 in Philadelphia. When the Emperor Dom Pedro II of Brazil clamped it to his ear, he was astonished. "My God!" the Emperor has been quoted as saying. "It talks!"

The phone did not, however, talk too persuasively as yet, and often trailed off into a fearful jumble of heterogeneous noises. And it is at this point that some of the early work of Thomas Edison becomes important. A Midwesterner from Ohio and Michigan, Edison had received his early training in the use of electrical circuits as a tramp operator for Western Union, and he had already improved the stock ticker. Thinking to get into the telephone business for itself, Western Union hired Edison as a free lance to add his bit of ingenuity to work already done by its own Elisha Gray, who actually had filed a caveat covering his own telephone invention a few hours after Bell. Working closely with Gray, Edison came up with a new carbon-actuated mouthpiece or microphone and an induction coil that greatly extended the range of the telephone circuit. This gave Western Union at least half of an original system and it promptly began competing with the Bell group. Bell brought suit in 1879 alleging patent infringement, and Western Union counter-charged that Elisha Gray and Edison had actually been first in all phases of the invention.

Eventually the squabble was composed in Bell's favor; and though Western Union continued to draw a 20 per cent royalty on the combined telephone patents, it withdrew from the business and stuck to its own wire service. Meanwhile the Bell group evolved into the great Bell System and the mighty American Telephone & Telegraph Co., which made the American long-distance grid the wonder of the world, and in the process became a far bigger behemoth than anything J. P. Morgan ever dreamed of. Yet thanks in part to policies laid down by its first president, Theodore N. Vail, A.T. & T. managed to keep "nationalizers" at arm's length, and has flourished as a unique private corporation doing the public's business.

Edison himself was to earn a quarter of a million dollars from his microphone, but in the late 1870's he had other things than improvements in the telephone on his mind. As usual with him one thing led to another. His work for Western Union in developing the carbon microphone started a train of thought: if sound could be produced by movement against a diaphragm, why couldn't it be *reproduced* by playing recorded indentations back again via a needle against a *second* diaphragm? Edison's own deafness had caused him to use a needle held between a diaphragm and his sensitive finger so that he could judge the amplitude of vibrations when he was tinkering with his telephonic devices. Thus his infirmity sparked the line of investigation that led to "stored" voices. Edison thought of his first phonograph device, consisting of embossed recordings on tinfoil, as an aid to all sorts of dictation, or for making phonographic "books" for blind people, or for various odds and ends including the teaching of spelling and elocution, the preservation of the sayings of great men, and as an auxiliary in the transmission of permanent records over the telephone. Almost casually Edison mentioned that it might also be "liberally devoted to music."

And then, having reaped a useful harvest of royalties by exhibiting the machine as a scientific curiosity, Edison forgot his first wholly original brainchild for ten years. A friend, Professor George F. Barker, had urged Edison to look into the uses of electricity for light, and when the inventor heard that Jablochkoff "candles," a Russian arc light, were being used to illuminate the Paris Exposition of 1878, he was off on a new career, which would in three decades transform the U.S. economy beyond recognition.

Edison was not the first American to use electricity for lighting: that distinction goes to Charles F. Brush of Cleveland and William Wallace and Moses G. Farmer of New England. These men had used ring-wound dynamos to light arc lamps on Cleveland streets, in John Wanamaker's big department store in Philadelphia, and in Naugatuck Valley brass mills. Brush had learned how to use automatic shunt coils to by-pass burned-out lamps, which made uninterrupted lighting from a central dynamo or generator a commercially feasible thing. But arc lamps, which were much too intense to be used in private homes, had a severely limited economic future. Edison, after a visit to Wallace's brass mill in Ansonia, which used the Wallace-Farmer lighting equipment, saw that lighting "had not gone so far but that I had a chance." The problem, as he saw it in an intuitive flash, was to "subdivide" light so that it could be brought into private houses. Few people in America thought this was practical, for electricians as yet had only an imperfect understanding of such things as "ladder" circuits, which could put out separate "rungs" into individual homes. And nobody knew the full range of possibilities in altering the relationships of the three electrical variables of force, amplitude, and resistance. Other inventors, seeking to produce a small lamp that would not burn out, were busy looking for a low-resistance filament that would withstand great heat without melting or exploding. But Edison proposed to discover a thin high-resistance filament that would take only a small amount of current off a main line. What he was looking for, on the hydraulic analogy, was the smallest possible household pipe for his water. With the amount of current stepped down for home use, the pipe wouldn't get much work—and the main conduit of power out in the street would have all the more fluid left for other end-appliance uses.

Having defied the great Lord Kelvin of England by elaborating the theory of the almost infinitely subdivided light, Edison had still to find the best material for his filaments and a method for properly sealing the bulb once it had been exhausted of its air. The story has frequently been told of how he tried platinum, nickel, carbon, molybdenum, and platinum again in a high vacuum to create bulbs that invariably burned out within an hour or two at most. So, too, has the story of the breakthrough—the making of a filament out of carbonized cotton thread in October of 1879 that burned for all of thirteen and one-half or forty hours, depending on whose memories of the glorious event are to be trusted. (Carbonized bristol board, bamboo, and, finally, ductile tungsten were later filament material.) The account of the perfecting of the bulb is so dramatic that it has quite obscured Edison's coincidental outlining of a complete light-and-power system, with a central dynamo station pumping its juice through underground wires to homes, offices, and factories. Edison worked out the details of cheap production of current in his notebooks, with aid from Professors Henry Rowland of Johns Hopkins and John Trowbridge of Harvard, a year before he finally succeeded in carbonizing a filament that would last long enough to be commercially useful.

It was around this time that J. P. Morgan got his first dividend from his advance to Edison. It took the form of a special back-yard installation complete with boiler, steam engine, and dynamo, which fed current to a lighting system in his Madison Avenue home. But such special home lighting was not what Morgan and other backers of Edison were after. They were waiting for "Pearl Street"—the site of Edison's first central power station, in downtown Manhattan —to come through. The Pearl Street project required entrepreneurial savoir faire of a high order, which the versatile Edison himself supplied. Jumbo dynamos had to be built, huge boilers and steam

Courtesy Consolidated Edison Co. of New York, Inc.

Dynamos at Edison's Pearl Street station, New York

engines had to be installed to provide the mechanical power to turn the dynamo armatures, switchboard and newfangled control instruments had to be created, an electric-current meter had to be invented to measure sales to individual buyers. At the same time City Hall had to be persuaded to permit the ripping up of streets for underground conduits.

Nor did troubles end here. When faulty governors on the original Porter-Allen steam engines used at Pearl Street caused the dynamos to give off eerie sparks and made the whole building vibrate horribly, Edison had to go looking for a different type of engine. And by the time Pearl Street was ready to deliver a small amount of current on a commercial basis to the principal stores from Fulton to Nassau streets, Edison had used up $600,000. Finally, on September 4, 1882, dressed in a Prince Albert and a white derby hat, Edison himself turned on the lights in the Morgan offices at the corner of Broad and Wall. Moments later, with clothes awry and his white hat discolored with grease, he was discovered underground wrestling to repair a circuit that had blown. The inventor-enterpriser who had devised the carbon-filament bulb and then manufactured a bewildering array of lamps, switches, fixtures, and heavier equipment was still his own mechanic.

Out of Pearl Street immense industrial rivers were to flow—and if Edison had stayed with any one of them he might have become a tycoon greater than Morgan or Rockefeller. As it was, his practice was to play along with a thing until it was well started, then to withdraw from it, using the profits to experiment with something new. In the eighties he had, as he said, to "push the system"— meaning that he had to turn promoter of lighting plants everywhere. He formed the Edison Co. for Isolated Lighting in 1881 (a subsidiary of the parent Edison Electric Light) to furnish individual power plants for factories and large department stores. He placed his young secretary from London, Samuel Insull, at the helm of the T. A. Edison Construction Department, which made credit available to small city lighting companies that could not find cash to buy generators and other central-station equipment. At Goerck Street in Manhattan, on the site of an old ship ironworks, the Edison Machine Works made generators.

Meanwhile Pearl Street became the central unit of the Morgan-backed Edison Illuminating Co., supplying current all over Manhattan. Edison Illuminating grew into Consolidated Edison, the prototype of central-station companies all over the U.S. A movement to "municipalize" central lighting companies made some headway before the turn of the century, but the unfortunate experience of Philadelphia with a municipal gas company (whose payrolls were loaded with the cousins and the retainers of the local machine politicians) exercised a somewhat dampening effect on the crusade for public ownership until the New Deal began building its big dams to harness the Tennessee and Columbia rivers. So the private power companies flourished and gradually evolved into great systems with connected physical facilities and interlocking finances.

To promote his own business interests Edison—and his successors—had to push simultaneously from two directions. As a missionary and showman, he persuaded many local capitalists to start operating companies. But many power stations had to be financed by equipment companies, which took stock in payment for dynamos. Since Edison's manufacturing patents were involved and could be had legitimately only by cross-licensing, the number of equipment companies was necessarily limited; and it may be for this reason that there was a so-called "trust" in equipment before there was a "power trust" in the field of providing current from central stations.

The original Edison equipment companies (Edison Lamp, the Edison Machine Works, and Bergmann & Co., which made small electrical appliances) were soon consolidated with the patent-holding Edison Electric Light into the Edison General Electric Co., with headquarters at Schenectady, New York. Morgan helped bankroll it, but Henry Villard, the brilliant promoter of the Northern Pacific Railroad, marketed a good deal of the company's stock to the Deutsche Bank of Berlin, which bought it for Siemens & Halske, the German electrical trust. With this German backing Villard became the first president of Edison General Electric.

There were other patents in the electrical field besides those of Edison, however, and two other great equipment companies managed to get a start in the late nineteenth century. They were helped by Edison's bullheadedness, which could be terrific at times. A partisan of direct current, Edison rejected the claims of the alternating-current system. It was his biggest mistake, for the high-voltage "A.C." could be transmitted cheaply over long distances, unlike "D.C.," and then stepped down by transformers for local distribution to houses and plants. The A.C. field was exploited by George Westinghouse, inventor of the air brake, who formed Westinghouse Electrical & Manufacturing Co. in 1885. Westinghouse bought up the U.S. rights to the European Gaulard-Gibbs transformer; it also held the patents to Nikola Tesla's induction motor, and the Tesla polyphase alternator, which made long-range transmission economically feasible.

Another believer in alternating current, Elihu Thomson of Philadelphia, invented a transformer of his own, which was taken up by New Britain, Connecticut, capitalists. The Thomson-Houston Co., like Westinghouse, not only made its own patented equipment but proceeded boldly to infringe Edison's patents in the incandescent-lighting field. It also dominated the sale of arc lights used in factories under patents held by Charles Brush. In time Thomson's company came under the control of a shoe salesman, Charles A. Coffin, who moved it to Lynn, Massachusetts.

Edison fought mightily to save his patents from continuing infringement by others, and eventually succeeded, but he also resented the time taken from his laboratory by litigations. Meanwhile, J. P. Morgan, watchdog for American investors in the Edison General Electric, began to distrust President Henry Villard's "brilliance" (perhaps because of Villard's failure in Northern Pacific). Morgan wanted a change, and in any event the time had come for mergers and cross-licensing of patents if the three big equipment companies were not to choke one another. So when the Thomson-Houston Co. refused to sell out, Morgan let the cards fall the other way: the Edison company was merged into Thomson-Houston. From this merger came, in 1892, the modern General Electric Co. While it was a blow to Edison's pride not to see his name in the final General Electric combination, he could hardly complain that J. P. Morgan or Charles Coffin had stolen his works. He had let them go voluntarily in order to free himself for other things.

G.E. became so heavily involved in the financing of public utilities (both street-railway and illuminating properties) that it almost went under in the depression of the nineties. To avoid bankruptcy it sold off many of its holdings, but soon found that in order to sell its equipment it had to take stock in other utility companies. Not wishing to operate forever as financier and investment banker, Charles Coffin brought Sidney Zollicoffer Mitchell to New York in 1905 to work out plans for the Electric Bond & Share Co. E.B. & S. was supposed to take G.E.'s utility "cats and dogs" off its hands and, after reviving them by good management, sell them at a profit to the public. Actually, E.B. & S. functioned more and more as a permanent holding company for utilities in widely separated areas. When, in 1924, G.E. divested itself completely of E.B. & S. by distributing it to its shareholders as a dividend, its market value was close to $117 million.

Electric Bond & Share was the prototype of many such holding companies, which though useful also became subject to much abuse. For the device lent itself to pyramiding and the milking of the underlying operating companies, as the public was to discover in 1932 when the billion-dollar empire built by Edison's old lieutenant, Samuel Insull, collapsed under the weight of its enormously inflated assets. Insull's failure (and others like it) led to the enforced divestment of many holding-company subsidiaries under New Deal legislation. Nevertheless, the holding company served its purpose: as Roger Babson said, "The utilities today owe more to Thomas A. Edison and Sidney Z. Mitchell than to any other men. . . . Mr. Mitchell provided means of financing Mr. Edison's inventions. One was the 'lock' and the other the 'key.' Either would have been helpless without the other."

The utilities brought not only light to the American city but a new form of transportation as well. Pioneered by Frank J. Sprague in Richmond, Virginia, in 1887 after he had quit Edison's employ, the trolley quickly endeared itself to millions who had merely endured the old shivering, oil-lighted horse cars. The trolley, like the central-power station, proved a spawning ground for new millionaires. The cynical Charles T. Yerkes ("It's the straphangers who pay the dividends") replaced the old horse-car lines of Chicago with 240 electrified miles and built the famous Loop through the city's heart. When Illinois politicians who had accepted some $1 million in bribes from Yerkes finally turned on him, he unloaded his decrepit lines on his eastern friends for $20 million and went off to England, where he died nearly bankrupt after attempts to make a killing in the London tubes.

Peter Widener and William Elkins, Philadelphians who had loaned Yerkes the money to get his start in Chicago, were as adept as their western protégé in getting franchises from ring-dominated city governments, but they did not practice skulduggery at the expense of the customer. An investor type of promoter, Widener built traction lines to last, contributed to the organization of U.S. Steel and American Tobacco, and earned the money that was ultimately to build the Widener Library at Harvard University. His

partner Elkins pioneered in introducing refrigeration into the produce business, controlled the refineries in Philadelphia where the
first gasoline was made, and as a real-estate man built thousands of
homes for potential straphangers as he and Widener extended their
trolley lines to the suburbs. In New York City, Widener and Elkins
were associated with William C. Whitney and Thomas Fortune
Ryan in operating the lucrative Broadway franchise, which became
the backbone of the Metropolitan Traction Co. in 1886.

Despite bankruptcies the trolleys (and the subways) made it
possible for the new millions of urbanized America to work in
great office buildings where Otis and Westinghouse elevators took
over the transport problem. They also made it possible for housewives to shop with ease at Frank W. Woolworth's spreading five-
and-ten-cent stores, or George L. Hartford's Great Atlantic &
Pacific Tea Co., or the big department stores such as Marshall
Field in Chicago, R. H. Macy in New York, Gimbel Brothers and
Wanamaker in New York and Philadelphia. When the trolleys
eventually went out of business, it was not because of financial high
jinks but because of the automobile, which was shortly to clog
downtown streets to such an extent that big chain stores have had
to expand to suburban shopping centers. Indeed, during the long
half-century of the trolley's reign, the big city reached its most effective point as a rational business unit.

While other people were busy making money out of trolleys and
all the industries that had grown out of the old Edison Illuminating
Co. (which later became Consolidated Edison), the inventor himself was off on new tangents. One was a new giant magnetic ore separator with which he hoped to revive the iron-mining industry in
New Jersey's northern mountains. Fortunately for both his bank
account and his peace of mind, he had two other inventions to fall
back on when open pit ore mining at the Mesabi in Minnesota made
his giant separator uneconomic. His phonograph, which attracted
little attention as a dictating machine, finally made its way as a
source of pleasure. After a ten-year lapse of interest, Edison perfected the tone of the instrument and introduced the diamond
needle. Over the years he made millions from his phonograph and
record sales despite competition from Victor Talking Machine—
"His Master's Voice."

The other invention that beguiled Edison after his retirement from active electrical manufacturing was his motion-picture camera, the kinetograph that took its succession of pictures on the long-strip celluloid George Eastman in Rochester had already developed for his Kodak. Edison designed a sprocket with teeth that could control the pace of the unwinding succession of photographed images, and tried without initial success to synchronize the film with sound effects from a phonograph. Placed in a cabinet with a peep-hole at the top, the visual mechanism became known as the kineto-scope, and was first used on Broadway in April of 1894 (the first day's business grossed $120). Soon the penny arcade, with rows of kinetoscopes, was an established feature on Broadway. When Thomas Armat, a Washington, D.C., camera amateur, made an improved projection machine called the Vitascope available to Edison, the way was opened for the premier showing of a "motion picture" at Koster and Bial's Music Hall in New York in 1896.

The first U.S. "theater" devoted to motion pictures alone was started, prophetically enough, in Los Angeles. But the first "continuous showing" (pictures from morning to midnight) came in an abandoned store in McKeesport, Pennsylvania. Within five years a host of nickelodeons—or nickelets—had sprung up all over the U.S. A Chicago furrier, Adolph Zukor, quit his fur business to team up with Marcus Loew in operating several theaters. Edison formed the Motion Picture Patents Co. in 1908, with a film-selling subsidiary, General Film, and allied himself with other companies such as Biograph and Vitagraph. But the so-called Edison picture "trust" never proved very formidable. Working with competing patents from Europe, and with films made with bootlegged Edison equipment, "independents" kept invading the field. The nickelets, with their tin-pan piano accompaniments, were succeeded by bigger theaters and by longer pictures climaxed by the success of David Wark Griffith's production of *Birth of a Nation* in 1914. By the middle 1920's producers like Goldwyn and De Mille were commonly spending $1 million on a single film for the big distributing chains such as Paramount. And in the late twenties and early thirties, Edison's old idea of adding sound to pictures suddenly became commercially practicable when A.T. & T. developed methods of synchronizing sound and sight tracking.

The development of radiobroadcasting and modern television owes an indirect debt to Edison's constant tinkering. Back in the early eighties the inventor noticed the leakage of current across a gap in his vacuum tube, and following this lead he developed the "Edison effect" lamp, a device that made use of the mysterious impulses (not yet called electronic) to rectify voltages. Thus he unwittingly became "the father of modern electronics." The Edison-effect lamp was studied in London by Sir John Ambrose Fleming in experiments that resulted in the so-called "Fleming valve," which the Italian inventor Guglielmo Marconi was eventually to use as a radio-wave detector. Though it was not perfectly understood for a long time, the new science of electronics set other investigators to work. In America, Lee De Forest turned the Edison effect and Fleming's valve to good advantage in making his audion tube, which was to bring commercial radio within reach. Taking off from the work of his predecessors, Irving Langmuir of General Electric perfected a high-vacuum tube that greatly improved the whole business of transmission and made good long-distance broadcasting possible. And, to cap the dazzling succession of electronic inventions, Major Edwin Howard Armstrong designed his amplifying regenerative circuit, which did away with earphones and so made household reception easy and pleasant.

The early electronics business, like electrical manufacturing, was beset by the incessant quarrels of litigious inventors. Order was eventually brought out of chaos by the old method of mergers and by the formation of patent pools to permit cross-licensing of necessary devices. Oddly, the U.S. government itself took the lead in promoting a radio trust, thinking that a big all-inclusive company was desirable to keep the British-owned Marconi system from getting control of the American airwaves. Called the Radio Corporation of America, it was set up in 1919 by Owen D. Young of the General Electric Co. and was cross-licensed to use patents held by G.E., by A.T. & T., and, at a later date, by Westinghouse Electric.

Radiobroadcasting was actually first undertaken by KDKA in Pittsburgh, a station that grew out of the after-hour "radio ham" avocations of Westinghouse Electric's Dr. Frank Conrad. In his private laboratory over a garage, Conrad had set up a wireless to get Arlington time signals from Washington. To amuse himself and to satisfy his humanitarian impulses, Conrad had started playing phonograph records over his radio to cheer sick radio amateurs in hospitals. When a Pittsburgh store started selling crudely made receivers to pick up the programs, Conrad proposed that Westinghouse go into the business of manufacturing receiving sets. Westinghouse thought well of the idea—and, to make a market for its product, it set up a broadcasting system, later called KDKA, which became famous by broadcasting the Harding-Cox election returns in 1920.

This success of KDKA whetted the appetite of the giants. In 1922, big A.T.&T. beamed the first sponsored broadcast from its own station WEAF in New York. Four years later it sold its stations and made available its studio-to-station telephone lines to the R.C.A. group, whose general manager, David Sarnoff, formed the National Broadcasting Co. to operate the network. When R.C.A. bought Victor Talking Machine, which made a high-grade combination radio-phonograph, it looked like the permanent monopolist of the U.S. radio industry. This development was checked, however, when William S. Paley, a Philadelphia cigar maker, financed the Columbia Broadcasting System, Inc. Soon other companies came into existence in the radio field. Sets were made by Zenith, Philco, and others—and, with the Federal Communications Commission parceling out wave lengths, small regional broadcasting networks began to share the air as affiliates of the bigger systems. In the forties television broadcasting was added to radio, but without any drastic realignment among the companies that had grown out of the seed planted by Edison on the day he noticed the puzzling "Edison effect."

The total effect of Thomas A. Edison, of course, went far beyond these new communication media. For modern electronics, the junior offshoot of electricity, has made possible such things as frequency modulation and the transistor; the great computers manufactured by Remington Rand and I.B.M.; and all sorts of control devices that affect the modern home and factory and have projected man into the age of space. Edison himself was not to see these wonders, and the millions he made in his later years through a family company, Thomas A. Edison, Inc., came chiefly from his phonograph and dictating-machine manufacture and his movie patents. His last fling came in the field of botanical cross-breeding when, with financing from Ford Motor and Firestone Tire & Rubber, he conducted thousands of experiments with the guayule plant and with honeysuckle, milkweed, and goldenrod in an attempt to develop a home-grown substitute for rubber from the East Indies. The development of cheap synthetic rubber from coal and oil derivatives rendered all these botanic experimentations commercially useless. But this in no way dimmed the homage that was paid to Edison as the folk hero of electricity when he died in 1931, two years after the fiftieth anniversary of his invention of the light bulb.

So pervasive is the force that was unleashed by Faraday and then applied by Edison that it is virtually impossible to imagine what the world would be like today without it. For a time it even looked as though electricity was to be the agency that would put the U.S. on automobile wheels. The first taxicabs in America were electrically propelled and small electric runabouts were popular in the early years of the century. When Thomas Edison turned his attention to experiments designed to perfect a good rechargeable long-life storage battery, it was with the idea of making a cheap electric runabout good for long-distance travel. But Edison was beaten out in this particular phase of his activity by his good friend Henry Ford, who came up with a better means of cheap transportation. It was Ford, using the gasoline-driven internal-combustion engine, who completed the job of taking the U.S. out of the age of steam, and gave the next decisive turn to American business.

11 F. O. B. Detroit

Durant's folly—the dream of 500,000 cars.

Duryea's "buggyaut" and the Merry Oldsmobile.

Ford's Model T rolls and reigns supreme for eighteen years.

The Chevy and Chrysler's Plymouth move up.

An enduring export: mass production.

THE destined founder of General Motors, William Crapo Durant, for whom the phrase "live wire" seems specifically to have been invented, was approaching forty when the twentieth century opened. The grandson of a lumber tycoon who had been the Civil War governor of Michigan, Billy Durant made his first million dollars in the carriage business in Flint. Thoroughly bored with the success of his Durant-Dort Carriage Co., he went off to New York to study the stock market, but a hurry call brought him racing back in 1904 to save his home town from a threatened business catastrophe. The automobile company started by David Dunbar Buick, a plumbing-supply man, was on the rocks—and Durant, as the wealthiest man in Flint, was asked to take it over.

Billy Durant knew nothing about automobiles. But he had been making a study of the trust movement, and he had big ideas: he wanted to become a Napoleon in some line of work. Getting himself one of the fifty-three Buicks that had been made in two years of the company's existence, he took off through the sand and mud of Michigan's cutover forest region to assure himself that he had a salable product. The Buick was probably no better and no worse than cars that were already being made in Detroit by Henry Ford,

202

or in the state capital of Lansing by Ransom Eli Olds, or by the precursors of the Willys-Overland company in Indianapolis, or by Alexander Winton in Cleveland, or by Thomas B. Jeffery in Kenosha, Wisconsin, who had already made money from the Rambler bicycle. It was the standing vaudeville joke of the times that for every hour devoted to coaxing speed from a primitive carburetor over bone-rattling roads at least two hours must be spent flat on one's back underneath the machine. The vaudevillians couldn't decide whether "get out and get under" or "get a horse" represented the utmost in derision as rubes seated on roadside fence rails tossed their taunts at the city slickers who had begun invading the countryside in their snorting devil wagons.

But Durant, an incorrigible optimist, was oblivious to irony. He decided that the Buick, which boasted a valve-in-head engine, was good enough to support his ambitions, and he poured enough money into the staggering company to buy personal control of it. Within two years he had raised Buick production from the sixteen or twenty-eight cars of 1904 (the accounts of the year differ) to the 2,295 of 1906. And he really began to make the Buick into a superior car. In a day when most automobiles were afflicted with broken rear axles with monotonous regularity because nobody in the Middle West understood automobile axle making, Durant enticed Charles Stewart Mott's Weston-Mott Axle Company to move to Flint from Utica, New York.

Mott, who in later years became the largest individual stockholder in General Motors, really knew how to make strong axles—and with Mott parts the Buick soon became known as the car that was superior to jarring bumps. In another shrewd move Durant made a deal with Albert Champion, the French racing driver, to manufacture his new AC porcelain spark plug for Buick. Meanwhile the capitalization of Buick had been increased from $75,000 to $1,500,000 by Durant's daring stock salesmanship, with Flint citizens subscribing half a million in a single day. The town of course boomed: to house the influx of Buick workers, Flint roominghouse proprietors began renting their beds in two shifts as the population proceeded to double in five years.

Intoxicated with his success, Billy Durant moved ahead in 1908 with his idea of creating an automobile trust. Lacking sufficient resources to buy out Henry Ford or Ransom Olds, each of whom asked for $3 million in cash, he journeyed east with Benjamin Briscoe of the Maxwell-Briscoe Co., and announced himself at J. P. Morgan & Co. with a boast that the time would come "when half a million automobiles a year will be running on the roads of this country." Curiously, this raised the hackles of Morgan partner George W. Perkins, the apostle of the "good trust" who was soon to bankroll Teddy Roosevelt's Progressive Party. Perkins promptly left the room. "If that fellow has any sense," he said, "he'll keep those observations to himself." But Perkins was wrong and Billy Durant was right in his analysis of the future of America. Unable to raise capital in Wall Street, the irrepressible Billy went back home and put together the combination of General Motors anyway, mostly by exchanges of stock.

G.M., which in 1960 boasted sales of over $12 billion, wasn't much in 1908 when its total capital amounted to only $2,000. Shortly, however, it swallowed up the Oldsmobile, the Oakland (now the Pontiac), and the Cadillac companies in addition to Durant's own Buick. (It also swallowed a lot of cats and dogs whose names are now forgotten.) Eventually it added Chevrolet to its empire—and with the relatively low-priced Chevy it finally outstripped Henry Ford. To harmonize its bulky components G.M. was forced to experiment with new managerial techniques in the realm of manufacturing. It was not the progenitor of "bigness" as such—that accolade, as we have seen, goes to Standard Oil and the Carnegie Steel Co. But in its ability to reconcile decentralized diversity of product (it was also to go into electric refrigerators and diesel engines in a later phase) with management control from the top, and to combine manufacturing skills with a scientific approach to marketing, G.M. set a new style and tone in American enterprise. By the late twenties it had begun to symbolize the automobile and automotive age itself.

The history of U.S. business from the turn of the century through the twenties cannot, of course, simply be tagged f.o.b. Detroit. The U.S. had its heavy industries well before the coming of the car, and Edison's breakthroughs in electricity were bound to transform American life in any case. Nevertheless, the automobile ballooned payrolls in steel, rubber, flat glass, and aluminum and helped turn places like Akron, Ohio, from small towns into burgeoning industrial cities. The car changed the whole pattern of the real-estate market, sparked new methods of consumer finance, obliterated old landmarks, and created new ones. World War I gave a powerful push forward to production, but in the unfolding drama of the century's economic development it at first appears as a kind of episode that is not nearly as important as the advent of the car. The war's effects were not to be fully apparent until the crash of 1929 and the coming of the Great Depression, when American business—by then committed to Detroit's mass-production methods—came up against new social and political challenges.

These developments lay some distance ahead when in 1908 Billy Durant was cold-shouldered by the House of Morgan because of Perkins' distrust of the automobile's potential and also because the Morgan "attorney general," Francis Stetson, didn't like the fact that Durant had been buying up Buick shares without telling his stockholders that a merger was contemplated. Durant, of course, had not presided at the birth of the automobile itself. Credit for making the first U.S. gasoline-driven car has generally been accorded to the Duryea brothers, Charles E. and J. Frank, of Springfield, Massachusetts, whose "buggyaut" made its first public street run in September of 1893. The second American car was made in 1894 by Elwood Haynes of Kokomo, Indiana. In his book *My Life and Work,* written with Samuel Crowther, Henry Ford challenges these claims by saying that his first successful car was rolled out of a brick shed in back of his home on Bagley Avenue, Detroit, in the spring of 1893; but historians, who have had access to Ford family papers and company records, are certain that Ford's initial breakthrough actually came some three years later. The first Detroit-made car was undoubtedly that of Charles Brady King, who beat Ford to the Detroit streets by some ninety days in 1896. King, incidentally, was one of Ford's early advisers and helpers. Actually, the whole argument about the "first" American car is a bit academic, for Europe led the way in making the automobile. In 1885, Gottlieb Daimler of Germany, adapting the principles of the Otto gas engine, designed a light-weight internal-combustion engine driven by gasoline fuel on which the modern automobile was to depend. And another German, Carl Benz, developed his car neck and neck with Daimler. Early European car-makers included the French firm of Panhard and Levassor, who took over German patents in France. French cars in particular were initially popular with the rich of Newport, and their import helped domesticate words like "chauffeur" and "garage," "tonneau" and "automobile" itself in the American language.

The reputedly idle rich, led by Willy K. Vanderbilt, also financed automobile racing, which led to improvements in engine compression and the durability of tires, and they helped organize the first U.S. automobile show at Madison Square Garden in 1900. Other things besides a rising "moneyed" and middle class were favorable as the century opened. The gasoline engine was to prove a compact and efficient power plant, which soon dominated the field despite the early vogue of electrically propelled vehicles and the formidable Stanley and White and Winton "steamers." Gasoline itself, for years an unused by-product of kerosene, became cheap and plentiful. Carriage-makers like Studebaker and the Fisher brothers and Billy Durant's own Durant-Dort of Flint readily reapplied their skills in the new horseless age. Perhaps most important, America was blessed with an inspired generation of mechanics who had put some 12 million bicycles on the road between 1880 and 1900. It was, in fact, two of these bicycle mechanics, Orville and Wilbur Wright, who showed the world in 1903 that a gasoline engine could lift a "flying machine" into the air. Taking off on December 17 at Kitty Hawk on the dunes of the North Carolina coast, with Orville Wright at the controls, the pioneer Wright machine actually flew under its own power for twelve seconds. Later in the day Wilbur Wright flew for almost a second longer; and before the day was done the plane managed to stay aloft on a fourth flight for fifty-nine seconds under Wilbur's control before careening to the ground and breaking the front rudder. These flights went virtually unreported at the time (only three papers in the United States deigned to mention them the next morning, and the Wright brothers' own home-town paper in Dayton, Ohio, the *Journal,* refused to give the story any space at all). Nevertheless, the power of the internal combustion engine had been demonstrated under the most exacting conditions.

But if the times were propitious for technological change in transportation, there remained the disconcerting fact that the U.S., even well into the 1900–10 decade, consisted of two civilizations, each of which seemed permanently walled off from the other. The towns were railroad-connected, but the American highway system had undergone a marked retrogression since the days of the first toll roads. Everywhere in eastern and middle America the country roads were impossible quagmires in early spring; in summer there were dust and deep ruts to contend with; in winter ice and snow frustrated the smooth tires of the time. Rich townsfolk, hankering for the nostalgic pleasures of the countryside, might dare these inconveniences first on bicycles and then in the early cars, equipping themselves with goggles and dusters for Sunday afternoon jaunts or for longer AAA-sponsored "Glidden tours" into the wilds of New Hampshire or Maine. Farmers, who couldn't afford the first cars anyway, were not disposed to vote a nickel for surfaced roads to help the pioneering Detroit and New England automobile "crack-pots." (The first rural mile of concrete pavement in the United States was not destined to be laid down until 1908, by the Road Commission of Wayne County, Michigan.) Yet paradoxically it was rural America that needed cars far' more than the city slickers who bought the first models.

The difficulties of bridging rural and urban America are well illustrated by the early career of Ransom Eli Olds, who, without disparagement to Henry Ford, was the first man to try to give the farmer what he needed. A machinist who had built a three-wheeled, steam-driven road vehicle as early as 1893, "Ranny" Olds had persuaded a Michigan copper-and-lumber millionaire, Samuel L. Smith, to finance the Olds Motor Works in Detroit in 1899. (Of $200,000 in paid-in capital, Olds himself contributed $400 and Smith the remainder.) Smith looked to make most of his money from marine engines, but Olds had it in mind to produce a one-cylinder buggy to retail for less than $700. Just as he was ready to begin its manufacture, the Olds factory in Detroit burned down; but the single completed model of the "curved dash" runabout— the "Merry Oldsmobile" of the popular song—was saved from the flames by a brave timekeeper. Without factory resources at his command, Olds proceeded to farm out the manufacture of his engines and parts to various firms in Detroit (the Dodge brothers, Horace and John, and Henry Leland of later Cadillac fame were among

Courtesy Detroit Public Library, Automotive History Collection

Ransom E. Olds

his first parts-makers). Moving his general assembly operations back to his home town of Lansing, Olds put together 600 of the "curved dash" economy models in 1901, 2,500 in 1902, 4,000 in 1903, and 5,000 in 1904.

This, if not mass production, was at least quantity production. But the farmer, as it turned out, could not make any particular use of the cheap curved-dash Oldsmobile because of its buggy-type construction which was not sturdy enough for rural ruts. In a race to get his car to New York in 1901 in time for the automobile show, an Olds driver, twenty-one-year-old Roy D. Chapin (later the boss of Hudson and a Cabinet officer under Hoover), had to leave the jolting, muddy highways of interior New York and take to the relatively smooth towpath of the Erie Canal, where he was held up by the mules. He managed to reach the door of the Waldorf-Astoria in seven and one-half days, so dirty and disheveled that he was shunted by a suspicious doorman to the service entrance. Not liking the long-term prospects of a car that had to seek out canal towpaths, copper man Smith insisted that Olds return to heavier and more expensive makes. Because of their basic disagreement, Olds departed from the company—which, however, would carry his fame through the years in the name of a G.M. division. He also gave his initials to the Reo Company, which in later years limited itself to the manufacture of trucks.

Other tinkerers backed by shoestring financiers were rapidly to appear and disappear on the American scene. The automobile graveyard is dotted with the names of hundreds of cars—Altham, Ajax, Crestmobile, Grant-Ferris, Lear, Mohawk, Niagara, Regas, Waterloo, Wolverine, Yale, Zentmobile are a few early casualties— that were never much more than a gleam in a mechanic's eye. But Roy Chapin and Howard Earle Coffin, graduates of the original Olds company, got the Hudson Motor Co. going with the help of $60,000 provided by Detroit department-store owner J. L. Hudson. John North Willys, a bicycle salesman, took the $80,000 worth of debts that represented the Overland Co. of Indianapolis, shifted the company's production to Toledo—and was off winging on the basis of the trust which dealers and parts-makers were willing to repose in his new Willys-Overland model. The success of Willys, which led to the parallel success of the Electric Autolite Co., quickly turned Toledo from a sleepy town into a modern manufacturing community. The Studebakers of South Bend, Indiana, convinced that wagons were on the way out, made a few cars on their own and acted as sales agent for a shoestring company called E-M-F, which had made $1,600,000 on 8,312 automobiles during the first seventeen months of its existence. Emboldened by the earnings on their stock interest in the E-M-F, the Studebaker company soon took over its manufacture. Packard was started in Warren, Ohio, by a cable manufacturer and was subsequently moved to Detroit by Henry Joy, the son of a Michigan Central Railroad lawyer. With capital provided by Detroiters, Joy made $1,300,000 on 1,188 expensive Packards in the single depression year of 1907.

But it was the coming in 1908 of Henry Ford's cheap and sturdy Model T that made the car available to all classes and that finally broke down the barrier between urban and rural America. The Ford saga has been told many times and from many angles, with Henry Ford himself providing a neat, rational explanation for every major decision made by his company. That the reasons were, for the most part, *ex post facto,* as is claimed by Ford's man Charles Sorensen, hardly makes any difference, for Ford, until he grew old and cantankerous, was a brilliantly intuitive man. Like an inspired somnambulist, he felt his way to his goals without knocking over the tables and the crockery. As the son of a Dearborn, Michigan, farmer, he hated farm work, preferring to hang around the blacksmith shop. His self-assigned homework consisted of taking watches apart and putting them together again—and when he was a young runaway mechanic in Detroit he eked out his board money by repairing watches at night. Called back from his first sojourn in the big city to take up forty acres of woodland offered to him by his father, he supported himself and his bride by setting up a portable sawmill. The farming he saw around him depressed him as 90 per cent waste motion; as he said later, "the worst factory in Europe is hardly as bad as the average farm barn. . . . A farmer doing his chores will walk up and down a rickety ladder a dozen times. He will carry water for years instead of putting in a few lengths of pipe."

One of Ford's most frequently asserted latter-day explanations was that it had always been his "most constant ambition" to develop the tractor power that would save the farmer from himself; cars were a secondary consideration. In the late eighties he made himself a steam car that ran, hoping to pull his own plow with it, but was forced to discard it as unsafe. He also built himself a miniature four-cycle gas engine, which he gave away. Moving to Detroit a second time to take a job as engineer and machinist for the Edison Illuminating Co., he angered his electricity-minded employer by continuing to experiment with gas engines. Though he won some fame as a racer with his own model, beating Alexander Winton at the Blue Ribbon Race Track in Grosse Pointe in 1901, he was still a seedy business failure at forty. A lumber dealer, William H. Murphy, had backed him successively in the Detroit Automobile Co. in

1899 and in the Henry Ford Automobile Co. in 1901. But when both companies failed to produce, Murphy broke with Ford and turned to Henry M. Leland, a veteran precision-tool-maker and apostle of interchangeable parts who had worked as a young man in the Colt gun factory in Connecticut and in the Brown & Sharpe Manufacturing Co. in Providence, Rhode Island. Leland and Murphy promptly changed the name of the first Henry Ford company to the Cadillac Automobile Co.

The day was saved for the disgruntled Ford when Barney Oldfield, a professional bicycle racer, won a second race from Alexander Winton at the tiller of a specially built Ford "999," which developed 80 h.p. Seated at the race track that day was Alexander Y. Malcomson, a Detroit coal dealer, who decided that he might well overlook the business failures of a man who could design so powerful a car. Malcomson brought others with him into the venture of giving Ford in 1903 a third shot at the manufacturing business: John S. Gray, a candy manufacturer and local bank president, took 105 shares and put in $10,500 in immediate cash; James Couzens, Malcomson's Canadian-born bookkeeper, added a borrowed $1,500 to his $900 savings for twenty-four shares; Couzens' schoolteacher sister Rosetta put in $100 for one share; two Malcomson-coal-company lawyers, John W. Anderson and Horace Rackham, invested $5,000 each; Albert Strelow, a carpenter, took fifty shares valued at $5,000 for providing the new company with the use of a one-story building; and the Dodge brothers, Horace and John, each got fifty shares for quitting Ransom Olds and devoting their parts-supply business to Ford. As for Malcomson and Ford, they assigned themselves 225 shares each.

This is the way automobile companies were capitalized when they and the century were young. With his capital in hand, Ford began feeling his way to producing a really cheap and durable car. One thing that helped him along was a chance occurrence in 1905 when he witnessed the smashup of a French car at the Palm Beach race track. Noticing a shiny piece of valve-strip stem lying near the wreck, Ford picked it up. It seemed both light and strong—and, when analyzed, it proved to be vanadium alloy steel, which had not yet been made in America. This gave Ford his cue. Finding a company in Canton, Ohio, that was willing to make the unfamiliar alloy, Ford had the basic material for critical stress parts that he needed for the lightweight Model T. During the 1908–09 season the Ford company continued to produce other models. But the Model T, as Ford himself put it, soon "swept them all out." Originally priced at $825 for the roadster and $850 for the touring car, it began an astonishing eighteen-year career with prices on some models eventually lowered to as little as $260. Production increased throughout World War I, even in the years after America's entry when Ford turned to the output of Eagle Boat subchasers and other war material. Late in 1918, Bernard Baruch, then head of the War Industries Board, threatened to cut Ford and other automobile makers off from their supply of automobile steel. But the war was over before the threat materialized and the Model T rolled on to make Ford a billionaire.

While the key to Ford's success was his ability to ferret out the mass market, other things also contributed. At the very beginning he and Couzens decided not to pay royalties on the famous Selden patent under which U.S. internal-combustion car engines were originally made—a decision upheld after a long court fight. For the rest Ford, never himself much more than a cut-and-try mechanic, borrowed heavily from others. The principles of mass production for which Ford has been given so much credit were well known before the Model T got started. The Pope Manufacturing Co. of Hartford had organized the production of bicycles and electric cars by assigning individuals to single repetitive tasks; Henry Leland of Cadillac had pioneered in the matter of interchangeable parts; and Olds and Durant were both ahead of Ford in making lavish use of suppliers. It was Walter E. Flanders, a hard-living, hard-drinking genius, who started Ford on the way to the modern assembly line by rearranging the machines at the Piquette Avenue plant in 1908. The moving production line, which was introduced at the Highland Park factory in 1913–14, and which was later carried to incredible pitches of assembly and subassembly refinement, was the work of many men including C. W. Avery, William Klann, Carl Emde, Charles E. Sorensen, and William Knudsen. Ford design, always more utilitarian than aesthetic, owed as much to the metallurgist C. Harold Wills as to Ford himself. In economic matters Ford's decision to raise the minimum wage to $5 per day has been attributed (with no direct denial by Ford himself) to his partner Couzens, who had become appalled by the inefficiencies created by labor turnover. Reporters who interviewed Ford soon after the event, however, have insisted that Couzens' suggestion of a $5 wage was meant ironically, and that Ford deserves credit for taking it up.

Despite the quarrels over "firsts," it was Henry Ford who fused all the basic mass production ideas together. In the end he not only outstripped all competitors but also acquired the means to buy out every last one of his financial partners. Strelow, the carpenter, and Malcomson both sold out early. Couzens left the company in 1915, not because of any business-policy discord but simply because he couldn't abide Ford's pacifistic attitude toward the war in Europe. When Ford eventually arranged to take over Couzens' stock in 1919, he paid $40 million for it (and Couzens had already had $11 million in dividends on his early investment of a very few thousand). Couzens' sister Rosetta, who sold out at the same time, collected $265,000 on her original $100, which had already brought her $90,000 in dividends. The estate of candy-maker Gray got $26 million on the original $10,500. As for Horace and John Dodge, who had precipitated Ford's decision to get rid of his minority stockholders by suing him for a distribution of earnings and by enjoining him from going ahead with the decision to build the big steelworks at the River Rouge in Dearborn, they departed with $12,500,000 each. They had already had more than $17 million each in dividends, much of which they had put to work in their own Dodge Motor Co., whose sturdy cars provided some competition for the Model T even though they were in a higher price range.

The financial strain on Ford that had been caused by buying his partners' stock and by building the huge plant at the Rouge was compounded by the 1920–21 postwar depression, but the Ford Motor Co. survived without giving hostages to the bankers, whom Ford always detested. Ford squeaked through by going full steam ahead with his factory runs and shipping huge numbers of cars— for cash—to his dealers, whose local credit was sufficient to carry them through the short depression period. The dealers groused about being badly used, but they had made such a good thing out of the Ford franchise for twelve golden years that virtually none of them cared to risk losing favor with the Dearborn autocrat. And what they lost in 1920–21 they soon recovered in 1922–24, when the Model T sold better than ever. Indeed, in 1924 Ford production ran to 1,600,000 units, representing a 51 per cent "penetration" of the total U.S. car market.

This, however, was the high point of popularity for the famous "Tin Lizzie," and well before this the tide had subtly begun to change. The Model T was the farmer's friend because of its durability, and in a masculine world it reigned supreme. But by the twenties—and even before—the American housewife had become a powerful factor in car buying, demanding amenities that Ford was reluctant to offer. Among the amenities was a self-starter, which was ultimately to replace the hand crank on all cars. Ford remained impervious to the general upgrading in quality, but other manufacturers, notably General Motors, capitalized on the new trend and eventually upset Ford's hold on the family car market.

G.M. itself had its full share of early growing pains, partly because Durant, while bringing together Buick, Oldsmobile, and Cadillac, had also cumbered it with many an unprofitable division including a head-lamp company with a fraudulent patent. In 1910, two years after he put the combination together, Durant himself lost control of it to two investment banking companies, Lee, Higginson and Co. of Boston and J. and W. Seligman of New York, because of a Buick bank debt of $7,000,000.

The bankers' representative in G.M. was James J. Storrow, a man who happened to have an interest in technology. Storrow hired the consulting firm of Arthur D. Little, Inc., of Cambridge, Mass., to advise him—and the consulting company came up with the study that resulted in the General Motors Research Department, which was to pay off fabulously over the years. Though Storrow was charged with carrying out the bankers' extremely stiff financial terms, his reorganization of the company was sufficiently canny to justify even the most seemingly exorbitant of fees. He gave Charles W. Nash his head as president of the company and Nash in turn made Walter P. Chrysler—a railroad mechanic with mechanical and electrical engineering knowledge learned from the International Correspondence Schools—the boss of Buick. Most important in a time of shakedown and change, Storrow had the good sense to continue Henry Leland in power at Cadillac. More than that, he heeded Leland's general advice. It was Leland who argued down the bankers when they proposed to slough off most of the G.M. divisions and concentrate on saving Buick alone. Because of Leland's prestige, G.M.'s full divisional structure was maintained.

By then a white-bearded patriarch of impressive mien, Leland had a bad conscience because a good friend, Byron T. Carter of the Carter Car Co., had been killed in the attempt to crank a balky car for a lady. This constituted a blot on the entire automobile business, which Leland was resolved to wipe out. Accordingly, he gave Charles F. Kettering of Dayton, Ohio, a commission to come up with a practical electric self-starter. Kettering had designed small electric motors for cash registers when in the employ of the National Cash Register Co. of Dayton, and, using an old barn as headquarters, he had recently formed the Dayton Engineering Laboratories Co. When Kettering offered some blueprints of a small motor designed to replace the hand crank, the G.M. directors summoned experts from General Electric, Westinghouse, and the German electrical trust of Siemens and Halske to inspect them. Unanimously the experts informed the directors that Kettering's device wouldn't work. But Leland persisted in spending money on Kettering's experiments. When the first Delco self-starter sparked a Cadillac motor on February 27, 1911, Leland gave Kettering a contract for four thousand self-starters even though the Dayton Engineering Laboratories had no manufacturing facilities. "Ket," as was to be his habit, carried the assignment through, thus forming a tie with G.M. that was to prove more and more fruitful in all departments of engineering as the years went by.

But it was not just G.M.'s technical know-how that was to prove decisive for its success. During the years of World War I it acquired both the car and the strong financial backing that were to make it the leader of the industry. Once more the story turns on the queer and volatile character of Durant. Banished by the bankers from the management of G.M., Durant nevertheless held on to his stock, and, equally important, acquired the rights to manufacture a car designed by a French racing driver, Louis Chevrolet. Using the Chevrolet Motor Co. of Delaware as a holding company for various activities including the production of Chevrolet cars, Durant steadily increased his holdings of G.M. by exchanging Chevrolet shares for G.M. stock. Presently he scented some powerful competition coming out of Wilmington where the du Ponts, who had profited heavily in 1914 and 1915 by the sale of powder to the Allies, were putting some capital into G.M. In 1915, Pierre du Pont became chairman of G.M. and the rule of the bankers was brought to an end. But actual control of G.M. resided in Durant's Chevrolet Motor Co.—a clear case of tail wagging dog. In a further reorganization in 1918 a newly incorporated G.M. absorbed the manufacturing facilities of Chevrolet—and Durant was ready for a second whirl as an automotive Napoleon.

Fearful of any ride on a Durant rocket, Nash and Leland both chose to quit, the one going to the newly formed Nash Motor Co. of Kenosha (successor to the Jeffery Co. and parent of the modern American Motors Corp.), and the other to form the Lincoln Motor Co., which was later bought by Ford. But Durant, recognizing a good thing in Leland's friend Kettering and in a Leland protégé named Alfred P. Sloan of the Hyatt Roller Bearing Co., proceeded to absorb "Boss Ket's" Dayton Engineering Laboratories and Sloan's own Hyatt into General Motors. Along with Delco and Hyatt, Durant picked off the New Departure Manufacturing Co., maker of ball bearings, and arranged for the purchase of a controlling interest in the Fisher Body Co. of Detroit. He also picked up the Guardian Refrigerator Co., which was to make the Frigidaire. And in 1919 he started the General Motors Acceptance Corp., which was to play such a large role in the development of mass installment selling.

Thus, as the twenties opened, the outlines of a new kind of automobile company, possessed of a broad line of cars, and with its fingers in all kinds of subsidiary equipment, were plainly discernible. Durant himself was not to enjoy the pay-off. Sales of all G.M. cars slacked off in the recession of 1920–21 and G.M. stock plummeted. Durant sought to support the market into which he had enticed his friends by buying heavily on margin, but soon reached the end of his resources. Fearing that his bankruptcy would hurt G.M., Pierre du Pont and his lieutenant, John J. Raskob, committed the du Pont Co. late in 1920 to purchasing Durant's 2,500,000 shares. With previous acquisitions, this gave du Pont a 27 per cent interest in

G.M.—an interest it is now being forced to relinquish under recent antitrust decisions. Considered risky at the time, the investment netted the du Ponts millions. Durant himself was not so fortunate. In the twenties he produced a car called the Star, and formed other companies, but his touch had deserted him. Overtaken finally by bankruptcy in the thirties, he was never to get a third chance in the big auto combination that his optimism had put together. Significantly, when he died in 1947 at eighty-six, he was trying to stage a comeback as one of the earliest supermarket promoters. He was also running a chain of bowling alleys.

Meanwhile General Motors rode up with the twenties, with Pierre du Pont calling the financial shots and Alfred P. Sloan emerging as its new organizing genius. Borrowing the line-and-staff principle that Standard Oil had used so effectively, Sloan left operating decisions to division heads, but kept pricing, research, and investment policies highly centralized, with committee work replacing Durant's improvisations. Realizing that the U.S. had grown sufficiently prosperous to pay extra for style, G.M. followed Roy Chapin of Hudson in allowing for more and more closed models at a price that was not too far away from the basic price of an open car. With "Boss" Kettering as head of research, it developed in conjunction with du Pont chemists a quick-drying spray so that it could offer cars in optional colors to the consumer.

While giving more car for the dollar, G.M. also set its cap to conquer the lower price field. In 1922 the Danish immigrant William Knudsen, who had left Ford, was put in charge of Chevrolet production, bringing with him all the arts of mass assembly. His goal was "vun for vun"—i.e., one Chevrolet for one Ford—and before too long he actually overshot it. Clinging to the Model T, Ford, as noted, had his last great run in 1924. In 1925 and 1926 sales began to slip and in 1927 even Ford had to admit that the era of feminine amenities had caught up with him. It was no longer a matter of "any color you want just so long as it is black." In 1927 Ford's production ran to 450,000 cars including the fifteen-millionth Model T unit. But Chevrolet sold 800,000 passenger cars, achieving a "two for vun" lead. After a nine-month shutdown Ford was back in business in 1928 with the Model A, a successful concession to

Alfred P. Sloan, Jr.

the glamour advertisements that were now crowding the magazines. But by then G.M., seizing time by the forelock, had become the acknowledged leader of the automobile world.

As a leader, however, G.M. had to fight for its position. For the twenties, flamboyant in most things, presented the American consumer with an extraordinary range of cars made by several companies. While the newer Fords jockeyed for first place with the Chevrolets, both found themselves chased in turn by a new contender. Walter P. Chrysler had cut loose from G.M. shortly after Durant's second take-over. In 1925 he founded the Chrysler Corp. within the corporate shell of the old Maxwell organization, and achieved quick success with a new high-compression engine developed by the famous engineering team of Fred M. Zeder, Carl Breer, and Owen Skelton. A hard-driving man who had an able financial adviser in B. E. Hutchinson, Chrysler added the flossy De Soto line to his original high-powered Chrysler, and then developed the low-priced Plymouth. One of the Chrysler coups was to purchase the Dodge Motor Co. from the Wall Street firm of Dillon, Read, which had bought it from the widows of the Dodge brothers in 1925. Since Dodge made trucks as well as medium-price cars, this gave Chrysler a full across-the-board representation in the business of selling transportation. It also gave him the foundry facilities needed to make the Plymouth. In 1929, when U.S. production of cars soared to a then all-time record of 4,500,000 units, Chrysler produced about 450,000 cars, Ford 1,475,000 and G.M. 1,900,000— with the balance shared by eight independents.

It would be twenty years before automobile production would surpass the 1929 peak. Between the stock-market crash of that year (to which speculation in auto shares contributed) and 1948 lie the "locust years" of the Great Depression, the upheavals of World War II, and some crucial economic history. But while subject to interruption, the automobile revolution, like the electrical revolution, could not be stopped. In a scant quarter century the mechanics of Dearborn and Detroit, Flint and Lansing, turned the car from a high-priced luxury into an everyday necessity, and the U.S. has never been the same since.

Oddly, though automobile production has become increasingly concentrated, with G.M. and Ford regularly taking 80 per cent of the market, it has actually worked in a profound sense to save America for the little man. Not for nothing has Christy Borth called the automobile the "power-plant and transportation tool of a free people." The sixty million cars that are now traveling the American roads mean that no one is chained to any single way of life. And the great automotive "oligopoly" (meaning "few companies to sell") has even served to "de-oligopolize" other sectors of the economy that were once considered lost to monopoly. For example, the voracious demands of the automobile manufacturers for varieties of steel—162 separate kinds went into a single automobile throughout the nineteen fifties—have helped to decentralize the steel industry by making it possible for specialty companies to exist and grow. The automobile supports scores of tool-makers not only in the Detroit area but in Rockford, Illinois, and in Cincinnati, Ohio. Almost every car has its radio, an immense boon to the electronics manufacturers. And even though the big auto companies like to own their own parts supply divisions, independent parts suppliers still account for hundreds of the separate 15,000 bits and pieces that go to make up a modern automobile.

For better or worse, the whole American landscape has been changed by the car, and not merely because of the popularity of outdoor advertising. One out of every six or seven Americans employed depends on the automobile or its passengers, and most of these people perforce have to be situated by the great American road. The motel business has had a phenomenal growth; so have moving picture drive-ins; so, despite the motels, has the resort hotel business. The growth of suburbia, made possible by the car, created the typical figure of George F. Babbitt, the gregarious and wistfully appealing "realtor" of Sinclair Lewis' Zenith. At a recent count more than half a million gasoline service stations lined the American highways or the street corners in American suburbs and towns. Because of the car-enforced development of the suburban shopping center, Sears, Roebuck, which once depended on selling by the mail order catalogue, has had to build itself anew around the big regional store specializing in appliances, hardware, paint, and tires.

The low-priced car and truck, which brought the farmer much closer to his customers and enabled him to market his foods while still fresh, combined with the electric refrigerator and Albert D. Lasker's pioneering advertising of the vitamins in such things as orange juice to change the American diet. But the car also has had a pervasive effect on the whole balance of the agricultural economy merely because it collaborated with the tractor to displace the horse. Because of the internal combustion engine, some eighteen million horses and mules have vanished along with stalls and stables —and the fifty million acres that were once required to feed them have become available to feed people. What with the increased effectiveness of modern agriculture, however, with its combination of chemical fertilizers and soil-replenishing legumes, the fifty million acres have contributed hugely to the agricultural surplus. The benefits deriving from the internal combustion engine, which might have released farmers to do other things, have been largely aborted by a social policy which has substituted government-financed storage bins for the stomachs of horses and mules. The internal combustion engine, however, stands as comforting insurance against famine if the population explosion ever makes it really necessary to feed humans from acres once devoted to sustaining the horse.

The automobile, in decentralizing the economy, has also had its paradoxical side effects in concentrating several other big industries, which is only to say that big and little enterprises grow together. Without Ford and General Motors there would be no Goodyear or Firestone as we know them today. The glass industry, originally a "blown in the bottle" handicraft, was revolutionized in the early twentieth century when Michael J. Owens perfected a machine that formed glass containers automatically. The demand of Detroit for windshields spurred on the process of mechanization and helped build Owens-Illinois, Libbey-Owens-Ford, and Pittsburgh Plate Glass into huge concerns. Automobile demand for aluminum has increased the size of the Mellons' Alcoa, now the leader of a Big Three in aluminum that includes Reynolds and Kaiser. The birth of the modern U.S. chemical industry dates from World War I, when this country was cut off from German dyestuffs, but its subsequent expansion depended to a ponderable extent on the requirements of the automobile age for paints, lacquers, synthetic rubber, and plastics.

World War I also opened up new international vistas to American banking and finance, but it is worth noting that almost from the first Detroit was as internationally minded as the bankers of Wall Street. Exports of U.S. cars rose from 50,000 in 1921 to some 400,000 in 1929. And automobile makers were among the first to understand the importance of overleaping tariff barriers by spreading their plants abroad, as G.M. did when it bought into the German firm of Opel, and as Ford did in England and Germany.

This internationalization of U.S. automotive investment is an interesting commentary on the ability of the human animal to get around his own man-made difficulties: *some* way around quotas and tariffs and currency conversion troubles must be found if the economic community of the West is to live. But the most important contribution of Detroit to the world goes far beyond the immediately tangible effects of G.M.'s and Ford's European market strategy. It lies in the philosophy of producing more for less. Exported as "Fordism" to Europe and other parts of the world, this philosophy has done more to bring closer the conquest of poverty than any other contemporary force or animating idea. The advent of mechanization can be painful, breaking up peasant economies and disrupting political institutions, but it is the only available instrumentality for changing underdeveloped countries into developed ones, and for the progressive enlargement of markets. Indeed, the European Common Market, so much in the headlines today, would be almost impossible to visualize had not mass production made its appeal to the French and German mind. From this point of view the expanding world of the fifties and the sixties is in a way a continuation of the twenties when Ford, G.M., and Chrysler raced up what seemed an open and continuous highway only to encounter the great roadblock which bore the historic label of "1929."

12 The New Frontier of the Depressed Thirties

Great expectations end in unprecedented world-wide deflation.

The New Deal restores "confidence" in just about everything except the profit system.

The "Big Three" of chemistry open up an astonishing world.

Optics, electronics, metal alloys, and the continuous-strip mill.

The aircraft industry sprouts its wartime wings.

ON the afternoon of October 24, 1929, Richard Whitney, brother of a Morgan partner, and himself acting president of the New York Stock Exchange, stalked to the U.S. Steel post and said bravely: "I bid 205 for 10,000." It was, as events proved, a wholly quixotic gesture. Five days later "Big Steel" closed at $174 for the day, and a general liquidation was on. The drop in stock values that began on Black Thursday was not to be halted even by a Morgan-Rockefeller consortium, and within a matter of weeks some $30 billion of paper value had gone up in smoke.

If 1929 had only marked a stock-market crash such as Wall Street had often experienced since brokers first gathered under the famous buttonwood tree in 1792, the history of the U.S. and the world might have been very different. After all, the destruction of paper values in tokens of ownership doesn't change a single machine tool, and paper values may come back. Black Thursday, however, was the prelude to a crisis of confidence in the whole business system that would persist in a virulent form until World War II began in 1939 and, indeed, still has ideological recurrences.

Plagued by the perplexing fact that the depression of 1929 failed to "bottom out" in a fairly short time as all previous U.S. depressions had done, commentators were temporarily at a loss for explanation. Soon, however, they came up with two theories to explain it all. The first theory was that 1929 was caused by wicked supporters of the "old order," bankers and businessmen who in their "Indian summer" were oblivious to the claims of common people. The second theory, first adumbrated by presidential candidate Franklin D. Roosevelt in his San Francisco Commonwealth Club speech of 1932 and later worked out in detail by American "Keynesians" such as Alvin Hansen, was that the American economy had become "mature" and could be kept going only by "controls" and a continual interjection of government funds, whether raised by taxes or conjured out of inflation.

Most writing about recent history is still shaped, consciously or otherwise, by a mixture of these two explanations, which have become a kind of orthodoxy. Yet at closer inspection neither theory will wash. We have already seen how the twenties rode to affluence with the rise of the automobile business. But there was much more to the twenties than motion on four wheels. The gains of the period, particularly during its first eight years, had been solid. Gross national product, that favorite yardstick of modern economists, rose from $72 billion in 1922 to $96 billion in 1928. Population increased, but per capita income jumped much faster, rising 30 per cent in the period. The 2,300,000 new families formed between 1921 and 1928 helped prodigiously to account for 3,500,000 new homes. Into the homes, new and old, went nine million new systems of electric wiring and six million new telephones. Savings deposits and life insurance doubled.

While the period has often been criticized for its "materiality," it also saw a flourishing of the arts not witnessed since the 1840's. Publishing itself became a bigger, if not a big, business and the spate of "little magazines" created new styles that were soon reflected in mass publications. True, the bellwether of the novelists, Sinclair Lewis, satirized the businessman unmercifully in *Babbitt*, signalizing an increasing distrust of the system by the intellectuals. But the derided "business civilization," which so troubled historian James Truslow Adams, was certainly not all careening automobiles and ambulatory drinking parties. As Russell Leffingwell, one of the derided bankers who were blamed for the crash, pointed out in a statement to the Pecora Committee in 1933, the twenties also had their courageous apostles of "a new and better world." Said Mr. Leffingwell: "Yet while we were living through the period it seemed that . . . our Federal Reserve System created in 1914 had put an end to banking panics which had periodically arrested every previous era of prosperity in modern history; that, possessed of a great continent with all the climates and all the natural resources, inhabited by an adventurous and hardy and industrious people; with the extraordinary development of communications, of telephone and telegraph and radio, of motorcars and of roads, electrical power, and all the manifold extensions of human activity; we had indeed entered upon a new phase in the life of the American people. . . . Our boast is that our effort during the whole postwar decade was constructively conceived toward the rehabilitation of America and the world after the war. . . . Were we after all wrong in our judgment that it would be possible to build . . . on the ruins left by the war? We think not."

If the twenties, which witnessed the emergence of the suburban way of life, were demonstrably something more than a period of prohibition-era looseness and wild stock gambling, the thirties, if revisited with open-eyed candor, offer even more startling surprises. What we recall, in this decade, is the impact of breadlines and bank failures followed by the cheerful tilt of Franklin D. Roosevelt's cigarette holder as our most sanguine of presidents presided over the explosion of the alphabet into such agencies as NRA, AAA, SEC, WPA, and TNEC. These made the headlines, and from such headlines the histories have been written. What the fog of conventional history tends to conceal is that the thirties were also a period in which vast new industrial enterprises were spawning, and in which businessmen, however much discouraged and restrained, placed their bets, sometimes small and sometimes enormous, on new and developing technologies.

Despite the popularity of the thesis that the building of America was finished, the decade of the thirties witnessed the coming of the streamlined and diesel-drawn train and the proliferation of the airlines with ever increasing payloads. It witnessed the building of huge Mult-au-matic turret lathes, the discovery of new cobalt and tungsten alloys, and the spread of the continuous wide-strip mill in the steel industry. The modern chemical industry surged forward, transforming the textile industry as synthetic fabrics continued to replace silk and cotton. Business houses and banks began to use electric calculating machines, punch-card filing systems, and other automated gadgets. The wooing of the customer continued as beer was "bottled" in tin cans and as George Gallup and Elmo Roper changed the art of pre-testing the market to an almost exact science. The pay-off of all this development came in 1941, when it was quickly discovered that our supposedly "mature" economy, far from "evenly rotating" in the manner of a textbook model, had been spinning off new things all along. Indeed, if it had not been for the industrial laboratories, the proving grounds, and the wind tunnels of the thirties, the U.S. might never have emerged victor in World War II.

It is this all-but-forgotten aspect of the so-called "gloomy decade" that constitutes the main line of business history and it is largely virgin territory. Compared to it, the crash of 1929 itself and its aftermath are well-trodden economic ground. Granted that an element of mystery will always surround what happened in 1929 and after, there are more reasonable explanations to be invoked for it than just a combination of "old order" folly and premature maturity. Part of the explanation lies deeply buried in World War I, which disrupted normal patterns of production in Europe, saddled the victors with monstrous debts and the defeated Germans with draining reparation payments, and broke down the serviceable gold-standard mechanism that had made international exchange of goods a progressively flourishing thing in the late nineteenth and early twentieth centuries. In the U.S. the war gave a vital stimulus to most phases of industry and helped expand a new middle class. But the war was also responsible for throwing American agriculture dangerously out of phase with the rest of the business system, piling up an enormous farm mortgage debt that could not be paid off out of subsequently declining wheat and cotton prices. Bernard Baruch as well as farm-bloc politicians like Senator Charles McNary of Oregon kept calling attention to the woeful state of the farmer, but few at the time listened. Neither were people much concerned by the fact that as early as 1925 the great postwar building boom had begun to peter out.

These developments suggest that the U.S. was due for a recession sometime during the late twenties even without the impact of stock-market panic. What masked the realities was a slow building up of speculative fever based on considerable monetary inflation. In view of huge gains in productivity many industrial prices should have fallen, thus easing the position of the farmer; instead they remained stable. As early as 1925, Secretary of Commerce Hoover was warning against the excesses of the Florida land boom, and had cautioned the authorities of the Federal Reserve System, created in 1914, against careless use of their new engine of money creation. These strictures went largely unheeded, partly as the result of events abroad. In 1925, Britain went back on the gold standard at the unrealistic prewar parity of $4.86 to the pound. As a result exports suffered, imports increased, and London found itself in great difficulties with its balance of payments. Accordingly, the Bank of England pleaded with Governor Benjamin Strong, head of the New York Federal Reserve Bank, to ease the situation by a money policy that would divert short-term funds from New York to London. And in the summer of 1927, partly to aid Britain, partly, too, to encourage lagging business at home, the Federal Reserve System took the momentous step of forcing a regime of easy money in the U.S. even though at the time it was actually losing gold.

Strong died in 1928, the victim of tuberculosis, and can scarcely be blamed for the full ravages of what Herbert Hoover has called the "Mississippi Bubble of 1927–29." But all evidence suggests that the heroic effort to shore up the international situation helped unleash the forces of domestic disorder. Between June, 1927, and September, 1929, brokers' loans in Wall Street rose from $3.5 billion to $8.5 billion, fed in part by the banks, and in much larger part as time went on by corporations seeking an outlet for their funds and by money from abroad. Stock prices soared from an index of 114 to 216. From Detroit the seven Fisher brothers carried the $300 million profit which they had derived from selling their factories to General Motors into Wall Street. Billy Durant, who had essayed a comeback with a new automobile company after the du Ponts had given him a good price for his G.M. stock, was already on the ground, ready to spark a bull consortium. From the West came Arthur Cutten, with his money from the wheat pit. These big-time operators, with others in their train, set off the first detonative phase of the big bull market. Soon the general public had caught the contagion, leaping to the chance of buying stocks on margins as low as 10 per cent. Though the number of shares listed on the New York Stock Market jumped from 221 million in 1920 to 757 million in 1929, the thirst for securities could not be slaked. Stocks were issued which represented little more than the pyramiding of paper values—the Blue Ridge Corp., Shenandoah Corp., Goldman Sachs Trading Corp., and many another glittering name. In vain government authorities tried to stem the tide. Though the Federal Reserve in 1929 raised its discount rate to 6 per cent, bankers like Chase's Albert H. Wiggin and National City's Charles E. Mitchell continued to make funds available for the hopelessly inflated securities, and in the last weeks of the madness brokers paid 20 per cent for borrowed funds.

Such a build-up could only have one end; indeed there had been plenty of informed prophetic warnings. In 1928 Kuhn, Loeb's Paul Warburg, one of the architects of the Federal Reserve System, spoke out against buying paper "accretions unrelated to . . . increases in plant." Bernard Baruch told his friends to get out while the getting was good, and Dwight Morrow, on leave from J. P. Morgan as U.S. Ambassador to Mexico, admonished an old Wall Street acquaintance that "you are on a gigantic spree, and unless you sober up promptly, you and the country are going to suffer painfully in 'the cold gray dawn of the morning after.' "

The chickens came home to roost quite as Warburg, Baruch, and Morrow had predicted. But the hangover, to shift the figure again, was no ordinary hangover. The crash in Wall Street proved to be much more than a wholly necessary correction of inflated values, and itself must be counted a partial cause of what proved to be a wholly unprecedented deflation. Between 1929 and mid-1932 wholesale prices fell some 35 per cent, production dropped from an index of 100 to 68, with output in the heavy industries falling much more than that, and unemployment rose from negligible proportions to some 11,500,000 in 1932 and a record 13 million in 1933.

Nothing like this had been seen before, and once more domestic and foreign influences reacted on each other. The real-estate debt situation lay like a dead weight over the construction industry as well as over the farmers, for throughout the twenties mortgages had been written without provision for periodic amortization of principal. Bank after bank rode into the thirties loaded up with tokens of debt that were almost completely frozen. As Secretary of the Treasury Andrew Mellon said to Hoover, "There is a mighty lot of real estate lying around the U.S. which does not know who owns it."

There were also unfortunately a lot of Peruvian and German bonds hanging around in U.S. bank vaults that soon were not worth owning by anybody. Throughout the twenties the U.S. had remained exclusively export- and tariff-minded, balancing its accounts abroad by huge injections of credit into Europe and Latin America. Even after the crash this flow of adrenalin was continued in a final burst of foreign lending. For the most part the money was poorly invested and served only to shore up but not strengthen Europe's shaky financial house. Britain remained in deep trouble, and conditions on the Continent were still worse. In May, 1931, the great Kreditanstalt of Vienna closed its doors— pushed over the brink, some said, by France's unwillingness to see Austria and Germany form a customs union. From Vienna the panic spread to Germany and so to a run on sterling. On September 21, 1931, Britain again abandoned the gold standard.

To parry this blow from Europe as well as to cope with growing unemployment at home, President Hoover in the White House, as is now pretty largely forgotten, used many of the governmental devices that a few years later were to be proclaimed as new and revolutionary. His Farm Board sought to prop up wheat prices; his Reconstruction Finance Corporation, set up in early 1932, strove to save weak banks; his Federal Reserve Board, under Governor Eugene Meyer, bought millions of "governments" in the open market. Less prudent in retrospect was the decision to raise taxes in 1932, though at the time it seemed the soul of discretion and necessary to maintain faith in the American dollar. In the event, the famous Hoover "corner" was nearly turned in the summer of 1932, European recovery set in, and almost all U.S. pundits agreed that the bottom had been reached. Came then another period of doubt and hesitation as battle was mounted for the national elections and rumors spread of currency devaluation. It proved one hesitation too much for the wobbly banking structure. In early 1933 the RFC was unable to bail out a key bank, the Union Guardian Trust Co. of Detroit, and its failure gave new impetus to the withdrawal of deposits from other banks. While Hoover and Roosevelt exchanged messages at cross-purposes the run became general. And on March 6, two days after the inauguration, and by executive order, the banking system of the richest nation of the world took a famous holiday.

The closing, however, proved momentary, and in the first hundred days of the New Deal there came a new wave of optimism. In many ways it seemed to be justified. President Roosevelt was magnificently right in seeing that confidence was the key to the situation, and his own courage and jaunty optimism—"there is nothing to fear but fear itself"—did much to break the mood of despair and national paralysis. But the baffling question, to which historians have paid all too little attention, is why business confidence was never fully restored, and why the great depression dragged on for six more painful years. In 1933, when F.D.R. gave his first fireside chat, there were some thirteen million unemployed in the U.S. As late as 1939 there were still nine million unemployed men and women, and on the record it was not Doctor New Deal but Doctor Win the War who, in Roosevelt's phrase, finally put the country back to work.

The explanation of this failure of the New Deal to accomplish its primary mission lies partly in Roosevelt's inability to decide for himself just what he was putting his confidence in. His far-reaching decision to follow Britain off gold was reflationary in purpose, but his subsequent failure to restore full redeemability of the currency, once the metal had been repriced, deprived the U.S. and the world of a needed monetary discipline. Many of his business reforms—notably his insistence on "truth in securities" and the setting up of the SEC—were long overdue; others were frankly punitive. With reason, businessmen came to ask themselves whether Roosevelt really understood a system where the hope of profit sparks expansion and investment. Or did he believe simply in centralizing decision and authority in boards and "planners" along the Potomac?

Courtesy his daughters, Mrs. Herberta J. Muth and Mrs. Walter S. Evans

"Mumbo Jumbo" cartoon by Herbert Johnson

The first important domestic creation of the New Deal, the NRA, was a total abnegation of the competitive market economy. A peacetime adaptation of Bernard Baruch's old War Industries Board of World War I days, the NRA appealed to some businessmen who preferred the cartel system of Europe to doing business competitively under the Sherman Act. Under General Hugh (Iron Pants) Johnson the new experiment made a tremendous noise. But with its price-fixing and market-allocating codes the NRA was a denial of the free system, and before it was thrown out by the Supreme Court its critics were referring to it as "Chamber of Commerce Fascism." Its inherent contradictions were later freely admitted by Administration intellectuals themselves when in Roosevelt's second term they set up the Temporary National Economic Committee to restore competitive pricing, while at the same time embracing the doctrine of Keynesian spending to restore purchasing power.

The difficulty with this new palliative was that its success depended uniquely on the restoration of profitability in the system. The Keynesians remembered that their master had argued against wage cuts; labor, he said, is seldom in a mood to take a cut-back. But he had certainly not called for money wage *increases* in a time of deflation when real wages were going up every time a retail price fell. To restore both profitability and purchasing power, the Keynesian formula called for a turn-about in prices through government spending as existing wage rates were maintained. Perversely, however, the American disciples of Keynes paid no heed to the role which profitability via rising prices pays in luring investment money from hiding. They overlooked the fact that money wage rates in manufacturing advanced some 43 per cent between 1933 and 1939 and *real* wages by an extraordinary 34 per cent, which, on Keynes's own theory, was detrimental to curing the surplus of labor. Some of this rise was no doubt to be expected in a period of partial recovery, but much of it flowed out of government-blessed wage boosts from an unprecedented surge of union organization. When NRA was buried, the provisions of its Section 7a were incorporated into the lopsided Wagner Act, which gave John L. Lewis, Walter Reuther, and others a free hunting license to push industrial unionism in the basic mass-production industries. In a free system labor has the incontestable right to organize and to bargain collectively; and it had exercised this right long before the New Deal. But the very rapidity of the spread of unionism in the thirties, beyond pushing up costs, was scarcely conducive to restoring business confidence. And the tactics of the sitdown strike, however effective in bringing companies like General Motors to heel, did nothing to encourage private investment in new industrial plant.

The pay-off story, indeed, is suggested by the figures for industrial profits and private investment—the key to industrial advance in a capitalist system. From their inflated peak of $8.3 billion in 1929, corporate profits after taxes plunged to minus $3.4 billion in 1932, recovered to $4.7 billion in 1937, and then collapsed again in 1938. Domestic investment followed the same pattern, falling from $16 billion in 1929 to a bare $900 million in 1932, rising to an $11.7-billion temporary peak in 1937, and then dropping back to $6.7 billion in the 1938 slide. Under such circumstances it is little wonder that the economy failed to pick up the huge pools of unemployed left by the crash and open new job opportunities for the growing labor force. To uncertainties at home must be added the facts that despite Cordell Hull's drive for a reciprocal lowering of tariffs the Roosevelt regime remained highly nationalistic in its orientation, that autarkic governments were everywhere sprouting in Europe, and that expanding world trade, based on freely convertible currencies, was hardly compatible with European and Asiatic preparations for coming military showdowns. Indeed, it was not until war orders from Europe broke the pattern that the famous Keynesian "multiplier" took hold.

Yet the magnitude of the response of U.S. business to the war is in itself refutation of the thesis that in the thirties businessmen simply sat on their hands and the economy reached "maturity." The really surprising thing about the decade, in fact, is that while investment was quantitatively lower than needed to restore full employment, it was *qualitatively* impressive. While many men were lamenting the disappearance of the old western frontier and the lack of a new "ladder" industry such as automobiles, technological advance continued without abatement, and the scientific revolution took hold. In time this revolution, gathering a momentum of its own, would produce frontier after frontier and ladder after ladder at a pace almost too dizzy to follow.

The big sleeper of the thirties was the chemical industry, which began its march toward making "anything out of anything." To use the term "sleeper" for the chemical thirties is to speak relatively, of course, for important companies had already begun to wheel themselves into place as far back as 1920. The first forward step came during World War I, when the British blockade of the central European powers cut America off from all sorts of German dyes, drugs, and synthetics. In early 1916, Lammot du Pont, whose M.I.T. degree was in mechanical engineering, took charge of a new "miscellaneous" department of his company that was destined to manufacture dyes, paints, lacquers, pyralin, and plastics. Included in the "miscellany" was synthetic indigo, for which $600,000 in powder profits was set aside to build a plant. Allied Chemical moved out from bulk inorganics into coke by-products and dyestuffs in addition to the older acids and alkalies; Union Carbide, whose newest division was busy with automobile antifreeze as early as 1920, took the leadership in the development of petrochemicals, a division of organic chemistry that is based on a straight-line chain of carbon atoms instead of the famous six-carbon benzene ring from which coal-tar products are derived.

The "Big Three" of du Pont, Allied Chemical, and Union Carbide all had to meet terrific development expenses throughout the twenties, but forged steadily ahead. Du Pont, an early rayon producer, took a pioneer position as a supplier of synthetic and semi-synthetic materials for both the textile and the container and wrapper industries. Because of its work in rayon the company had formed a tie with the French Comptoir de Textiles Artificiels, which had financed a Swiss-born French chemist, Jacques Edwin Brandenberger, in the development of cellophane. In 1926 two du Pont chemists, William Hale Charch and Karl Edwin Prindle, found a way to waterproof cellophane—and with the new water-proofed magical wrapper the company really went to town. ("You're the tops, you're cellophane," sang Cole Porter.) By 1933 the demand for cellophane was so heavy that du Pont, not wishing to tie up too much capital in any single product, licensed the Sylvania Industrial Corp. to produce the stuff.

The du Pont triumph in waterproofed cellophane was merely one of a number of accomplishments that took the company pretty much out of the munitions business long before Senator Gerald Nye and his war-profits investigating committee of the thirties traduced the big Wilmington concern as a "merchant of death." Its tie with General Motors strengthened this tendency, providing an additional outlet and a stimulus for its new chemical skills. Early in the twenties a General Motors research team headed by

Thomas Midgley and Charles Kettering, neither of whom was a chemist, discovered that tetraethyl lead would eliminate the "knock" from gasoline. The practical process of safely distilling tetraethyl lead in commercial quantities was developed by a Clark University professor, Dr. Charles A. Kraus, and his assistant, Dr. Conrad C. Callis, for the Standard Oil Co. of New Jersey, which shortly combined with General Motors to set up a joint subsidiary, the Ethyl Gasoline Corp. Lacking facilities to make its own tetraethyl lead in quantity, the Ethyl company turned to the du Ponts, who proceeded to supply it in large and profitable amounts. And in the thirties a du Pont-G.M. subsidiary provided dichlorodifluoromethane (Freon), another Midgley-Kettering product, for the refrigerant that went into G.M.'s Frigidaires.

Success with such items as rayon and waterproofed cellophane spurred the du Ponts to the most important decision of their latter-day existence as a company, which was to enter the field of pure— or fundamental—research. To head the new program, Dr. Wallace H. Carothers was plucked in 1928 from the faculty of Harvard University, where he had already distinguished himself with his studies of the structure of substances of high molecular weight. Once ensconced in his du Pont laboratory, where he had an annual fund of $250,000 to play with, Dr. Carothers began working on the synthesis of the long-chain—or polymerizing—molecules that form the basic building blocks of living tissue. In April of 1930, when people everywhere were despairing of the ability of private enterprise to turn up new and profitable lines, Dr. Carothers and his crew of assistants watched as the first "thread" of a new long-chain substance, silk-like and strong, was drawn out of a laboratory still. Four years later Carothers and his team had succeeded in getting a synthetic filament that was proof against attack by heat, solvents, and water. And four years after this, in 1938, nylon was at last ready to go in a pilot plant. Altogether, the du Ponts spent $27 million—$6 million for research, $21 million for plant—to put nylon on the market. The first pair of nylon stockings was offered for sale in May of 1940—and by 1941 du Pont operating capacity for nylon was more than two million miles of yarn a day. Some 400 textile mills, cut off from their sources of raw silk for stockings by the attack on Pearl Harbor, grabbed for the stuff. Nylon also went into toothbrush bristles, tennis racquets, fishing rods, and self-lubricating bearings.

Other du Pont triumphs of the thirties included Lucite, synthesized musk oil (a basis for fine perfumes), and the merchandising of neoprene, the basis for a synthetic rubber. Meanwhile Union Carbide, which had bought the Bakelite Co., the earliest hard-plastic manufacturer in the country, for $11 million in stock, was also expanding its oxygen and acetylene plants, and proliferating with chemicals and alloys. Behind Allied Chemical & Dye and Union Carbide & Carbon there were a profusion of lesser companies: Dow Chemical, a bulk chlorine producer, which perfected styrene for synthetic rubber; American Cyanamid, the first developer of a nitrogen-fixation process; Monsanto, which moved by way of coal-tar-based organics into petrochemicals and plastics; and the oil companies, which developed the Houdry catalytic-cracking process. In addition, there were fertilizer companies which possessed the industrial skills that would erupt in a vast array of fungicides, herbicides, soil conditioners, defoliants, and insecticides after World War II. In 1934 agricultural-chemical production amounted to 100 million pounds; after the war the poundage would soar to a yearly two billion.

While chemistry was leaping out of the test tubes of the thirties, industrial physics was hardly quiescent, and there were also developments on that strange frontier where physics and chemistry meet. Rumors of an atom-smashing cyclotron came from the University of California laboratory of Dr. Ernest O. Lawrence, and this suggested new sources of industrial power. General Electric, on the advice of Dr. Arthur H. Compton, went into fluorescent lighting; Carrier went ahead with air conditioning. Electronics hit a commercial plateau period in the thirties as radio continued to prosper; but Vladimir Zworykin of R.C.A. worked throughout the decade to clarify the television image projected by his iconoscope, and Philo Farnsworth, a free lance, developed independent television patents. The FCC, which professed to have protective feelings about the average citizen's investment in his radio receiving set, dawdled over granting a commercial television license until 1940—so the first leap forward in putting television sets into homes was postponed by government fiat. But in Britain, where there were fewer shackles in such matters, the first electronic television system was set up in 1936.

Standing at the crossroads where optics and chemistry come together, the Eastman Kodak Co. worked all through the twenties and early thirties on the problem of making color photography a commercial proposition. The first processes all had flaws, and it remained for two concert musicians, Leo Godowsky and Leopold Mannes, who had made photography a hobby, to come up with a three-color dye-coupling developing process and a film that was no more complicated to use than the traditional black-and-white. Invited to join the Kodak organization at a good salary-cum-patent-royalty figure, Mannes and Godowsky perfected the color film that was finally put on the market by Eastman under the name of Kodachrome in 1935. Eastman also kept a close watch on the development of a synthetic light-polarizing material, obtaining the rights to the use of Edwin H. Land's invention as it related to photographic filters. The sagacious Land, a young Harvard student when he started work on his polarizer, also licensed American Optical and Bausch & Lomb to use his patents in making sunglasses and optical instruments and went on to form the Polaroid Corp. for himself.

Despite the depression in heavy industries in the thirties, Alcoa made the continuous casting of aluminum standard practice. The hot continuous rolling of wide-strip steel was pioneered by the American Rolling Mill Co.'s John B. Tytus, who had first installed his cylinders at an Ashland, Kentucky, subsidiary of Armco as early as 1923. The son of a paper manufacturer, Tytus had watched huge rolls of paper emerging in a long strip from the mills of his father. In a roughly analogous way he adapted this to the making of steel sheet. Tytus' patents gave Armco a long headstart on the rest of the steel community, but in the thirties other companies, while honoring Armco's patents, began to catch up. National Steel, a relatively small company, was the first to introduce the Steckel mill, a system for rolling extra-thin steel sheets. Under tough Ernest Weir, National Steel boldly moved into the Detroit area, making handsome profits while older-line companies were floundering, and introduced new and needed competition into the entire industry.

Harold Ickes's public-works program helped shore up a depressed market for heavy structural steel. But as the thirties progressed, private orders also started to flush the mills into larger activity. Kettering of General Motors, whose hobby was a diesel yacht, had perfected a diesel-electric engine that could be used also to pull railroad cars—and just as the railroad business seemed to be on the verge of floundering because of high costs, it was suddenly discovered that high-speed diesel-drawn trains could make money. Western roads such as the Burlington, the Union Pacific, and the Santa Fe started diesel-drawn streamlined service, and soon the eastern roads were following suit with both diesel and electric streamliners. Within a few short years, with 48,000 miles of high-speed tracks available in the U.S., the rolling stock of the roads had taken on a modern appearance.

Next to chemistry, it was the aviation business that really marked the decade of the thirties for its own. Although the Wright brothers had flown as early as 1903, which was the same year in which the Ford Motor Co. got its start, the airplane had taken much longer than the automobile to realize its potential. The U.S. Army got interested in the airplane around 1908, but neither the military strategists nor the tacticians seemed to know what the plane might be used for in wartime. In 1917 the automobile men, notably Howard Coffin of Hudson, John N. Willys, Ford, and Henry Leland, made Liberty engines for aircraft. American planes, however, were not manufactured in time to affect the issue over the battle lines in France.

Thus it happened that American aces like Eddie Rickenbacker flew British and French planes over the World War I trenches. They returned to the U.S. hoping to make a true business out of air transport. In 1923, Juan Terry Trippe, just a year after his belated graduation from Yale, quit his job as a bond salesman and, with his friend John Hambleton, bid a total of $4,500 for nine Navy flying boats that were about to be junked. Trading off some of these planes for better models, Trippe and Hambleton tried running a plane taxi service around New York, only to find themselves going broke. In 1925, however, the Kelly Air Mail Act authorized the Post Office Department to sign contracts with private companies for carrying mail at rates running up to $3 a pound, which made

Wide World Photos

Juan Terry Trippe

commercial flying a real possibility. Helped by Cornelius Vanderbilt Whitney and William H. Vanderbilt, Trippe and Hambleton
scraped up enough cash to start Eastern Air Transport. This company joined forces with Colonial Airways to become Colonial Air
Transport, which started to carry New York to Boston mail.

At just about the same time Charles Lindbergh, then an Army reserve flyer, began carrying the mail for the Robertson Aircraft Corp. on the St. Louis–Chicago run.

Between them, as it turned out, Trippe and Lindbergh did more than any other two individuals to set the U.S. on the road to the development of air transport. Visiting Havana in 1927, Trippe sewed up an exclusive landing permit from President Machado of Cuba, which gave him control of the bottleneck to the Caribbean region and so made Pan American Airways a possibility. And in that same year Lindbergh made his solo flight across the Atlantic, hitting Le Bourget field near Paris right on the nose. Lindbergh's flight sparked increasing interest in Wall Street, as evidenced by the growth of holding companies like North American Aviation Inc. It also led to the formation of domestic carriers like United Air Lines and Eastern (originally called Pitcairn after its founder). Meanwhile, T.W.A. developed as a midcontinental carrier, and Cyrus Rowlett—or "C.R."—Smith began to build American Airlines into a transcontinental company. Other big domestic airlines were built in the thirties, and scores of "feeders" were consolidated with them.

Looking beyond the continental limits of the U.S., Trippe's Pan American Airways had things pretty much to itself at the start. Running his own private diplomatic service, Trippe negotiated flight-landing agreements with strategic countries on both the west and east coasts of South America. When mollifying deals were necessary, he shared arrangements with local airlines (often run by Germans) as well as with the Grace steamship interests. But always he pushed the claims of Pan American Airways as a "chosen instrument," able to deliver service that lesser aspirants could not guarantee to postmaster generals. With a shrewd sense of public relations as well as of flying skills, he employed Lindbergh to pioneer some of his first Caribbean routes. Despite some stockholder recalcitrance, he pushed Pan American across the Pacific in the mid-thirties, establishing airports on lonely islands that turned out to have inestimable military value when war came.

Pan American service to the Philippines and Macao and Hong Kong off the coast of China had been reduced pretty much to routine operations well before the commercial conquest of the

Atlantic, which was held up until 1939 because of disagreements between London and Washington over the right to airport facilities spotted along the British approaches to the North American continent. Eventually the diplomatic snarls were straightened out, and Pan Am spanned the Atlantic just in time to set a pattern of operations for the thousands of military transport planes that would shortly be carrying soldiers and civilian V.I.P.'s to London and Lisbon on the edge of the Nazis' Fortress Europa.

The development of aviation in the thirties did more than open the vital air routes. To produce planes for Pan American and the domestic big four, airframe companies began to dot the U.S., including Martin at Baltimore, Boeing at Seattle, Douglas at Santa Monica, all of which created a vast new demand for the Mellons' aluminum. Donald Douglas' famous DC-3 first took to the air in 1936. With its retractable landing gear, its variable-pitch propeller, and its 180-mile-an-hour cruising speed, the DC-3 was among the first planes to make passengers feel like something more than unprofitable additions to baggage, and later it turned into the great and beloved workhorse of World War II. Meanwhile huge Sikorsky, Martin, and Boeing clippers came to discharge Pan American passengers, mail, and cargo at the ends of the earth in Auckland, New Zealand, and later in the Congo. Into these planes went myriad instruments produced by old and new companies such as Sperry Gyroscope and Collins Radio. And Curtiss-Wright and United Aircraft turned out radial motors of ever increasing horsepower until the piston engine itself began to give place to the jet.

This whole complex of engineering skills helped beleaguered Britain in 1939 and likewise helped produce the "miracle" of production after Pearl Harbor. When President Roosevelt in a famous defense message called for 20,000 planes, the skeptics laughed. But in the course of the war an industry that, in the preceding twenty years, had made fewer than 30,000 planes was able to turn out some 300,000 with an assist from Detroit. The ability of the economy to make air power a reality was only one manifestation of its latent strength. Once firm war orders were placed, military paraphernalia of all types poured off the production lines. In 1918 General von Hindenburg in defeat had remarked sadly of the U.S. industrial effort under Baruch's War Industries Board:

"Those men understood war." In World War II this accolade was doubly applicable. The automobile industry alone produced 200,-000 tanks and gun carriages, 450,000 aircraft engines, 2,300,000 machine guns, and some 2,600,000 Army trucks, while continuing with its left hand to turn out the spare parts to keep some 26 million cars on the roads.

Thus the Great Depression ended on a new affirmation of industrial power, and under the impact of mobilization unemployment vanished as if by sleight of hand. Political veterans who remember the struggles of the thirties are quick to argue, of course, that the rapid achievement of full and overfull employment proves that they were right all along in their assertion that the private economy had become hopelessly static and could only be revitalized by vast dosages of government spending and government "investment." Yet had the economy of the thirties been really "mature" it would simply not have been able to produce a new type of goods when the war button was pressed. Moreover, it should be observed that war spending involved a huge social as well as financial cost. For to lessen the worst ravages of inflation the U.S. had to impose all manner of controls and, in fact, adopted an authoritarian economic system. With its ration cards and multiplying directives from Washington agencies, such a system would not be accepted for peacetime use in a free society.

The Keynesian analysis, when properly understood and qualified, adds a useful dimension to economic discourse. But in its more radical interpretation it obscures the problem of combining general stability with the flexibility and decentralization of the market economy. The reconciliation of large defense spending, made necessary by the Russian danger, with limited constitutional government and with voluntary economic enterprise became, as we shall see, a challenge of the fifties. It was a challenge that remained with us as we reached out to shoot the moon.

13 The Modern World of Enterprise

Industry delivers the LST's, bombers, proximity fuses, and Spam.

It reconverts to automobiles, refrigerators, and radio sets and to suburban split-levels.

Diversification breeds new competition.

R. and D. spins out transistors, antibiotics, rare alloys, and space vehicles.

Despite various threats and stumbling blocks the international market widens.

Early in the 1950's commentators on the American scene began to notice a new phenomenon: the depression-born animus against the free-market system was disappearing. To use the cliché that was soon to be in everyone's mouth, the "image" of business was shifting from nefarious to good. The change in the climate of opinion manifested itself in the unlikeliest quarters: even old New Deal stalwarts seemed to be altering their view. For example, David Lilienthal, former boss of the government-owned TVA, was loud in his praise of the accomplishments of large private corporations; and ex-brain-truster Adolf Berle, now the prophet of an ethical and socially beneficent business system, no longer read the doom of the free market in the statistical tea leaves that he liked periodically to consult.

The popularity of the new image of business went hand in hand with the rise of a new "conservatism"—though to many it seemed that the new stirrings were not conservative at all, but simply a resurgence of the old liberalism of the nineteenth century, which believed that individuals could best solve their problems by trusting to voluntary associations. The labels, in any case, did not matter much. Always pragmatic, the American people—and not a few of their pundits—had simply responded to the pressures that were intimately affecting their lives. A free economy based on private property looked better and better as the much-touted European variants of socialism failed to bring in the millenium. True, the U.S. government continued to assume a big role in the economy because of the continuing demands of the cold war. But government spending hardly accounted for the buoyancy that the American system had displayed since World War II in complete defiance of depression-born fears of "economic maturity." The animating force in the economy was private-business enterprise, which paid the government bills, produced the sinews of defense, and satisfied the greatest linked consumer and private-investment demand that the world had ever witnessed.

The figures themselves made for dramatic reading, especially in perspective of the prewar years. Between 1946 and 1961 gross national product, estimated in constant dollars, jumped 60 per cent to $521 billion. Population exploded from 141 million to 185 million. Meanwhile, owing to advancing productivity, real per capita income rose, and families with income of over $4,000 multiplied from 50 per cent to 67 per cent of all families in the country. Behind the bare statistics there loomed a success story, no matter how told, whether in the continued prosperity of great industrial corporations like General Motors and Jersey Standard, or great life-insurance companies like Metropolitan Life, or huge and resourceful banks like Chase Manhattan in New York and the Giannini chain on the Pacific coast, or simply in terms of the vastly variegated little fellow, as any glance at the yellow pages of the telephone directory for any U.S. city will attest. The rich had got richer, the poor had got richer, too—and as for the middle class, it now bade fair to include practically everybody. Admittedly, the 1945–62 period had seen five economic dips, but they had all been of a mild nature. If that is the worst the business cycle could do, the free-market system had little to fear from a candid comparison with any other system anywhere.

This new dynamism in the economy, which contrasted so sharply with the depressed thirties, was prefigured in the response that business made to the exigencies of World War II. At the very outset of the war the head of the Bank of England sarcastically suggested to Ambassador Joseph P. Kennedy that it would take God Almighty to handle industrial mobilization in America. God not being available, a succession of mere human beings from the great specialty corporations of America managed to do that job. In Washington men like William Knudsen, Donald Nelson, and Ferdinand Eberstadt, assisted by a labor leader or two, wrestled with such things as priorities, allocations, and price and wage controls, which in the event proved necessary for all-out war. But these controls would have been no more than paper plans had it not been for the response of American industry all down the line. As no other war had ever been, this was a war of production dependent on the skill of industrialists. General George C. Marshall put the contrast succinctly—and a trifle wistfully—at Teheran in 1943. "My military education and experience in the First World War," he told the Combined Chiefs of Staff and their Russian counterparts, "have all been on roads, rivers, and railroads. During the last two years I have had to learn all over again. Prior to the present war I had never heard of any landing craft except a rubber boat. Now I think of little else."

Marshall was thinking, specifically, of the top priority item of that pre-D-Day year, which was the creation of a flotilla designed to take an army across the English Channel. Landing craft, far from being a uniform product, broke down into a succession of LST's, LCIL's, LCT's, LCM's, LCVP's, LCC's, LSD's, and LSMR's. (No rubber boats here.) They had to be built to disgorge tanks and huge mobile guns and trucks, and they had to come complete with their proper adjuncts—i.e., elaborate artificial harbors. The LST, built specifically to transport tanks, was 327 feet long and fifty feet wide. Another landing craft, the LCIL, had an engine with an 1,800 horse power thrust.

To make the landing craft, and the fighter planes to protect them as they moved in huge convoy on D-Day, and the big bombers to bomb the enemy's rear area communications, and the armament for the soldiers aboard the landing craft, and the cans of Spam to feed the soldiers, and the miles of three-inch gasoline pipe that were laid under the English Channel from the Isle of Wight to Cherbourg to keep the tanks rolling through France after the landing craft had done their job, and the thousand-and-one other quantity and quality items needed for invasion on such a colossal scale, had entailed prodigies of dovetailed scheduling. But once an item had been decided upon and its general nature disclosed, the substitutes for God Almighty in Washington could trust the mock-up experts in Cleveland, Schenectady, or wherever to provide the model, and from there on the production of the item was a familiar technological and administrative process. Scientists and military experts reporting to the National Defense Research Committee and, later, the OSRD (Office of Scientific Research and Development) might turn up the "wonder weapon of the war," the proximity fuse. From then on it was a matter of orders: Sylvania Electric turned a proved know-how to the assembly of delicate tubes made by Western Electric and Raytheon, ceramic chambers made by Globe-Union, Inc., of Milwaukee, batteries from Union Carbide, and triggering devices from Bell Labs.

To expand capacities for war production, General Electric, for example, spent $78 million of its own capital in 1942, to which was added $112 million of government money. General Motors, du Pont, Union Carbide—all the other "blue chips"—were engaged in similar single-hearted channeling of energies facilitated by similar government-assisted expansion. Du Pont, plunging into the intricacies of nuclear physics, took a $1 profit from the government to build the atomic installation of Hanford on the Columbia River and a pilot enterprise at Oak Ridge in Tennessee. And there were the "new men," such as Henry Kaiser with his cargo ships, and Andrew Jackson Higgins of New Orleans with his PT boats; and the small men, such as Gus Swebelius of New Haven, Connecticut, with his first-rate small arms. In addition and essential to the whole effort were the subcontractors, thousands upon thousands of them, from the small valleys of New England to the small towns of Michigan and Ohio.

Everyone was in the war—or the war effort, as the incantative understatement of the day had it. And then, suddenly, everyone was out of the war, and the private economy was up against another great test. Between 1944 and 1947 government expenditures plunged down from $95 billion per year to $39 billion, and predictions were rife that there would be a return to eight million or 12 million unemployed. To the surprise of depression-born prophets, nothing like this happened; the economy simply rode through the stop signals. Far from being hampered by war-induced hangovers, the American industrialist had come out of five years of military production with a renewed belief in his strength and creativity. The war itself had been an incredible forcing house, demanding prodigies of lithe and sudden adaptation—and if the industrialist had been able to move one way under pressure in 1941 and 1942, he saw no technological difficulties in moving just as fast in an opposite direction in 1946. Despite taxes and inflation-induced costs, the postwar businessman forsook the wailing wall of the thirties and avidly adapted himself to the new world.

The first conversion success involved the satisfaction of primal needs, and in satisfying them the country did well, if not superlatively well. One section, that of the Texas-Oklahoma Southwest, with its oil and its beef cattle and its cotton ("The world is naked," cried Lamar Fleming, president of the big Houston cotton-factoring concern of Anderson, Clayton, after the war), was suddenly prolific of a whole new crop of millionaires, earning for itself the envious title of "land of the Big Rich." The fact that the Southwest prospered by hanging on to the increment of its industry—in the form of the oil-depletion allowance and multiplying beef herds— offered a suggestively piquant commentary on the still prevailing theory that government redistribution of wealth through high taxation is necessary to keep a modern economy going. With capital to play with, the Texans raised the serrated skylines of Houston and Dallas; and the force of their new money was felt far away in Wall Street, where Texas-born Murchisons and Richardsons proved they could best even the Morgans and the Vanderbilts in proxy battles for the control of old American corporations. "Better Texas than taxes" was a sharp comment of the time.

The big job of conversion and of absorbing some 12 million men from the armed services fell squarely on industry itself. Not every businessman made the right guesses about the tastes of the consumer market. Robert Young, the Texas-born boss of the Chesapeake and Ohio Railroad, hoped to lure travelers back to the railroads by offering first-run movies shown aboard a fast-speeding "Train X," but the public refused to respond to his ideas even after he had gained control of the New York Central. Henry Kaiser managed to come out of the war with a promising aluminum business, but he badly underestimated the difficulties of gaining a permanent foothold in the automobile market. In general, however, the great mass-production industries prospered—thanks no little to tremendous pent-up consumer demand for goods of all kinds. By 1949, car production was back to 5,100,000 or past its 1929 record. Steel production held up. The biggest force in the postwar economy was the resurgence of private investment, which had fallen to minimal proportions during the war years, but rose to $43 billion in 1948, pushed to over $60 billion in the late fifties, and in 1960 rose to over $70 billion.

It was this great surge of private-investment spending, fed by profits and by depreciation, that kept the economy moving in high gear and opened up new frontiers of technological advance and rising real incomes. In the advance, corporations had, of course, become bigger than ever. They had also become increasingly limber. The standard criticism of the big American corporation is that it "administers" its prices (in tacit collusion with other members of a Big Three or a Big Five), that it prefers "profitable and comfortable stagnation" (the phrase is John Kenneth Galbraith's) to adventurous pioneering, and that it seeks to throttle competition. But all aspects of the criticism were belied by the actual behavior of the corporation in the fifties.

Prior to the mid-fifties, for instance, the charge that the automobile industry was "profitably and comfortably" committed to the big tail-finned car at an "administered" high price could still be maintained without provoking more than a halfhearted denial. But the specter of a possible mass importation of the German Volkswagens and British Hillman Minxes in the fifties soon made mincemeat of the contention that price and significant model competition had disappeared forever from the Detroit scene. Partly because of high gasoline taxes, partly because of parking congestion in cities, the great American customer wanted a smaller car. And, with his disposable income nibbled away even in the lower income-tax brackets, he wanted to spend less money not only for gasoline but on buying the car in the first instance. George Romney, with his American Motors' Rambler "compacts," was the first to give the customer what he wanted. But even without the imaginative prod

Photo by Francis Miller, Life, copyright 1962 Time Inc.

George W. Romney

of Mr. Romney, the Big Three would still have had in time to accede to customer demand to produce such compacts as the Falcon, Corvair, and Valiant.

The great electrical price-fixing conspiracy, which came to light in 1961, would seem to prove that the impulse to cartelize business had not entirely disappeared. But most American corporations, far from seeking protection against competition by way of cartel agreements, endeavored to get off the hook of saturated markets by planned diversification. Even companies that were irrevocably committed to one type of product tried periodically to "remake" their markets. The competition between substitutes—between stainless steel, coated steel, aluminum, wood, plaster-board, brick, cinder and cement blocks, and a whole host of plastics, for example—was fierce, and there were so many companies involved in providing viable alternatives in most areas that there could be no possibility of an effective and lasting cartel agreement even if one were desired.

As for mergers, which were undertaken in the 1890–1910 period in hopes of achieving an almost complete monopoly, they were now pursued for competitive motives that were wholly in keeping with the spirit of the Sherman Antitrust Act. Railroads sought "horizontal" mergers with other railroads in order to get into a position to maintain themselves in a transportation world that was increasingly dominated by trucks, buses, private automobiles, and airplanes. The Ford Motor Co. sought a "vertical" merger with certain component units of the Electric Autolite Co. in order to compete with General Motors, which owned its own spark-plug division. The Snyder Co. of Detroit bought a company making pharmaceutical equipment and filling machinery in order to wriggle free of total dependence on the machine-tool purchases of the automobile companies. Other enterprises mixed mergers with internal diversification. The oil companies, with a commitment in petrochemicals, invaded the territory of the old-line chemical companies by an incursion into nitrogen. And the du Pont Co., baffled by the government's objection to its part ownership of General Motors, licensed nylon manufacture to Chemstrand and let out cellophane to Olin Mathieson as it put development capital, not into new nylon and cellophane capacity, but into such things as Orlon and Delrin.

To provide the needed diversification when saturation threatened, the modern corporation continued to put ever greater effort into R. and D. (research and development). It also pursued R. and D. to keep its older products in competitive trim. R. and D. resulted in the oxygen process, which cut the cost of making steel. It developed the process of turning taconite ore into pellets that can be used as a high-grade blast furnace feed. In the coal industry, R. and D. had not only mechanized the mines as fast as labor costs rose, but resulted in the pulverization and liquefaction of coal for delivery over long distances through pipes. Much of the money for R. and D. was provided for ostensibly restricted purposes by the government, which had its own military-atomic and space-age requirements to worry about. Nevertheless, R. and D. resulted in a hundred new things in the consumer markets, from power steering to powerful antibiotics, and from Fiberglas sailboats to stereophonic phonograph records.

Paced by technology and rising demand, most industries in the economy showed expansion but at sharply different rates. Steel, chemicals, oil, aluminum all moved up with the gross national product, and the growth of the utilities, especially in areas like Florida and the Southwest, made comparative kilowatt figures from the Soviet Union look tame. Other lines of business, such as cotton textiles, continued to suffer from the competition of new products; railroads, despite piggyback trucking and hopes of mergers, were enmeshed in chronic overregulation; and even the airlines, the star performers of the thirties, had a hard time making money out of their extremely expensive jet fleets. The biggest and most spectacular gains were made, of course, by the high-technology industries, with the electronics industry leading the van and developing at a rate that would have caused even so sanguine a pioneer as Thomas A. Edison to rub his eyes with amazement. In 1939 factory sales of electronic equipment of all kinds amounted to less than $400 million; in 1960 the figure reached $10 billion, to which $5 billion more would have to be added to account for broadcasting revenues, servicing, and distribution. No other segment of the economy could match this for the postwar period.

An industry that has been called the "multiple non-industry," simply because it forms a part of so many things, electronics has been all over the place. Military developments, underwritten by government, have found their civilian uses—and vice versa. Methods of mass production of the printed circuit were developed by the Bureau of Standards for the proximity fuse, which in itself is a tiny transmitter-receiver that has to be housed in the nose of a shell. Once the war was over, Philco, Motorola, and other radio-set makers pounced upon the printed circuit as a substitute for wired circuits in commercial radio. Radar, used in the air and on the sea for detection purposes in wartime, became a standby of police forces for trapping speeding motorists. Advanced microwave radar was employed by the military for weapons control and by ships and planes for storm spotting as well as general navigation. ENIAC, the first "giant electronic brain," was put together by J. Presper Eckert and John W. Mauchly, who formed the Eckert-Mauchly Computer Corp., for Army Ordnance in 1946. Such computers were subsequently produced by Remington Rand (UNIVAC), Thomas Watson's I.B.M., and others, and were leased or sold to the Bureau of the Census, the insurance companies, and the larger banks and utility companies.

Basically, the various computers and communications control devices were adaptations of old discoveries. But the postwar period brought forth one electronic invention that added a new dimension to the business. This was the tiny transistor, which was produced by Dr. William Shockley and a team of Bell Labs scientists in 1948. The transistor, a three-electrode "tube" of solid matter that could be substituted for the glass vacuum tube, met all the requirements for the "miniaturization" needed to give real impetus to the rocket and missile age. Using a rare metal, germanium, for their solid semi-conductor material, Dr. Shockley and his team won the Nobel Prize for their patents, which were assigned to Western Electric for use in work for A.T. & T. and for general license to the trade. By 1951 any company could obtain use of the transistor patents by paying $25,000 advance on royalties.

Texas Instruments, which, as Geophysical Service Inc. had been in the oil exploration field, was among the early users of the Shockley patents. With his license in hand, T.I.'s President John Erik Jonsson, the son of a Swedish immigrant, bought up talent on a big scale—and within two years his company had brought down the price of a germanium transistor from $16 to $2.50. Sales multiplied—and after 1954, when T.I. made the first practical silicon transistor, the market really took off. With its better resistance to extremes of heat and cold and its longer life, the silicon transistor took some of the hazard out of space age experimentation. In an electronics market that had a compounded growth of some 15 per cent a year, T.I. showed a 40 per cent annual growth. Its 1954 sales were $24,500,000; its 1961 figure was $235 million—and the profit therefrom had grown more than forty-six times the 1948–50 base. In 1960 T.I. stock sold for sixty-five times earnings. As the sixties unfolded, T.I. and other electronics companies encountered tougher going. But the show was a gorgeous one, making possible the whole vast new enterprise of space exploration.

Roughly, the companies involved in electronics could be shuffled into three groups. One group specialized in components such as transistors, capacitors, vacuum tubes and so on: representatives of this type of company included Texas Instruments, Varian Associates, Litton Industries, Transitron and older companies like Sprague Electric in New England and Standard Kollsman in California. Another group stuck largely to end products (I.B.M. and Sperry Rand with their computers, Beckman Instruments with its powerful analytic tool, the mass spectrometer; and Minneapolis-Honeywell with its data processing systems and its "first complete automatic programing system for computer control of industrial process"). Aircraft manufacturers moved sidewise—or shifted entirely—into the end-product electronic field: Boeing and North American and Northrop had their missile projects, and the Glenn Martin Co. (now part of Martin-Marietta) dropped air frames for missiles and controlled spacecraft entirely. Finally, there were the middle-type companies which made some of almost everything in the electronic line—old companies like R.C.A., Sylvania, G.E., and Philco, which was absorbed by the Ford Motor Co. As for Ford, it had already committed itself to space work with its Aeronutronic Division, which was hard at work on a lunar capsule.

In 1960 government orders sopped up $5 billion worth of electronics, missiles alone accounting for $4 billion. Meanwhile civilian markets—old and new—were ponderable. Television sets remained in the five-million to six-million-a-year area, grossing around $1 billion. Color television, after years of disappointment, had become a practical reality. The Teco subsidiary of Zenith Corp. held licenses for pay-as-you-see television patents and awaited only the permission of the FCC to develop a whole new and promising field. Meanwhile electronics penetrated into the factory and production line. Much of the early postwar development of automation was electrically, not electronically controlled: the big Cross Co. "transfer-matic" lines for machining the automobile cylinder block, which are as long as a football field, had not been run by electronic signaling and "feedback" devices. But continuous-process industries such as petroleum, chemicals, and paper used electronically guided flow systems. And after the Korean War electronics began to be applied to the automation of hard-goods manufacture.

While electronics was the star of the postwar business world, it was not the only great performer. Without any big governmental R. and D. subsidy, drug manufacturers took off on their own, jumping their sales from $300 million in 1939 to an almost incredible $3.3 billion in 1961. The $410 million that the public spent on antibiotics alone in 1961 represented more money than was spent for all types of drugs in 1939—as did the $350 million spent on synthetic vitamins. Though the sums involved would, on the face of things, argue that medical costs had been skyrocketing, the prices for such "wonder drugs" as penicillin dropped and dropped over the years. As for preventives such as the Salk polio vaccine, the cost of almost total immunization in any community represented only a few cents per child. What the whole phenomenon suggested is that the drug industry had been getting money for the prevention or quick cure of diseases that used to go to doctors for long and often far more expensive cures; pneumonia was now eradicated within the week, and tuberculosis in most cases no longer demanded long sanitorium treatment. All this contributed significantly to keeping people healthy and able to enjoy the good life that rising incomes made possible.

This rise was spectacular by almost any standard, and the good life—sometimes called "keeping down with the Joneses"—had become a commonplace. Entering the 1960's, American society could no longer be represented by a pyramid, with the few at the top having most of the purchasing power and the millions at the bottom having little. Modern society is "bunched in the middle," financially speaking: some 47 per cent of all non-farm families in 1959 had after-tax cash incomes of $5,000 to $10,000 a year. The "proletarian" worker was disappearing; the old "blue-collar" man, now a machine watcher, lived as often as not in a split-level "ranch house" next to a white-collar contemporary. Blue collar's diversions were likely to be skiing, bowling, boating—which created big business in themselves.

It was sometimes charged, of course, that the American people spent too much on wasteful luxuries and an assortment of *kitsch*, or junk, but the indictment was scarcely borne out by the statistics. In 1959, for instance, the after-tax income of the U.S. was $336 billion, three-fourths of which went for food, housing, clothes, and transportation. The remaining quarter went into savings ($24 billion), medical expenses ($19 billion), support of private religious and welfare institutions ($4 billion), private education ($4 billion), and "personal" business such as bank charges and interest on loans ($17 billion)—and $16 billion for movies, sports, reading, gardening, travel, and related hobbies. With expenditures for education and medicine rising in relation to spending for amusements, it was apparent that the U.S. economy, even in the midst of fabulous production, had been a relatively austere one. It might have done with a little more "waste" and "frivolity." And Madison Avenue, far from deserving censure for trying to promote consumption, should have been praised for doing its best under difficult circumstances.

The sober affluence of the new middle class was in itself a stabilizing factor in the economy: with 60 million cars on the road it took a yearly production of six million cars in the early sixties merely to meet replacement demands. At the same time, of course, American taste was constantly changing, with people buying electric blankets one year and the next switching to good paperback books or high-fidelity records or wall-to-wall carpeting. This constant change in the use of "discretionary income" gave the economy its unique dynamism, and precluded almost by definition attempts to control it from a central watchtower—only low-grade economies can be so directed and this at enormous social cost. The great virtue of the American market system was that the consumer vote still had a controlling influence over the flow of demand and to a significant degree over the flow of profits and hence investment. In 1961 some 450,000 new businesses were born in the hope of turning a profit by catering to changing consumer taste, while an almost equal number closed their doors because they had failed to meet the market test. Such a system might appear less tidy than the great centrally controlled economies. But the untidiness was only a surface manifestation hiding an inner order and discipline.

Because of America's quick responses to changing human needs, U. S. citizens at the beginning of the sixties had every reason to take pride in their $560 billion gross-product system. Along Wall Street they talked of "the soaring sixties." But the sixties, as things turned out, did not behave in accordance with the prophecies. Economics, to a great extent, creates and conditions sociology, but there are times when the cause-and-effect order is reversed; and the sixties were to prove just such a time. President John F. Kennedy took over from Eisenhower in 1961 with a promise to "get America moving again." He should have construed his mandate as one to keep America moving.

Move it did, but its very prosperity created problems that could not have been foreseen in a simpler time. The vast amounts of capital that had moved abroad (the Marshall Plan, Point Four, the rise of the multinational corporation) created sticky balance of payments situations. For a short period, dollars tended to flow back to buy the product of American factories, but once Japan and West Germany had been rebuilt, and the Common Market had managed to rid the West European world of tariffs and quotas that did not consort with narrow boundaries, the U. S. system was placed on notice that it must compete as it had never competed before. The dollars that had been coming home became the Eurodollar and stayed abroad to finance foreign subsidiaries. General Motors made its Opel cars in West Germany, Ford its Cortinas in Britain, Chrysler had its Simca connection in France. This was competition, but the reflex of a Europe chockablock with liquid dollar claims was a run on Fort Knox. The "gold drain" was among the first hard economic problems to face the Kennedy administration.

The Bretton Woods money system had been set up to soften and defer balance of payment troubles. The hope was that the trading nations of the West would discipline their home economies in time to remain evenly competitive. This hope was never realized in Britain, and in the sixties it faded in America. Discipline would have required the cooperation of the labor movement to pursue collective bargaining within limits imposed by the unit productivity of the individual worker. Two young steel union economists, Harold Ruttenberg and Joe Scanlon, tried to tell that to Phil Murray, the head of the United Steelworkers, in the late forties, but the hold of the Gompers formula—"More"—was too strong to be lightly set aside. In Detroit Walter Reuther continued to push the idea that purchasing power depends on ever rising hourly wage rates. So the incrustations on the U. S. system grew as wages and fringe benefits went beyond productivity. The working man who kept his job was better off than ever even in a time of rising inflation, but the steel union lost a third of its membership as Europe and Japan, getting the jump on America with the new oxygen furnaces, made steel at better competitive rates.

Instead of Marx conquering the world, it was the enterprising American who had rammed home his lesson all too well. In the sixties we lost our overseas electronics markets to Japanese companies such as Sony. Remington and Underwood typewriter trademarks gave way to the Italian Olivetti; Hollywood gasped for life as France, Britain, Italy, and even Yugoslavia made better and cheaper films; the German Volkswagen and the Japanese Toyota and Datsun squeezed the high-powered and oversized Detroit car out of foreign markets and even invaded the U. S. in ever increasing numbers; and Hong Kong textiles were all over the place. Only in airplanes and computers did we continue to hold our old lead. The Boeing 747 remained in great demand (the German Lufthansa began using it as a transatlantic freighter), and the Red Chinese signaled their return to the world community by bidding for Boeing's smaller 707. But Boeing itself, made fearful by the retraction of government support for the giant supersonic, the SST, felt constrained to make provision for manufacturing planes in Japan and Italy. IBM was still the great name in jumbo-sized computers, but the Japanese had made big inroads in the mini-computer market, and it was only a question of time before they would go for the bigger stuff. In the meantime we had suddenly had to face up to our growing energy shortages. The need for oil from the Persian Gulf and liquified natural gas from Algeria threatened to add progressively to our balance of payment woes. It remained a matter of pride to realize that American international companies had been dominant factors in developing Saudi Arabian oil fields, but this did not keep the price of oil from rising as we lagged in exploiting new sources on our mainland, in Alaska, and on our continental offshore shelves.

In spite of our international troubles we had become a trillion-dollar economy. Our very affluence, however, created disturbing expectations. The consumer, with money in his pocket and a bigger margin of time in which to enjoy life, started to ask finicky questions about quality. Ralph Nader, a far greater master of public relations than Ivy Lee and Edward Bernays, put himself at the head of a consumers' lobby, with rather mixed impact on the economy. The consumers' movement is here to stay, and it will put new life into Better Business Bureaus and the journalism that has built its success on the pioneering of such magazines as *Consumer Reports*. But "Naderism" killed off a small economy-type car, the rear-engine Corvair, that had already been made roadworthy by correction of its original defects. Moreover, Nader zealotry, a good thing on balance as long as it sticks to proselytizing within the free market, could have disastrous inhibiting effects if it were to result in a super-agency designed to police the American corporation. Ever since the formation of the Interstate Commerce Commission in the eighteen-eighties, the lesson of government regulation is that it creates more problems than it solves. The natural history of a regulatory agency, as the late Robert Young often complained, is that it becomes prey to politics. As often as not, the industry to be regulated manages to get working control of the agency itself. The collapse of the eastern railroads in the sixties was a pointed commentary on the regulatory idea. The consumer of mass travel would manifestly be better off today if railroads had been left free to tear up unused tracks, to trim the crews of Diesel trains, and to combine in order to compete with trucks and airplanes. The merger of the New York Central and the Pennsylvania might have worked if it had come a generation earlier with a good railroad man such as Alfred Perlman in charge of combined operations.

Environmentalism, the natural complement of the consumer movement, has also proved a mixed blessing. The ecologists, busy with their stop signals, perform a necessary warning service. Common sense should tell us that it is dangerous to construct atomic energy plants along the line of the San Andreas fault in California, or to drill indiscriminately for oil in the geologically unstable bottom of the Santa Barbara Channel. Moreover, there is more than sentimentalism involved in the protection of endangered species from soil and water pollution and the ravaging of fragile landscapes such as the Alaskan tundra. The trouble with the ecologists is that they have overdone it; instead of producing a healthy wariness, they have unleashed an unhealthy fear.

The sum total is not a safer or more habitable world. If, for lack of an oil pipe line across Alaska to the sea (or, better, a longer pipe line across Canada to Midwest markets), we lack the economic strength to pursue a successful Middle East diplomacy, the result could be atomic warfare, with its practically universal poisoning of the atmosphere. The answer to the ecologists is not to hold back on investment; it is to add the necessary ingredient of safety engineering to economic development. Surely American enterprise is up to providing insulation for hot oil in the Arctic. Even better, it has been suggested that oil might be forced through a buried cross-tundra pipe line in a cold brine solution that would not do damage to the heritage of either caribou or Eskimo.

The jumbo tanker, according to Dr. Edward Teller, is more of a menace to the ecology of the oceans than any offshore drilling rig. So it is no service to the human race, Americans included, to prohibit drilling for oil off the New England coast; lack of offshore oil merely means building more tankers for the long voyage from Kuwait or Libya. As for the tankers themselves, they could be built with detachable bunker units, which could be floated off and towed to shore in case of mishap on the high seas.

Lacking oil, and worried about the atmospheric pollution that comes from burning coal, we should be pushing the development of clean atomic generating plants. Dr. Teller, who laments the slowdown caused by worries over possible atomic pollution, suggests that many hazards might be eliminated by putting nuclear power plants underground. As for coal itself it will surely come back into favor some day when R. and D. learns to gasify it in the seams or close to the minehead for a cleaner energy.

The damage that we have done to ourselves through over-fearful surveillance extends to the drug industry, which has fallen behind the West German's in inventiveness. Nobody wants another thalidomide, but if the test of a new drug were that it should have no side effects, penicillin would never have come on the market. As one exasperated chemist put it, if the marketing of a single effective drug is to be postponed for political reasons for as much as a year, the resulting deaths could make the thalidomide damage seem negligible by comparison.

In the late sixties many an undesirable government interventionist chicken came home to roost. The farm legislation of the nineteen-thirties did not stop American agriculture from becoming the most productive in the world. But the hidden cost of subsidizing the big producer (the small farmer, lacking acres to put into the soil bank, was arithmetically eliminated from the largesse) was to be reckoned in the spread of the northern city slum. Traveling between Columbia and Beaufort in South Carolina, for example, or in southeastern Alabama, one is appalled at the emptiness of a land which Swiss or Dutch peasants could make inordinately fruitful. The people, pushed off acres that have been progressively turned over to twenty-year tree crops, have crowded into the decaying areas of Detroit, Chicago, Washington, and New York. The pressure of the slums, in turn, has exacerbated the flight to the suburbs. The sociological distortion has been accompanied by a distortion of investment and consumer patterns: we have had too many resources tied up in big-power cars, in miles of asphalt, and in a sprawl that is not a really effective decentralization. The fault goes back to the failure of Henry Wallace, Roosevelt's secretary of Agriculture, to provide a cut-off point to big farm subsidies: instead of helping the family farm, he pushed a bigger concentration of fertilizer, feed, and machinery funds into the hands of the more wealthy producers. The resulting displacement of populations led directly to our big city woes, the proliferation of our Harlems and our Bedford-Stuyvesants and the sad saga of the modern drug culture, with its attendant crime, that is making our biggest cities uninhabitable.

Capitalism, which did not create the problem of forced-draft migratory patterns, does its best to mitigate it. Despite everything, the income for black families rose by 99.6 per cent in the sixties while the income for white families went up by 69 per cent. According to statisticians Ben Wattenberg and Richard Scammon, a slim majority of black Americans are now properly to be described as middle class people. The improvement has come about even though minimum-wage laws have hurt teen-age blacks who, more than white apprentices of the same age, have been unable to get jobs at the legally imposed rates.

Photo by John Loengard, Life, *copyright 1962 Time Inc.*

Thomas J. Watson, Jr.

With the changing urban-rural balance, whole industries have come into being to take advantage of the new suburbias. The shopping center has become omnipresent: Houston's Galleria, for example, has not only taken retail trade away from "downtown," it has also provided a new cultural and recreational base. The largest Sears Roebuck and J. C. Penney stores are to be found in Woodfield Mall, twenty-five miles northwest of Chicago. U. S. Gypsum, for example, has promoted nine shopping centers; the Arlen Realty and Development Company promotes the Korvette discount chain, and new linear "downtowns" along the beltways around big metropolises force the building of new peripheral roads designed to by-pass the older by-passes. Meanwhile, the Holiday Inn, far from "downtown," becomes the center for business meetings, and industrial as well as scholarly seminars are held in rural retreats in the Poconos of Pennsylvania or the foothills of Virginia's Blue Ridge country.

With the coming of the computer and its memory banks the "knowledge industry" and the communications industry have taken on new dimensions. Xerox, with its 4000 copier, pushed its astounding profits to new highs in 1973. With all the difficulties taken out of copying, the Authors Guild took an understandable fright that piecemeal pirating of authors' material might, at some future time, kill the reprint business. Along with Xerox, the Eastman Kodak Company and National Cash Register have become interested in the possibilities of allying microfilm to retrieval systems. An entire journal might be mailed on microfilm at the cost of a single first class letter. In the newer world the newspaper and magazine business would assuredly suffer, but the newest printing processes are enabling newspapers to by-pass the old-style composing room; and the day may come when printers will be compelled to become paste-up artists as the linotype machine becomes an antique.

At the beginning of the seventies, R. and D. was running at $27 billion a year. But it had suddenly hit a series of dry wells: where were the 1970 equivalents of the jet aircraft, the computer or the TV to float new "ladder industries"? Cable TV promised a profitable refinement of an established business, as did the communications satellites that were being pushed into orbit to "bounce" news and entertainment across the hemispheres. But the changes in communications dimensions did not help the 100,000 U. S. scientists, engineers, and technicians who were reportedly out of work in April of 1972. The system needed a new buoyancy, but where was the necessary sense of adventure to be found in the anti-business climate that had been cultivated by the consumer movement, the spread of ecological fears, the disasters to the American dollar, and the inability or unwillingness of the big labor leaders to watch the productivity "tilt light"?

In spite of reverses, the hope of enterprise will be rekindled. The secrets of getting safe and cheap energy out of the hydrogen atom will someday be unlocked. Communism has been unable to feed its millions; the universal Marxist revolution, once the hope of the Maoists and the disciples of Ché Guevara, has had to be postponed as propitiatory Red envoys come begging wheat. We have had the Cuban and Chilean debacles, but they have been more than offset by the West German and the Japanese "miracles."

The enterpriser's adventure really goes on and on, in a world setting. When the first settlers reached Virginia tidewater and the rocky New England coast, local enterprise was conditioned by British mercantilism and restriction. The taming of a wilderness and the setting up of a new form of limited government under the Constitution led on to a major breakthrough. In successive chapters of this history we have watched the results: the development of the West, the laying down of the rails, the rise of Henry Ford, the spread of mass production. Perhaps the biggest achievement of business was to stage its most impressive show in a high-tax postwar era when the socialists were confidently expecting its downfall and a return to the Depression of the thirties.

Only yesterday our airspace companies were making fighter planes. Now, with the success of the Apollo "moonshooting" program behind them, they are embarked on a space lab technological adventure that will pick up despite all momentary checks. Man's Promethean instinct will be satisfied. Yet, while the exploration of space will continue to yield new secrets in metalworking and in the scope of electronic control and communication, the biggest contribution of American enterprise still lies on the surface of the planet called Earth. The market economy offers the only form of organization that is compatible with freedom. Its success has been made plain through two and one half centuries on the North American continent. It will defend itself in its homeland even as it triumphs in the extended West European Common Market, in the new Japanese-Australian iron-and-steel Axis, and in the various Taiwans, Hong Kongs, Ivory Coasts, and Brazils that have had the sense to free the enterpriser to work his assured magic.

Bibliography

NOTE: The material used in the preparation of this book ranges widely—as the story of American business itself does—over the economic, social, and political life of the United States. The following list of sources and recommended reading includes, therefore, the work of historians, biographers, and statisticians, company reports and autobiographies, and even the evidence presented by some novelists. Some works, however, are so broad in scope and contain so much basic material that is indispensable to the study of the development of a business civilization (and were so continuously consulted and referred to) that they are listed separately—under *I. General*—at the start of this bibliography, followed by a list of the other sections to which certain books particularly apply. Other sources have been grouped under eight broad subject and period headings. Generally these headings do not refer to specific chapters but follow their chronological sequence.

I. GENERAL

DOCUMENTARY GUIDES AND ENCYCLOPEDIAS: Adams, J. T., and Coleman, R. V. (eds.): *Dictionary of American History* (5 vols., 1940; secs. II through VIII); Bogart, E. L., and Thompson, C. M. (eds.): *Readings in the Economic History of the United States* (1916; secs. II through VII); Daniells, Lorna M.: *Studies in Enterprise* (1957; secs. II through IX); Flugel, F., and Faulkner, H. U. (eds.): *Readings in the Economic and Social History of the United States 1773–1829* (1929; secs. II, III, IV); *Historical Statistics of the United States 1789–1957*, Department of Commerce (secs. II through IX); Johnson, Allen, and Malone, Dumas (eds.): *Dictionary of American Biography* (11 vols., 1957–1958; secs. II through IX); Larson, Henrietta M.: *Guide to Business History* (1948; secs. III through VIII); Paullin, C. O.: *Atlas of the Historical Geography of the United States* (1932; secs. II through V); Seligman, E. R. A. (ed.): *Encyclopedia of the Social Sciences* (15 vols., 1930–1935; secs. II through VII).

HISTORIES: Beard, C. A., and Beard, M. R.: *The Rise of American Civilization* (4 vols., 1927, 1941, and 1942; secs. III through VII); Bining, Arthur Cecil: *The Rise of American Economic Life* (1955; secs. V through VIII); Bishop, J. Leander: *A History of American Manufactures from 1608 to 1860* (2 vols., 1864); Clark, Victor S.: *History of Manufactures in the United States* (3 vols., 1929; secs. II through VII); Cochran, Thomas C., and Miller, William: *The Age of Enterprise* (1942; secs. II through VI); Cochran, Thomas C.: *Basic History of American Business* (1959; secs. V, VI, VIII); Dewey, David Rich: *Financial History of the United States*

(1936; secs. II through VIII); Faulkner, Harold U.: *American Economic History* (1960 new ed.; secs. III through VIII); Gras, N. S. B., and Larson, H. M.: *Casebook in American Business History* (1939; secs. II through VII); Hacker, Louis M.: *American Capitalism. Its Promise and Accomplishment* (1957; secs. IV through VIII); Hacker, Louis M.: *The Triumph of American Capitalism* (1940; secs. V through VIII); Johnson, E. R., Van Meter, I. W., Huebner, G. G., and Hanchett, D. S.: *History of Domestic and Foreign Commerce* (2 vols., 1915; secs. II through VII); Schlesinger, A. M., and Fox, D. R.: *History of American Life* (13 vols., 1927–1948; secs. III through VIII); Soule, George: *Economic Forces in American History* (1952; secs. IV through VII).

SERIES AND PERIODICALS: Dorfman, Joseph: *The Economic Mind in American Civilization* (5 vols., 1946–1959); Faulkner, H. U., and others: *Economic History of the United States* (7 vols., 1945–1961, see subject headings for specific titles); *Federal Reserve Bulletin* (1915–1961); *Fortune* magazine (1930–1961); Gabriel, R. H. (ed.): *The Pageant of America* (15 vols., 1925–1929); Johnson, Allen (ed. vols. 1–50), and Nevins, Allan (ed. vols. 51–56): *Chronicles of America* (56 vols., 1919–1940); *Journal of Economic History* (1951–1960); *Journal of Economic and Business History* (1928–1932).

II. COLONIAL AND REVOLUTIONARY TIMES: PLANTERS, MERCHANTS, BANKERS AND EARLY INDUSTRIALISTS

Adams, James Truslow: *Provincial Society* (1938); Allan, Herbert S.: *John Hancock* (1945); Augur, Helen: *The Secret War of Independence* (1955); Barrett, W., and Scovill, J. A.: *The Old Merchants of New York City* (1963); Beard, Miriam: *A History of the Business Man* (1938); Beatty, Richard C.: *William Byrd of Westover* (1932); Bishop, J. Leander: *A History of American Manufactures from 1608 to 1860* (vol. 1, 1864); Coleman, R. V.: *Liberty and Property* (1951); Davis, Joseph Stancliffe: *Essays in the Earlier History of American Corporations* (2 vols., 1917); Diamond, Sigmund: *The Reputation of the American Business Man* (1955); *Documents Relative to the Colonial History of the State of New York* (vols. III, IV; 1853); Dos Passos, John: *Prospects of a Golden Age* (1959); Dos Passos, John: *The Men Who Made the Nation* (1957); East, Robert Abraham: *Business Enterprise in the American Revolutionary Era* (1938); Ferguson, E. James: *The Power of the Purse: A History of American Public Finance 1776–1790* (1961); Fiske, John: *The Critical Period of American History 1783–1789* (1899); Forbes, Esther: *Paul Revere and the World He Lived in* (1942); Hacker, Louis M.: *Alexander Hamilton in the American Tradition* (1957); Hedges, James Blaine: *The Browns of Providence Plantation* (vol. 1, 1952); Hirsch, A. H.: *The Huguenots of South Carolina* (1928); Hunt, Freeman: *Lives of American Merchants* (2 vols., 1844); Keir, Malcolm: *March of Commerce* (Pageant of America series, 1927); Knollenberg, Bernhard: *Origin of the American Revolution* (1960); Marquand, John P.: *Timothy Dexter Revisited* (1960); Marvin, Winthrop L.: *The American Merchant Marine* (1902); Minnigerode, Meade: *Certain Rich Men* (1927);

Morison, Samuel Eliot: *Maritime History of Massachusetts 1783–1860* (1921); Morison, Samuel Eliot: *Sources and Documents Illustrating the American Revolution 1764–1788 and the Formation of the Federal Constitution* (1953); Nettels, Curtis P.: *The Money Supply of the American Colonies Before 1720* (1934); Paine, R. D.: *The Ships and Sailors of Old Salem* (1908); Prussing, Eugene E.: *The Estate of George Washington, Deceased* (1927); Ripley, W. S.: *The Financial History of Virginia, 1609* (1776); Ritter, Halsted L.: *George Washington as a Business Man* (1931); Robert, Joseph C.: *The Story of Tobacco in America* (1949); Rossiter, Clinton: *Seedtime of the Republic* (1953); Schlesinger, A. M.: *The Colonial Merchants and the American Revolution* (1957); Smith, Bradford: *Bradford of Plymouth* (1951); Spears, John R.: *The American Slave Trade* (1901); Stone, William L.: *The Centennial History of New York City, from the Discovery to the Present Day* (1876); Sumner, William G.: *The Financier and the Finances of the American Revolution* (vols. I and II, 1892); Sumner, William G.: *Robert Morris* (1892); Trevelyan, G. M.: *English Social History* (1942); Trow, Charles E.: *The Old Shipmasters of Salem* (1905); Van Doren, Carl: *Benjamin Franklin* (1938); Wallace, David Duncan: *Life of Henry Laurens* (1915); Weeden, William B.: *Economic and Social History of New England* (2 vols., 1891); Wildes, H. E.: *Lonely Midas: The Story of Stephen Girard* (1943); Young, E. M.: *Robert Morris, Forgotten Patriot* (1950).
See also general sources indicated for this section.

III. THE PROGRESS OF INVENTION, INDUSTRY, AND BUSINESS TO THE CIVIL WAR

Adams, Henry: *History of the United States During the Administrations of Jefferson and Madison* (9 vols., 1889–91); Beals, Carleton: *Our Yankee Heritage* (1952); Bolles, A. S.: *Industrial History of the United States* (1887); Bramson, Roy T. L.: *Highlights in the History of American Mass Production* (1945); Burlingame, Roger: *Engines of Democracy* (1940); Burlingame, Roger: *March of the Iron Men* (1938); Byrn, E. W.: *The Progress of Invention in the Nineteenth Century* (1900); Cameron, E. H.: *Samuel Slater: Father of American Manufactures* (1960); *The Collins Company—One Hundred Years* (1926); Crow, Carl: *The Great American Customer* (1943); Davis, Joseph Stancliffe: *Essays in the Earlier History of American Corporations* (2 vols., 1917); Edwards, William B.: *The Story of Colt's Revolver: A Biography of Colonel Samuel Colt* (1953); Greenslet, Ferris: *The Lowells and Their Seven Worlds* (1946); Hazard, E. B.: *The Organization of the Boot and Shoe Industry in Massachusetts Before 1873* (1921); Holbrook, Stewart H.: *Holy Old Mackinaw* (1938); Holbrook, Stewart H.: *Lost Men of American History* (1946); Hunt, Freeman: *Lives of American Merchants* (2 vols., 1844); Irving, Washington: *Astoria* (N.D.); Kaempffert, Waldemar: *Popular History of American Inventions* (1924); Lathrop, William G.: *The Brass Industry* (1926); May, Earl C.: *Principio to Wheeling 1715–1945—A Pageant of Iron and Steel* (1945); Myers, Margaret G.: *The New York Money Market* (1931); Nevins, Allan, and Mirsky, Jeannette: *The World of Eli Whitney* (1952); Nevins, Allan: *Abram S.*

Hewitt with Some Account of Peter Cooper (1935); Porter, Kenneth: *John Jacob Astor, Business Man* (2 vols., 1931); Rohan, Jack: *Yankee Arms-Maker; The Incredible Career of Samuel Colt* (1935); Singer, C., and others (eds.): *A History of Technology* (vols. III, IV, V, 1958); Thompson, Holland: *The Age of Invention* (Chronicles of America series, 1921); Ware, Caroline F.: *The Early New England Cotton Manufacture* (1931); Weeden, William B.: *Economic and Social History of New England* (2 vols., 1891); Weeks, Lyman Horace: *History of Paper Manufacturing in the United States* (1916); Wilson, Mitchell: *American Science and Invention* (1960); Woodward, Helen: *The Lady Persuaders* (1960).
See also general sources indicated for this section.

IV. GEOGRAPHICAL EXPANSION AND THE EARLIER EVOLUTION OF TRANSPORTATION IN THE NINETEENTH CENTURY

Albion, Robert G.: *The Rise of New York Port 1815–1860* (1939); Beals, Carleton: *Our Yankee Heritage* (1952); Beard, Miriam: *History of the Business Man* (1938); Bidwell, Percy Wells, and Falconer, John I.: *History of Agriculture in the Northern United States, 1620–1860* (1941); Bristol Brass Corporation: *Bristol Fashion* (1950); Burlingame, Roger: *Engines of Democracy* (1940); Burlingame, Roger: *March of the Iron Men* (1938); Carter, C. E.: *When Railroads Were New* (1909); Chalmers, Harvey II: *The Birth of the Erie Canal* (1960); Clark, William H.: *Railroads and Rivers* (1939); Diamond, Sigmund: *The Reputation of the American Business Man* (1955); Dunbar, Seymour: *History of Travel in America* (1937); Flexner, James T.: *Steamboats Come True* (1944); Garrett, Garet: *The American Story* (1955); Holbrook, Stewart H.: *The Story of American Railroads* (1947); Hoyt, Edwin P.: *The Vanderbilts and Their Fortunes* (1962); Hulbert, Archer B.: *The Paths of Inland Commerce* (Chronicles of America series, 1921); Hunter, Louis C.: *Steamboats on the Western Rivers* (1949); Irving, Washington: *Astoria* (N.D.); Jones, C. L.: *Economic History of the Anthracite Tidewater Canals* (1908); Keir, Malcolm: *March of Commerce* (Pageant of America series, 1927); Larkin, Oliver W.: *Samuel F. B. Morse* (1954); Marvin, Winthrop L.: *The American Merchant Marine* (1902); Minnigerode, Meade: *Certain Rich Men* (1927); Morison, Samuel Eliot: *Maritime History of Massachusetts 1783–1860* (1921); Nevins, Allan: *Abram S. Hewitt with Some Account of Peter Cooper* (1935); Porter, Kenneth W.: *John Jacob Astor, Business Man* (2 vols., 1931); Robbins, R. M.: *Our Landed Heritage: The Public Domain 1776–1936* (1942); Smith, Henry Justin: *Chicago's Great Century 1833–1933* (1933); Taylor, George Rogers: *The Transportation Revolution 1815–1860* (1958); Thompson, Slason: *A Short History of American Railways* (1925); Twain, Mark (psd. Clemens, Samuel L.): *Life on the Mississippi* (1883); Weeden, William B.: *Economic and Social History of New England* (2 vols., 1891); Wilson, Mitchell: *American Science and Invention* (1960).
See also general sources indicated for this section.

V. THE CIVIL WAR, THE COMING OF INDUSTRIALISM

Allen, Hugh: *Rubber's Home Town* (1949); Appel, Joseph A.: *The Business Biography of John Wanamaker* (1930); Bolles, A. S.: *Industrial History of the United States* (1887); Borth, Christy: *Masters of Mass Production* (1945); Borth, Christy: *True Steel* (1941); Bruce, P. A.: *The Rise of the New South* (1905); Bruce, Robert J.: *1877: Year of Violence* (1959); Burlingame, Roger: *Engines of Democracy* (1940); Burlingame, Roger: *March of the Iron Men* (1938); Business History Review-Staff of eds.: *Oil's First Century* (1960); Crow, Carl: *The Great American Customer* (1943); Dodd, William E.: *The Cotton Kingdom* (1920); Dorian, Max: *The du Ponts from Gunpowder to Nylon* (1962); Eckenrode, H. J., and Edmonds, P. W.: *E. H. Harriman* (1933); Erickson, Charlotte: *American Industry and the European Immigrant 1860–1885* (1957); Fite, Emerson D.: *Social and Industrial Conditions in the North During the Civil War* (1910); Fritz, John: *Autobiography of John Fritz* (1912); Giddens, Paul H.: *The Birth of the Oil Industry* (1938); Girdler, Tom, in collaboration with Boyden Sparkes: *Bootstraps: The Autobiography of Tom M. Girdler* (1943); Hacker, Louis M., and Hendrick, Benjamin B.: *The United States Since 1865* (1932); Helper, Hinton Rowan: *The Impending Crisis* (1857); Hendrick, Burton J.: *Life of Andrew Carnegie* (2 vols., 1932); Henry, Robert Selph: *This Fascinating Railroad Business* (1942); Holbrook, Stewart H.: *Holy Old Mackinaw* (1938); Holbrook, Stewart H.: *Iron Brew* (1939); Holbrook, Stewart H.: *The Story of American Railroads* (1947); Hough, Emerson: *The Passing of the Frontier, A Chronicle of the Old West* (Chronicles of America series, 1920); Howells, William Dean: *The Rise of Silas Lapham* (1889); Hoyt, Edwin P.: *The Vanderbilts and Their Fortunes* (1962); Jennings, W. W.: *Twenty Giants of American Business* (1953); Keir, Malcolm: *March of Commerce* (Pageant of America series, 1927); Kirkland, Edward C.: *Men, Cities and Transportation 1820–1900* (2 vols., 1948); Lane, Wheaton J.: *Commodore Vanderbilt* (1942); Lewis, Lloyd, and Smith, Henry Justin: *Chicago. The History of Its Reputation* (1929); Lewis, Oscar: *The Big Four* (1938); Lewton, Frederick L.: *A Brief History of the Sewing Machine* (1929); Longstreet, Stephen: *A Century on Wheels: The Story of Studebaker* (1952); Mahoney, Tom: *The Great Merchants* (1955); Minnigerode, Meade: *Certain Rich Men* (1927); Morley, Felix: *Freedom and Federalism* (1959); Nevins, Allan: *Abram S. Hewitt with Some Account of Peter Cooper* (1935); Osborn, Norris G. (ed.): *History of Connecticut* (4 vols., 1925); Redlich, Fritz: *History of American Business Leaders*, Vol. I: *Iron and Steel* (1940); Robbins, R. M.: *Our Landed Heritage: the Public Domain 1776–1936* (1942); Thompson, Holland: *The New South* (Chronicles of America series, 1919); Twain, Mark, and Warner, Charles Dudley: *The Gilded Age* (1873); Wasson, Gordon: *The Hall Carbine Affair* (1948); Webb, Walter Prescott: *The Great Plains* (1931); Weeks, Lyman Horace: *History of Paper Manufacturing in the United States* (1916); Wilkins, Thurman: *Clarence King* (1958); Wright, C. D.: *Industrial Revolution in the United States* (1897).
See also general sources indicated for this section.

VI. TRUSTS, THE GROWTH OF BIG ENTERPRISE, AND THE RISE OF THE NEW YORK MONEY MARKET

Allen, Frederick Lewis: *The Great Pierpont Morgan* (1948); Allen, William H.: *Rockefeller: Giant, Dwarf, Symbol* (1936); Appel, Joseph A.: *The Business Biography of John Wanamaker* (1930); Baruch, Bernard: *My Own Story* (vol. 1, 1957); Beard, Miriam: *A History of the Business Man* (1938); Bogue, Allan G.: *Money at Interest. The Farm Mortgage on the Middle Border* (1955); Business History Review-Staff of eds.: *Oil's First Century* (1960); Corey, Lewis: *The House of Morgan* (1930); Diamond, Sigmund: *The Reputation of the American Business Man* (1955); Eckenrode, H. J., and Edmonds, P. W.: *E. H. Harriman* (1933); Flynn, John T.: *God's Gold* (1932); Henry, Robert Selph: *This Fascinating Railroad Business* (1942); Hidy, Ralph, and Hidy, Muriel: *Pioneering in Big Business* (vol. 1, 1955); Holbrook, Stewart H.: *The Age of the Moguls* (1953); Holbrook, Stewart H.: *James J. Hill* (1955); Holbrook, Stewart H.: *The Story of American Railroads* (1947); Hoyt, Edwin P.: *The Vanderbilts and Their Fortunes* (1962); Josephson, Matthew: *The Politicos 1865–1896* (1938); Josephson, Matthew: *The Robber Barons* (1934); Kennan, George: *E. H. Harriman, A Biography* (1922); Lloyd, Henry Demarest: *Wealth Against Commonwealth* (1894); Medbery, J. K.: *Men and Mysteries of Wall Street* (1870); Minnigerode, Meade: *Certain Rich Men* (1927); Moody, John: *The Masters of Capital* (Chronicles of America series, 1919); Moody, John: *The Railroad Builders* (Chronicles of America series, 1921); Moody, John: *The Truth About the Trusts* (1904); Myers, Gustavus: *History of the Great American Fortunes* (1936); Nevins, Allan: *John D. Rockefeller: A Biography* (2 vols., 1940); Redlich, Fritz: *The Molding of American Banking—Men and Ideas* (1951); Satterlee, Herbert L.: *J. Pierpont Morgan* (1939); Tarbell, Ida M.: *History of the Standard Oil Company* (1904); Twain, Mark, and Warner, Charles Dudley: *The Gilded Age* (1873); Winkler, John K.: *The First Billion: The Stillmans and the National City Bank* (1934); Winkler, John K.: *John D. Rockefeller, a Portrait in Oils* (1929); Winkler, John K.: *Morgan the Magnificent* (1930); Winkler John K.: *Tobacco Tycoon. The Story of James Buchanan Duke* (1942). See also general sources indicated for this section.

VII. THE MAKING OF THE CITIES: THE COMING OF ELECTRICITY, THE TELEPHONE, NEW TRANSPORTATION

Barnard, Harry: *Independent Man; the Life of Senator James Couzens* (1958); Borth, Christy: *The Automobile: Power Plant and Transportation of a Free People* (1952); Borth, Christy: *Wheels of Freedom* (1960); Boyd, T. A.: *Professional Amateur: The Biography of Charles F. Kettering* (1957); Casson, H. N.: *History of the Telephone* (1910); Costain, Thomas B.: *The Chord of Steel* (1960); Danelian, Noobar Retheos: *A. T. & T.: the Story of Industrial Conquest* (1939); Forbes, C. B.: *Men Who Are Making America* (1917); Ford, Henry, with Crowther, Samuel: *My Life and Work* (1922); *Fortune* magazine: February, 1930; January, 1931; January, April, May, 1932; December, 1933; November, December, 1934; January, May,

1935; March, April, May, June, 1936; February, December, 1938; January, 1939; Garrett, Garet: *The American Omen* (1928); Garrett, Garet: *The Wild Wheel* (1952); Jewkes, John, Sawers, David, and Stillerman, Richard: *The Sources of Invention* (1959); Josephson, Matthew: *Thomas A. Edison* (1961); Hendrick, Burton J.: *The Age of Big Business* (Chronicles of America series, 1919); Kennedy, E. D.: *The Automobile Industry* (1941); Kettering, Charles F., and Boyd, T. A. (ed.): *Prophet of Progress: Selections from the Speeches of Charles F. Kettering* (1961); Kirkland, Edward C.: *A History of Economic Life* (1940); Kirkland, Edward C.: *Industry Comes of Age* (1961); Lessing, Lawrence: *Man of High Fidelity: Edwin Howard Armstrong* (1956); Maurer, Herrymon: *Great Enterprise* (1955); Merz, Charles: *And Then Came Ford* (1929); Mitchell, Sidney Alexander: *S. Z. Mitchell and the Electrical Industry* (1960); Morris, Lloyd: *Not So Long Ago* (1949); Mumford, Lewis: *The Brown Decades* (1931); Nevins, Allan, and Hill, Frank E.: *Ford: The Times, The Man, The Company* (vol. 1, 1954); Nevins, Allan, and Hill, Frank E.: *Ford: Expansion and Challenge 1915–1933* (vol. II, 1957); Pound, Arthur: *The Automobile and an American City* (1962); Pound, Arthur: *The Turning Wheel* (1934); Rae, John B.: *American Automobile Manufacturers* (1959); Ramsay, M. L.: *Pyramids of Power* (1937); Russell, Dean: *Men, Motors and Markets* (1959); Shannon, Fred A.: *Economic History of the People of the United States* (1934); Sorensen, Charles E.: *My Forty Years with Ford* (1956); Sullivan, Mark: *Our Times: The Turn of the Century* (1926); Sullivan, Mark: *Our Times: The War Begins* (1932); Sullivan, Mark: *Our Times: America Finding Herself* (1929); Thompson, Holland: *The Age of Invention* (Chronicles of America series, 1921); Tunnard, Christopher, and Reed, Henry Hope: *American Skyline* (1956); Walker, James Blaine: *The Epic of American Industry* (1949); Winkler, John K.: *The du Pont Dynasty* (1935). See also general sources indicated for this section.

VIII. THE FIRST DECADES OF THE TWENTIETH CENTURY, THE GREAT BOOM OF THE TWENTIES AND THE DEPRESSION OF THE THIRTIES

Allen, Frederick Lewis: *The Big Change* (1952); Allen, Frederick Lewis: *The Lords of Creation* (1935); Allen, Frederick Lewis: *Only Yesterday* (1931); Baruch, Bernard: *My Own Story—The Public Years* (vol. II, 1960); Borth, Christy: *True Steel* (1941); Brandeis, Louis D.: *Other People's Money and How the Bankers Use It* (1932); Chandler, Lester V.: *Benjamin Strong, Central Banker* (1958); Corey, Lewis: *The Decline of American Capitalism* (1934); Danelian, Noobar Retheos: *A. T. and T.: The Story of Industrial Conquest* (1939); Davis, Forrest: *What Price Wall Street* (1932); Dulles, Foster Rhea: *The United States Since 1865* (1959); Dutton, William S.: *Du Pont—140 Years* (1942); *Fortune* magazine: February, 1930; January, 1931; January, April, May, 1932; December, 1933; November, December, 1934; January, May, 1935; March, April, May, June, 1936; February, December, 1938; January, 1939; Graves, Lloyd M.: *The Great Depression and Beyond* (1932); Gunther, John: *Taken at the Flood* (1960); Hacker, Louis M., and Hendrick, Benjamin B.: *The United States Since 1865*

(1932); Hoover, Herbert: *The Memoirs of Herbert Hoover* (vols. I and II, 1952); Jewkes, John, Sawyers, David, and Stillerman, Richard: *The Sources of Invention* (1959); Josephson, Matthew: *Empire of the Air* (1944); Kahn, E. J., Jr.: *The Big Drink: The Story of Coca-Cola* (1960); Kelly, Fred C. (ed.): *Miracle at Kitty Hawk* (1951): Kelly, Fred C.: *The Wright Brothers* (1943); Kennedy, E. D.: *Dividends to Pay* (1939); Lessing, Lawrence: *Man of High Fidelity: Edwin Howard Armstrong* (1956); Maurer, Herrymon: *Great Enterprise. Growth and Behavior of the Big Corporation* (1955); Mitchell, Broadus: *Depression Decade* (1947); O'Connor, Harvey: *Mellon's Millions* (1933); Peterson, William H.: *The Great Farm Problem* (1959); Richberg, Donald R.: *The Rainbow* (1936); Sakolski, Aaron M.: *The Great American Land Bubble* (1932); Schlesinger, A. M., Jr.: *The Politics of Upheaval* (1960); Smith, Henry Ladd: *Airways Abroad* (1950); Snyder, Carl: *Capitalism, the Creator* (1940); Sullivan, Mark: *Our Times—The War Begins* (1932); Tebbel, John: *The Inheritors* (1962); Warren, Harris G.: *Herbert Hoover and the Great Depression* (1959); Yoder, Dale, and Davies, George R.: *Depression and Recovery* (1934).
See also general sources indicated for this section.

IX. BUSINESS: ITS ROLE IN WORLD WAR II AND BEYOND

Dorfman, Joseph: *The Economic Mind in American Civilization* (vols. IV and V, 1946); Drucker, Peter: *The Future of Industrial Man* (1942); *Economic Reports of the President* (1947 through 1962); *Fortune* magazine (editors of): *The Changing American Market* (1955); *Fortune* magazine (editors of): *Markets of the Sixties* (1960); *Fortune* magazine (editors of): *The Mighty Force of Research* (1956); Galbraith, John Kenneth: *The Affluent Society* (1958); Galbraith, John Kenneth: *American Capitalism* (1952); Galbraith, John Kenneth: *The Liberal Hour* (1960); Glover, John G., and Lagai, Rudolph L. (eds.): *The Development of American Industries* (1959); Harper, F. A.: *Why Wages Rise* (1957); Janeway, Eliot: *The Struggle for Survival—A Chronicle of American Mobilization in World War II* (Chronicles of America series, 1951); Kahn, E. J., Jr.: *The Big Drink: The Story of Coca-Cola* (1960); Kaplan, A. D. H.: *Big Enterprise in a Competitive System* (1954); Land, Emory S.: *Winning the War with Ships* (1958); Mahoney, Tom: *The Story of George Romney* (1960); Maurer, Herrymon: *Great Enterprise. Growth and Behavior of the Big Corporation* (1955); Mazur, Paul: *The Standards We Raise* (1953); Robinson, Claude: *Understanding Profits* (1961); Standard & Poor: *Industry Surveys* (vols. I, II, 1955–1961; *Wall Street Journal* (editors of): *The New Millionaires and How They Made Their Fortunes* (1961); Walton, Francis: *The Miracle of World War II* (1956).
For the 1960's, see issues of *Fortune* magazine and of *Barron's National Business & Financial Weekly*.

Index

Abbott, Horace, 129
Acme Oil Co., 152
Adams, James Truslow, 225
Adams, John, 28, 61
Adams, John Quincy, 66
Adams, Sam, 24
Adams Express Co., 181
Aetna Fire Insurance Co., 168
Africa, trade with, 3, 12, 17, 26, 44, 46
Air conditioning, 236
Airplanes and airlines, 206, 238–241
Allen, Ethan, 112
Allied Chemical Corp., 234, 236
Almy & Brown Co., 53–55
Aluminum Company of America, 221, 237
Aluminum industry, 183–184
Amalgamated Copper Co., 180
American Airlines, 240
American Bridge Co., 177
American Can Co., 166
American Cyanamid Co., 236
American Hide & Leather Co., 180
American Motors Corp., 248
American Optical Co., 237
American Revolution, 10, 16, 18, 24–42, 44
American Rolling Mill Co., 237
American Smelting & Refining Co., 180
American Steel & Wire Co., 177, 179
American Sugar Refining Co., 165, 174, 180
American Telephone & Telegraph Co., 181, 186, 189, 198–199, 252, 262
American Tin Plate Co., 177
American Tobacco Co., 165, 174, 196
Anderson, John W., 211
Anderson, Joseph Reed, 128
Andrews, Samuel, 150
Appleton, Nathan, 55
Archbold, John D., 152
Arkwright, Sir Richard, 53
Arlen Realty Co., 262

Armour, Philip D., 125
Armstrong, Maj. Edwin H., 199
Aspinwall, William, 142
Astor, John Jacob, 83–84
Astor, William B., 142
Atlas Portland Cement Co., 180
Augur, Helen, 30
Automation, 107–108
Automobile industry, 102, 183, 202–222, 242, 248
Avery, C. W., 212
Aviation industry, 238–241
Ax industry, 88–89, 92, 99, 112

Babbitt, 220, 224
Babbitt, Benjamin T., 101
Babson, Roger, 196
Baker, George F., 173, 181
Baldwin Locomotive Works, 181
Baltimore & Ohio Railroad, 74–76, 145, 172
Baltimore Turnpike, 65–66
Banking, growth of, 129–130, 166, 182
Bankers Trust Co., 181
Bank of the United States, 39, 40, 66, 78, 120
Barker, George F., 190
Barnum, Phineas T., 142
Baruch, Bernard, 184, 212, 228, 231
Bausch & Lomb Optical Co., 237
Bell, Alexander Graham, 188
Bell Telephone Co., 189
Bell Telephone Laboratories, 246, 252
Benz, Carl, 205
Berle, Adolf, 243
Bernays, Edward, 256
Bessemer process, 116–118, 128, 145, 156, 159–160
Bethlehem Steel Co., 117, 129, 183, 256
Bicycles, 206, 212
Biddle, Nicholas, 120
Big business, 146–162, 204, 243
Bingham, William, 86

273

Bishop, Japhet, 142
Bishop, J. Leander, 113
Bissell, George H., 149
Blake, Lyman R., 111
Blanchard, Thomas, 102
Bland-Allison Act, 182
Blue Ridge Corp., 228
Boeing Airplane Co., 241
Bond sales, 130–132, 138, 169
Boone, Daniel, 63
Borden, Gail, 110
Borth, Christie, 220
Boston Associates, 56
Boston Massacre, 10
Boston Tea Party, 10, 24, 29
Bowditch, Nathaniel, 47, 56
Bowdoin, George S., 173
Bradford, William, 2
Brandeis, Louis, 181
Brandenberger, Jacques Edwin, 234
Brass industry, 57, 59, 190
Breed, Ebenezer, 111
Breer, Carl, 219
Brewster, James, 102
Briscoe, Benjamin, 204
British Mercantile Plan, 26, 262
British Navy, 7, 10–11, 17, 44–45
Brown, George, 74
Brown, Capt. James, 11
Brown, Moses, 53
Brown, Nicholas & Co., 11
Brown, Obadiah, 11
Brown, Sylvanus, 55
Brown & Sharpe Mfg. Co., 211
Brown University, 12
Brush, Charles F., 190, 195
Bryan, William Jennings, 165, 182
Buell, Abel, 61
Buick, David D., 202
Bulfinch, Charles, 45, 47
Burgess, Hugh, 104
Byrd, William, II, 20

Cadillac automobile, 92, 204, 207, 211
Calhoun, John C., 132
Callis, Dr. Conrad C., 235
Cambria Iron Works, 117, 158–159
Canals, era of, 66–67, 70
Candee, L. Co., 103
Canning industry, 110
Capital, 7–8, 43–62, 122, 138, 184–201
Capital expenditures, 122, 262
Carnegie, Andrew, 117, 145, 156–162

Carnegie, Thomas M., 157–159
Carothers, Dr. Wallace, 235
Carr, Albert Z., 153
Carrier Corp., 236
Carter, Byron T., 215
Carter, Robert, 21
Cartwright, Edmund, 53
Cattle, 137–138
Cellophane, 234, 250
Central Pacific Railroad, 134–137
Champion, Albert, 203
Chapin, Roy D., 208, 217
Charch, William Hale, 234
Chase, Salmon P., 129
Chase Manhattan Bank, 244
Chase National Bank, 181
Chemical industry, 233–234, 237
Chemstrand Corp., 250
Chesapeake & Ohio Railroad, 76, 172, 248
Cheves, Langdon, 120
Chevrolet car, 204, 215–217
Chicago, Burlington & Quincy Railroad, 175–176
Chicago, growth of, 64, 73–74, 79–80, 97, 125
China clipper trade, 44–45, 47, 49
Chinese labor, Central Pacific, 135
Chrysler, Walter P., 214, 219
Civil War, 81, 119–139
Clark, Edward, 109
Clark, V. S., 57
Clay, Henry, 66, 100, 133
Clinton, De Witt, 66–67
Clipper ships, 44–45
Clock industry, 61, 64, 93
Clothing industry, 124
Coal mining, 69, 71
Cochran, Thomas, 166
Codfish trade, 6, 29
Coffee trade, 18, 46
Coffin, Charles A., 195
Coffin, Howard Earle, 209, 238
Coggeswell, William L., 142
Coleman, William, 158
Colles, Christopher, 66
Collins Co. of Collinsville, 88, 92, 99
Collins Radio Co., 241
Colonial Air Transport, 239
Colonial trade, 1–23
Colt, Samuel, 61, 84, 89, 91–92
Colt revolver, 81, 90–92, 99, 128, 137
Columbia Broadcasting System, 200
Columbus Oil Co., 157
Commonwealth Edison Co., 186

Communism, 263
Compact car, 249–250
Competition, suppression of, 150–153
Compton, Arthur H., 236
Computers, 252–253
Comstock Lode, 126, 134
Conestoga wagon, 65
Conrad, Dr. Frank, 199–200
Consolidated Edison Co., 186, 193
Consolidated Tobacco Co., 174, 180
Constitution, U.S., 36, 38, 55
Cook, Capt. James, 47
Cooke, Jay, 130–132, 138, 169
Cooper, Peter, 75–76, 105–106, 113–116
Copper industry, 57, 184
Cornell, Ezra, 106, 115
Corporation, first U.S., 41
Cort, Henry, 112
Coster, Charles H., 173
Cotton gin, 60
Cotton industry, 5, 48, 55, 69, 83, 120–121
Couzens, James, 211, 213
Coxe, Tench, 40
Crédit Mobilier, 134, 140
Crocker, Charles, 134
Crompton, Samuel, 53
Cross Co., 253
Crowther, Samuel, 205
Cumberland Road, 63, 66
Currency problems, 31, 34, 82
Curtiss-Wright Corp., 241
Cushing, John P., 49
Custis, John Parke, 23
Cutten, Arthur, 228
Cyclotron, 236

Dabney, Charles H., 169
Daimler, Gottlieb, 205
Dale, Sir Thomas, 2
Davis, Ari, 107
Davis, Jefferson, 120
Davis, Phineas, 76
Davison, Henry P., 181, 183
Day, Benjamin Henry, 104
Dayton Engineering Laboratories Co. (Delco), 215–216
Deane, Silas, 30–31
Declaration of Independence, 10
Deere, John, 94
De Forest, Lee, 199
Delco self-starter, 215–216
De Mille, Cecil B., 198
Depew, Chauncey, 172
Derby, Elias Hasket, 45–47

Derby, Richard, 7, 10
Derby Turnpike, 65
Detroit, growth of, 73–74, 202–222
Dickens, Charles, 70
Diesel-electric locomotives, 238
Dill, James B., 174
Dillon, Read & Co., 219
Disston saws, 88–89
Dodd, Samuel C. T., 153
Dodd, William E., 122
Dodge, Gen. Grenville, 135
Dodge brothers, 207, 211, 213, 219
Douglas Aircraft Co., Inc., 241
Dow Chemical Co., 236
Drake, Col. E. L., 149
Drew, Daniel, 77, 141, 143, 145
Drug industry, 254
Duer, William, 39, 44
Duke, James B., 174
Dunne, Peter Finley, 164
Du Pont, Lammot, 127, 234
Du Pont, Pierre, 216–217
Du Pont de Nemours, I. E. Co., 101, 126, 129, 181, 216, 228, 246, 250
Durant, William C., 183, 202, 214–215, 228
Duryea brothers, 205
Dynamo, 186, 190, 192

Eastern Air Transport, 239
Eastman, George, 198
Eastman Kodak Co., 237
Eaton, Maj. Amos Beebe, 92–93
Echert, J. Presper, 252
Edison, Thomas A., 50, 147, 173, 184–201, 251
Edison effect, 199
Edison Electric Light Co., 193–194
Eisenhower Administration, 256
Electric Autolite Co., 209, 250
Electric automobile, 201
Electric Bond & Share Co., 195–196
Electric light and power, 185–198
Electronics industry, 199, 236, 251
Elkins, William, 196
Emde, Carl, 212
Emerson, Ralph Waldo, 100
Emery, Lewis, Jr., 155
Enfield rifle, 92
Equitable Life Insurance Co., 181
Ericcson, John, 129
Erie Canal, 36, 66–68, 74–77
Erie Railroad, 143, 169–170
Erskine, Robert, 113
Ethyl Gasoline Corp., 235

European capital, 166
European Common Market, 222, 260
Evans, Oliver, 42, 51–52
Evaporated milk, 110
Explosives industry, 101, 126

Fabbri, Egisto P., 173
Factory, rise of, 81–99
Fairfax, Lord Thomas, 22
Faneuil Hall, Boston, 10
Faraday, Michael, 186, 201
Farm Board, 229
Farmer, Moses G., 190
Farming, 35, 83, 88–99, 124–125
Farnsworth, Philo T., 236
Federal Communications Commission, 253
Federal Reserve System, 183, 225–228
Federal Steel Co., 160, 177
Field, Cyrus W., 105
Firearms, 61, 89–92, 127–128, 168
Firestone Tire & Rubber Co., 201, 222
First National Bank of N. Y., 173, 179, 181
Fisher, George, 108
Fisher Body Co., 206, 216
Fishing industry, 3, 7, 112
Fisk, James, 141, 143, 145, 169
Fitch, John, 50, 71
Fitzhugh, William, 20
Flagler, Henry M., 150, 153
Flanders, Walter E., 212
Fleming, Sir John A., 199
Fleming, Lamar, 247
Florida land boom, 227
Flour milling, 22, 52–53
Fluorescent lighting, 236
Food, farm mechanization and, 124
Forbes, Esther, 29
Forbes, John Murray, 49
Forbes, Robert Bennet, 49
Ford, Henry, 183, 202, 205, 207, 210–214, 263
Ford Motor Co., 201, 210–214, 238, 250, 253, 256
Franklin, Benjamin, 29–30, 50
Frasch, Herman, 155
Free enterprise, 1–23
Free Silver campaign, 165
French and Indian War, 23, 28
Frick, Henry Clay, 158
Frigidaire, 216, 235
Fritz, John, 117, 129
Frontier, expansion of, 81–99

Fuller, John, 90
Fulton, Robert, 51, 71
Fur trade, 83–84

Galbraith, John Kenneth, 248
Galey, John H., 155
Gallatin, Albert, 65
Gallup, George, 226
Garrett, Garet, 81
Gary, Elbert H., 177–179
Gasoline, 197, 201, 205, 220
Gates, John W., 177, 179
Geddes, James, 68
General Electric Co., 186, 195, 199, 215, 236, 253, 262
General Film Co., 198
General Motors Acceptance Corp., 216
General Motors Corp., 183, 202, 204, 214, 228, 234, 244, 246, 256, 262
Ghent, W. J., 179
Gibbons, Thomas, 72
Gilded Age, 78–79, 140–162
Gimbel Brothers, 197
Girard, Stephen, 16, 34, 44, 49
Glass industry, 221
Godey, Louis Antoine, 110
Godfrey, Charles H., 173
Godowsky, Leo, 237
Gold mining, 48, 92, 98, 126
Gold standard, 43–44, 164, 182, 260
Goldwyn, Samuel, 198
Goodlow, Daniel R., 122
Goodyear, Charles, 103, 111
Goodyear Tire & Rubber Co., 221
Gould, Jay, 141, 143, 145, 169
Government agencies, 225
Government bonds, 130–132, 138, 169
Government contracts, 224, 253
Government spending, 242, 259
Grant, Ulysses S., 130, 132
Gray, Elisha, 189
Gray, John S., 211, 213
Gray, Robert, 48
Great Atlantic & Pacific Tea Co., 197
Great Depression, 205, 219, 224, 242
Great Lakes shipping, 80, 125, 160
Great Northern Railroad, 138, 175–177
Great Western Iron Co., 117
Greenbacks, 130, 138
Greene, Nathanael, 31
Griffith, David Wark, 198
Grilley brothers, 59
Griswold, J. W., 129

Gross national product, 224, 244, 256, 259
Guaranty Trust Co., 181
Guffey, Col. J. M., 155
Gulf Oil Co., 155, 183

Hacker, Louis, 40
Hackley, Charles H., 87
Hadley, Arthur Twining, 163
Haggerty, John, 142
Hale, Sarah Josepha, 110
Hall, Charles Martin, 183
Hambleton, John, 238
Hamilton, Alexander, 33, 37–41, 91
Hamilton, Dr. Alexander, 2
Hancock, John, 10, 24, 29
Hancock, Thomas, 8–10
Hansen, Alvin, 224
Hargreaves, James, 53
Harkness, S. D., 150
Harnden, William, 101
Harper & Brothers, 116
Harriman, Edward H., 174, 177
Harrison, Richard, 30
Hartford, George L., 197
Harvard University, 9, 56, 196, 238
Harvey, Charles T., 80
Hasenclever, Peter, 113
Havemeyer, Henry O., 174
Haynes, Elwood, 205
Hays, John Coffee, 90
Hearst, William Randolph, 126
Helper, Hinton Rowan, 122
Hendrick, Burton J., 142, 158
Henry, Joseph, 187
Henry, William, 71
Hewes, George Robert, 24
Hewitt, Abram S., 114, 128
Higgins, Andrew Jackson, 246
Hill, James Jerome, 138, 175
Hindenburg, Paul von, 241–242
Hoe, Richard March, 103–104
Holbrook, Stewart, 86
Holding companies, 195
Homestead Act, 133
Homestead strike, 165
Hood, Thomas, 107
Hoover, Herbert C., 227, 229
Hopkins, Mark, 134
Hopkins, Samuel, 12
Houdry Process Corp., 236
Howe, Elias, 107–111
Howe, F. W., 93
Howells, William Dean, 141–142
Hubbard, Gardiner G., 188

Hudson, J. L., 209
Hull, Cordell, 233
Hunt, Walter, 108
Hunter, S. V. A., 111
Huntington, Collis P., 134
Hussey, Obed, 96
Hutchinson, B. E., 219
Hyatt Roller Bearing Co., 216

IBM, 257
Ice industry, 101–102
Illinois Central Railroad, 116, 125, 174
Incomes, 1960's, 254
Indians, 35, 63–64, 83–84, 137, 187
Indigo, 17–18, 27–28, 234
Industrial revolution, American, 62
Inflation, 34, 82–83, 138
Inland Steel Co., 183
Insull, Samuel, 193, 196
Insurance companies, 101
Interchangeable parts, 61, 211–212
Interlocking directorates, 69, 181
Internal-combustion engine, 201, 221
International Business Machines Corp., 200, 252, 262
International Harvester Co., 98, 181
International Mercantile Marine Co., 180–181
International Paper Co., 166
Invention, rise of, 43–62, 185–201
Investment capital, 49–50, 138
Iron and steel industries, 12, 16, 57, 71, 80, 111–118, 128–129, 133
Irving, Washington, 83

Jackson, Andrew, 40, 66, 81, 106, 129
Jackson, Patrick Tracy, 55
Jefferson, Peter, 22
Jefferson, Thomas, 19, 27, 36, 47, 61, 65–66, 94, 132
Jeffery, Thomas B., 203
Johnson, Herbert, 231
Johnson, Gen. Hugh S., 231–232
Jones, Capt. Bill, 158–159
Jones & Laughlin Steel Corp., 117, 183
Joy, Henry, 209
Judah, Theodore, 134
Juniata iron works, Pittsburgh, 117

Kaiser, Henry J., 246, 248
Kaiser Aluminum & Chemical Corp., 221
Kansas Pacific Railroad, 135–137
KDKA, radio station, 199–200
Kelly, William, 117, 128

Kendall, Amos, 106
Kennedy Administration, 256
Kentucky, expansion of, 28
Kerosene, 147, 150
Kettering, Charles F., 215, 217, 235, 238
Keynesian economics, 44, 224, 232, 242
Kidd, Capt. William, 14
Kidder, Peabody & Co., 179
Kier, Dr. Samuel, 101, 149
King, Charles Brady, 205
Klann, William, 212
Kloman, Andrew, 117, 156–158
Knox, Gen. Henry, 44
Knudsen, William, 212, 217, 245
Korean War, 254
Kraus, Dr. Charles A., 235
Kuhn, Loeb & Co., 165, 174, 181, 183, 228

La Follette, Robert, 87
Laissez faire, 27
Lamont, Thomas F., 181
Lancaster Pike, 40, 65
Land, Edwin H., 237
Land, government sale of, 81–82
Land boom, Florida, 227
Lane, John, 94
Langmuir, Irving, 199
Lasker, Albert D., 221
Latrobe brothers, 76
Laurens, Henry, 18
Lawrence, Ernest O., 236
Ledyard, John, 47
Lee, Ivy, 147, 258
Lee, Higginson & Co., 214
Lee, Gen. Robert E., 132
Leeds, William B., 179
Leffingwell, Russell, 225
Lehigh Coal and Navigation Co., 69
Leland, Henry M., 207, 211–216, 238
Lenox, James, 142
Lewis, John L., 232
Lewis, Sinclair, 220, 224
Libby-Owens-Ford Glass Co., 221
Liberty, tradition of, 25
Liberty engines, 238
Lilienthal, David, 243
Lincoln, Abraham, 100, 120, 128, 132
Lincoln Motor Co., 216
Lind, Jenny, 142
Lindbergh, Charles A., 240
Lindsay, David, 13
Little, Arthur D., Inc., 214
Little, Jacob, 101

Living standards, 1960's, 254
Livingston, Philip, 112
Livingston, Robert R., 71
Locke, John, 27
Locomotives, 74–75, 128–129, 144, 238
Loew, Marcus, 198
Louisiana Purchase, 82
Lowell, Francis Cabot, 55–56, 61, 107
Lowrey, Grosvenor, 185
Lucas, Eliza, 17
Luchich (Lucas), Anthony, 155
Lucite, 236
Lumber industry, 85–89

McCormick, Cyrus Hall, 95–99
McCormick reaper, 96–97
McCoy, Joseph G., 137
McKay, Donald, 45
McKay, Gordon, 111
McKinley, William, 165, 182
McNary, Charles, 227
Machine gun, 128
Machine tools, 41, 61, 93, 102, 226
Macy, R. H., Co., 197
Madison, James, 38, 47, 132
Maine, industry in, 5, 86
Malcolmson, Alexander Y., 211, 213
"Manifest destiny," 81, 118
Mannes, Leopold, 237
Marconi, Guglielmo, 199
Marshall, Gen. George C., 245
Marshall, Chief Justice John, 72
Marshall Plan, 256
Martin Company, 253
Mass production, 60–61, 92, 205, 208, 212
Mauchly, John W., 252
Meason, Isaac, 117
Meat industry, 125
Mellon, Andrew, 155, 183, 229
Mercantilism, 25, 28, 262
"Merchant princes," 142
Mergers, 250
Merrill, Charles, 87
Merritt brothers, 179
Mesabi ore fields, 160, 163, 179, 197
Metalworking industry, 57, 61, 93, 102
Metropolitan Life Insurance Co., 244
Metropolitan Traction Co., 197
Mexican War, 90–91, 106, 121–122
Meyer, Eugene, 229
Michigan Central Railroad, 49
Middle class, 255
Midgley, Thomas, 235
Milk, evaporated, 110

Miller, Phineas, 60
Mitchell, Sidney Zollicoffer, 195
Mix, Jonathan, 102
Money power, rise of, 163–184
Monitor and *Merrimac*, 128
Monopolies, 151–154, 181
Monsanto Chemical Co., 236
Moody, John, 145, 180
Moody, Paul, 56
Morgan, J. P., 127, 156, 161, 163–165, 167–185, 189, 191, 195, 204, 228
Morgan, Junius Spencer, 168
Morgan-Rockefeller interests, 179–183
Mormons, 126, 135
Morrill Tariff, 130, 133
Morris, Robert, 16, 31, 39, 44
Morrow, Dwight, 228
Morse, Jedidiah, 105
Morse, Samuel F. B., 81, 104–106, 187
Mott, Charles Stewart, 203
Muckraking, 179, 181
Murphy, William H., 210
Mutual Life Insurance Co., 181
Myers, Gustavus, 83

Nader, Ralph, 258
Nail industry, 50, 113
Nash, Charles W., 214, 216
National Broadcasting Co., 200
National Cash Register Co., 215
National City Bank, 181, 183, 228
National Steel Co., 183, 237
National Tube Co., 177
Naugatuck Valley, Conn., 59, 61, 65, 190
Nelson, Donald, 245
Newbold, Charles, 94
New Deal, 193, 196, 230–233, 243
New England, industry in, 1, 3, 44, 47, 55–56, 93
New York, New Haven & Hartford Railroad, 145, 181
New York Central Railroad, 77, 143–148, 152, 171, 248, 258
New York City, growth of, 2, 13, 40, 68
New York Stock Exchange, 176, 223, 228
Non-Intercourse Act, 48
North, Simeon, 61
North American Aviation, Inc., 240, 262
Northern Pacific Railroad, 138, 172, 175–177, 194
Northern Securities Co., 179

NRA (National Recovery Act), 231–232
Nye, Gerald, 234
Nylon, 235–236, 250

Oak Ridge, Tenn., 246
Office of Scientific Research and Development, 246
Ogden, Col. Aaron, 72
Ogden, William B., 79, 97
Ohio, expansion of, 28, 39
Oil well, first, 149
Olds, Ransom Eli, 203, 207–209, 211
Oldfield, Barney, 211
Olin Mathieson Chemical Corp., 250
Oliver, James, 94
Oregon territory, 48, 82
Otis, James, 27
Otis Elevator Co., 186
Otto cycle gas engine, 205
Owens, Michael J., 221

Pacific Gas & Electric Co., 186
Pacific Mail Steamship Co., 135
Packard Motor Car Co., 209
Paine, Thomas, 32
Paley, William S., 200
Pan American Airways, 240–241
Panic of 1837, 83; of 1873, 138, 140; of 1907, 182
Paper money, 34, 39, 82
Parker, Daniel, 44
Pattison brothers, 58–59
Peabody, George, 168
Peabody, Joseph, 47
Pearl Harbor attack, 241
Peavey, Joseph, 86
Penn, William, 2, 114
Pennsylvania, iron industry, 16, 133; oil industry, 126, 149
Pennsylvania Railroad, 79, 116–117, 145–146, 157–158, 171–172, 258
Pepperrell, Sir William, 4–5
Perkins, George W., 183, 204
Perkins, Jacob, 50
Perkins, Thomas Handasyd, 49, 74
Petroleum industry, 101, 126, 146–156
Pharmaceutical industry, 254
Phelps, Anson G., 59
Phelps Dodge Corp., 59
Philadelphia, growth of, 2, 16, 36, 49, 130, 138, 193, 196
Philco Corp., 200, 253
Phoenix Iron Works, 128
Phonograph, 189–190, 197

Photography, 59, 198, 237
Pinckney, Mrs. Charles, 17
Piper, J. L., 157
Pitts, Lendall, 24
Pittsburgh Plate Glass Co., 221
Plastics industry, 234–235
Polaroid Corp., 237
Polk, James K., 92
polymerization, 235
Pope Manufacturing Co., 212
Population increase, 224
Porter brothers, 59
Postwar reconversion, 247
Potomac Co., 36
Powel, Samuel, 16
Price fixing, 154–155, 165, 231, 249
Principio Iron Works, 22
Prindle, Karl Edwin, 234
Printing presses, 103–104
Private enterprise, 1–23
Progressive Party, 204
Proximity fuse, 246
Public utilities, 186, 195–196
Pujo Committee, 182–183
Pullman, George M., 79, 97
Pullman Palace Car Co., 165, 181
Pure Oil Co., 155
Putnam, Col. Israel, 29
Putnam, Silas, 50

Quakers, 2, 113

Rackham, Horace, 211
Radar, 251–252
Radio Corporation of America, 186, 199, 236, 253
Radio industry, 199–200, 220
Railroad industry, 74, 79–80, 114, 133–134, 138, 144, 146, 159, 170–177
Ramsey, Joseph A., 170
Randolph, Edward, 3
Raskob, John J., 216
Raytheon Co., 246
Reaper, 96–99
Rebates, 146, 152
Reconstruction Finance Corp., 229
Reed, Daniel G., 179
Reed, Ezekiel, 50
Refrigeration, 102, 221
Remington Rand Corp., 200, 252
Reo Co., 209
"Report on Manufactures," 40–41
Research and development, 155, 250–253
Reuther, Walter, 232, 257

Revere, Paul, 11, 24, 57–59
Revolutionary War, see American Revolution
Revolver, 89–92, 128
Reynolds Aluminum Co., 221
Rickenbacker, Eddie, 238
Roads, 35, 63–64, 206–207, 220
Robbins & Lawrence Co., 93
Roberts, George B., 172
Robinson, Moncure, 70
Rockefeller, John D., 146–156, 163, 175, 179–183, 257
Rockefeller, William, 175
Rodney, Adm. George B., 30
Roebling, John A., 115
Rolfe, John, 21
Romney, George, 249
Roosevelt, Franklin D., 224–225, 230, 241
Roosevelt, Nicholas, 71
Roosevelt, Theodore, 177, 204
Root, Elisha King, 89, 91, 93
Roper, Elmo, 226
Rowe, John, 9
Rowland, Henry, 191
Royal Dutch Shell Co., 156
Rubber industry, 103, 201
Rumsey, James, 51, 71
Russell, George R., 48
Ryan, Thomas Fortune, 174, 194

Salem, Mass., industry in, 3, 10, 45–46, 49
Sanders, Thomas, 188
Sarnoff, David, 200
Schiff, Jacob, 166, 174, 181
Schlesinger, Arthur M., 28
Schoenberger, Dr. Peter, 117
Schuyler, Gen. Philip, 66
Schuyler, Robert, 145
Schwab, Charles M., 160
Scott, Thomas A., 145, 157
Securities and Exchange Commission, 231
Self-starter, 215
Seligman, J. & W. Co., 165, 214
Seward, William Henry, 118
Sewing machine, 81, 107–111, 123–124, 262
Shaw, Maj. Samuel, 44
Shays' Rebellion, 37
Shell Oil Co., 156
Sherman, William Tecumseh, 119
Sherman Antitrust Act, 155, 165, 250
Sherman Silver Purchase Act, 182

Shiffler, Aaron, 157
Shockley, Dr. William, 252
Shoe industry, 110–111, 124
Sholes, Christopher, 186
Shreve, Henry, 73
Siemens-Halske firm, 195, 215
Silliman, Benjamin, 149
Silver, 57, 126, 182
Singer, Isaac Merrit, 109, 262
Skelton, Owen, 219
Slater, Samuel, 42, 53–55, 57, 61, 107
Slavery and slave trade, 3, 12–13, 17, 21, 60, 120–122
Sloan, Alfred P., 216–218
Smibert, John, 6
Smith, Adam, 25, 40, 133
Smith, Cyrus Rowlett, 240
Smith, Sydney, 70
Snyder Co., 250
Solomon, Haym, 36
Sorensen, Charles, 210
Soviet Union, 251
Space age, 262
Spanish-American War, 177
Spencer, Samuel, 173
Sperry Rand Corp., 241, 253
Spindletop oil field, 155
Spinning jenny, 53
Spotswood, Col. Alexander, 112
Sprague, Frank, 196
Stamp Act, 10, 28
Standard Kollsman Industries, Inc., 253
Standard Oil Co., 146–156, 180, 183
Standard Oil Co. of N. J., 154, 235, 244
Standard Oil Co. of Ohio, 154
Stanford, Leland, 134
Stanton, Edwin M., 98, 128
State banks, 82, 129–130
Steamboats, 50, 71
Steam engine, 71
Steel industry, 80, 156–160, 183, 220
Stephenson, George, 74
Stetson, Francis Lynde, 173, 205
Stevens, Col. John, 71–72, 74, 77
Stevens, Robert L., 77, 114
Stevens, Thaddeus, 132
Stewart, A. T. & Co., 123, 142
Stiegel, Henry W., "Baron von," 12
Stiles, Ezra, 12
Stillman, James, 175
Stock market, 101, 146, 176; crash of 1929, 219, 223, 225, 277
Storrow, James J., 214
Streetcar, electric, 196

Strelow, Albert, 211, 213
Strong, Benjamin, 227
Strutt, Jedediah, 53
Studebaker brothers, 102, 129, 206, 209
Sturgis, Bill, 48
Stuyvesant, Peter, 13
Sugar trade, 25–26, 174
Sumner, Charles, 132
Sun Oil Co., 155, 183
Swebelius, Gus, 246
Sylvania Electric Products Co., 246, 253
Synthetics, 201, 235–236, 250

Tariff, 41, 120, 122
Taxes, 259–260
Taylor, Moses, 165, 175
Tea trade, 24–26, 28–29
Telegraph, 81, 105–106, 188
Telephone, 188
Television, 199, 236, 253
Terry, Eli, 64
Tesla, Nikola, 194
Texaco, Inc., 155, 183
Texas, settlement of, 89–91, 120, 137
Texas Instruments, Inc., 252
Textile industry, 53–57, 107, 234
Thimonnier, Barthélemy, 108
Thomas, Philip Evan, 74
Thomas, William, 109
Thompson, Jeremiah, 68
Thomson, Elihu, 195
Thomson, Frank, 172
Thomson, J. Edgar, 145–146, 158–159
Thorndike, Israel, 47
Tobacco industry, 18–21, 27–28, 121
Tom Thumb, 76, 105–106, 113, 116
Town, Ithiel, 102
Townsend, James, 149
Townshend Acts, 18, 28
Transatlantic cable, 105–106
Transistors, 252
Trans World Airlines, 240
Tredegar Iron Works, 128
Trenton (N. J.) iron mills, 114–117, 128
Trippe, Juan Terry, 238
Trowbridge, John, 191
Trusts, 165, 174, 177, 180, 183
Tryon, W. K. & Co., 90
Tudor, Frederic, 101
TVA, 193, 243
Twain, Mark, 73, 78–79, 140
Typewriter, 186
Tytus, John B., 237

Union Carbide Corp., 234, 236, 246
Union Pacific Railroad, 133, 137, 174–175
United Aircraft Corp., 241
United Air Lines, 240
United Shoe Machinery, 111
United States Rubber Co., 166
United States Steel Corp., 156, 161, 163–165, 177, 223

Vail, Theodore N., 189
Van Bibber, Abraham, 30
Vanderbilt, Cornelius, 72, 77, 101, 138, 141–144, 171
Vanderbilt, William H., 144, 170–171, 206, 239
Vanderlip, Frank A., 183
Varian Associates, 253
Villard, Henry, 194, 195

Wadsworth, Jeremiah, 31, 44
Wages, 166, 232
Wagner Act, 232
Walker, Capt. Samuel, 91
Wallace, Henry, 260
Wallace, William, 190
Wall Street, 101, 165, 167, 181–182, 185, 204, 216, 222–223, 228, 246
Walpole, Robert, 26
Wanamaker, John, 190, 197
Warburg, Paul M., 183, 228
Ward, Capt. Eber B., 160
Warner, Charles Dudley, 78–79, 140
War of 1812, 40, 47–48, 67, 69, 72, 85, 94, 129
Washburn, Cadwallader C., 87
Washington, George, 10, 16, 22–23, 30–31, 36, 38, 60, 113, 144
Watson, Elkanah, 66
Watson, Thomas J., 252, 261
Webb, Walter Prescott, 137
Webster, Daniel, 72, 100, 121
Weeden, William B., 10
Weir, Ernest, 237
Welch, Sylvester, 70
Wells Fargo Express Co., 101, 135
Western Electric Co., 246, 252

Western Union Co., 106, 141, 187, 189
West Indies trade, 5, 7, 10, 22, 26, 32, 44–45, 101
Westinghouse, George, 194
Westinghouse Electric Corp., 186, 199–200, 215
Whaling industry, 10, 34, 46, 49, 59, 147
Wheat growing, 96–99, 125
White, Josiah, 69
White, William Allen, 141
Whitney, Cornelius Vanderbilt, 239
Whitney, Eli, 42, 51, 59–62, 64, 89, 92, 107
Whitney, Richard, 223
Whitney, William C., 197
Widener, Peter, 196
Wiggin, Albert H., 228
Wilkinson, David, 55
Wilkinson, Jeremiah, 50
Willing, Thomas, 16, 31, 39
Wills, C. Harold, 212
Willys, John North, 209, 238
Willys-Overland Co., 203, 209
Winslow, J. A., 129
Winthrop, John, Jr., 112
Winton, Alexander, 203, 210
Wood, Jethro, 94
Woolworth, Frank W., 197
World War I, 212, 231, 233, 238
World War II, 219, 226, 233, 236, 241, 244–246, 259
Wright, Benjamin, 68
Wright, J. Hood, 173
Wright brothers, 206, 238

Yale University, 12, 60, 149, 163
Yankee traders, 43, 48, 50, 59, 64
Yerkes, Charles T., 196
Young, Brigham, 135
Young, Owen D., 199
Young, Robert, 248, 258

Zeder, Fred M., 219
Zenith Radio Corp., 200, 253
Zukor, Adolph, 198
Zworykin, Vladimir, 236

About the Author

JOHN CHAMBERLAIN is a critic, journalist, and editor, who is currently on the staff of the *Wall Street Journal*. A graduate of Yale, he has long been associated with many of America's leading newspapers and magazines, including *Fortune, Life, The Freeman, National Review, Barron's Weekly, The New York Times, The Saturday Review*, and *Harper's Magazine*. John Chamberlain has also been writing a regular column for the King Features Syndicate for the last twelve years.

74 75 76 77 10 9 8 7 6 5 4 3 2 1